PRAY *the*
SCRIPTURES
BIBLE

Psalms and
Proverbs

GOD'S
WORD.
TRANSLATION

PRAY *the*
SCRIPTURES
BIBLE

*Psalms and
Proverbs*

BETHANYHOUSE
Minneapolis, Minnesota

Pray the Scriptures Bible: Psalms and Proverbs
Prayers © 2011 Kevin Johnson

GOD'S WORD®
© 1995 by God's Word to the Nations
Used by permission of Baker Publishing Group. All rights reserved.

Published by Bethany House Publishers
11400 Hampshire Avenue South
Minneapolis, Minnesota 55438

Bethany House Publishers is a division of
Baker Publishing Group, Grand Rapids, Michigan

ISBN 978-0-7642-0859-1

Printed in the United States of America

Library of Congress Cataloging-in-Publication Data is available for this title.

In keeping with biblical principles of creation stewardship, Baker Publishing Group advocates the responsible use of our natural resources. As a member of the Green Press Initiative, our company uses recycled paper when possible. The text paper of this book is comprised of 30% post-consumer waste.

green press INITIATIVE

Preface

God's Word ® Translation

God's Word® Translation (GW), produced by God's Word to the Nations Mission Society, fills a need that has remained unmet by English Bibles: to translate the Bible from the Hebrew, Aramaic, and Greek texts to their closest natural English equivalent.

GW consciously combines scholarly fidelity with natural English. Because it was translated by a committee of biblical scholars, GW is an accurate, trustworthy translation. Because of the involvement of English reviewers at every stage of the translation process, GW reads like contemporary literature.

Closest Natural Equivalence

Like many Bibles published before it, *God's Word* has been translated directly from the Hebrew, Aramaic, and Greek texts. Unlike many Bibles before it, however, GW used a translation theory that reflects the advancement of translation theory and practice.

Closest natural equivalent (CNE) translation provides readers with a meaning in the target language that is equivalent to that of the source language. It seeks to express that meaning naturally, in a way that a native English speaker would speak or write. Finally, it expresses the meaning with a style that preserves many of the characteristics of the source text.

However, CNE does not attempt to make all books or passages function on the same level. The more difficult books of the Bible are translated to the same level of difficulty as the original languages. In addition, abstract concepts in Greek and Hebrew are translated into abstract concepts in English, and concrete concepts remain concrete in translation.

This translation theory is designed to avoid the awkwardness and inaccuracy associated with formal-equivalent translations, and to avoid the loss of meaning and oversimplification associated with functional-equivalent translations.

Translation Process

The first consideration for the translators of GW was to find equivalent English ways of expressing the meaning of the original text, ensuring that the translation is faithful to the meaning of the source text. The next consideration was readability; the meaning is expressed in natural English by using common English punctuation, capitalization, grammar, and vocabulary. The third consideration was to choose the natural equivalent that most closely reflects the style of the Hebrew, Aramaic, or Greek text. At the core of this effort was a full-time translation team composed of biblical scholars who served as translators, English experts who actively reviewed English style with scholars at every stage of the translation process, and professional production personnel who oversaw the work. The basic process is outlined below.

Translation

In the first step of this process, a biblical scholar used the principles of closest natural equivalence to produce an initial translation of one of the books of the Bible. During this time, the translator was able to consult with the rest of the translation team as needed.

English Review

With the initial draft of a book completed, an expert in English style reviewed the translator's text and suggested changes. The English reviewer was concerned primarily with a natural English rendering. Additionally, the English reviewer electronically searched the entire translation to ensure that any proposed revisions would not destroy the translation's consistency.

The translator and the English reviewer then worked together to produce a second draft that improved both the naturalness and accuracy of the translation. Upon completion of the second draft, the translator and English reviewer served as resources for the rest of the editorial process.

Peer Review

After the English review process, the second draft was circulated to the other full-time translators and English reviewers for comments. This peer review stage allowed the other members of the translation team to compare the draft with their own work, offer suggestions for further improvement, and maintain consistency from one book of the Bible to another.

Technical Review

The translator and English reviewer incorporated all appropriate suggestions offered in the peer review stage to produce a third draft. This draft was then submitted to a number of scholarly technical reviewers, who submitted written suggestions for improvements in the translation.

Review by Book Editorial Committee

The next step in the process produced a fourth draft of the text. Taking into account the comments of the technical reviewers, a book editorial committee met to read and discuss the text for each book of the Bible.

The final step for the book editorial committee was reading the text aloud. Since the Bible is read not only silently but also aloud in worship and instructional settings, having a Bible translation that can be immediately grasped by the listener or reader and understood without the benefit of rereading was an important consideration.

Review by Consultative Committee

After the members of the book editorial committee finished their work, they passed the fourth draft to the members of the consultative committee. This group of more than fifty Christian leaders from various denominations submitted comments and suggestions.

Review by Old Testament, New Testament, and Bible Editorial Committees

The final editorial changes were made when all the books of the Bible had been completed or were near completion. Old and New Testament committees and, finally, a Bible editorial committee approved the accuracy and readability of the text.

Features of *God's Word* ®
Layout

The features that distinguish *God's Word* from other Bible translations are designed to aid readers. The most obvious of these is the open, single-column format.

In prose, GW looks like other works of literature. It contains frequent paragraphing. Whenever a different speaker's words are quoted, a new paragraph begins. Lists, genealogies, and long prayers are formatted to help readers recognize the thought pattern of the text. The prose style of GW favors concise, clear sentences. While avoiding very long, complicated sentences, which characterize many English Bible translations, GW strives to vary the word arrangement in a natural way. Doing this enhances readability and brings the Scriptures to life.

The books that are primarily poetry in GW are instantly recognized by their format. The single-column format enables readers to recognize parallel thoughts in parallel lines of poetry. In a single-column, across-the-page layout, a variety of indentations are possible. The translators have used indentation to indicate the relationship of one line to others in the same context. This enables a person reading the Bible in English to appreciate the Bible's poetry in much the same way as a person reading the Bible in the original languages of Hebrew, Aramaic, or Greek.

Punctuation, Capitalization

In English, meaning is conveyed not only by words but also by punctuation. However, no punctuation existed in ancient Hebrew and Greek writing, and words were used where English would use punctuation marks. *GOD'S WORD* strives to use standard English punctuation wherever possible. At times this means that a punctuation mark or paragraph break represents the meaning that could only be expressed in words in Hebrew or Greek.

Italics are also used as they would be in other printed English texts: for foreign words or to indicate that a word is used as a word. (GW never uses italics to indicate emphasis.)

Wherever possible, GW has supplied information in headings or half-brackets to identify the speaker in quoted material. To minimize the confusion produced by quotations within quotations, quotation marks are used sparingly. For instance, they are not used after formulaic statements such as "This is what the LORD says: . . . ."

Contractions can fit comfortably into many English sentences. Certainly, "Don't you care that we're going to die" is more natural than, "Do you not care that we are going to die?" GW achieves a warmer style by using contractions where appropriate. But uncontracted words are used in contexts that require special emphasis.

GW capitalizes the first letter in proper nouns and sentences and all the letters in the word LORD when it represents *Yahweh*, the name of God in the Old Testament. Some religious literature chooses to capitalize pronouns that refer to the deity. As in the original languages, GW does not capitalize any pronouns (unless they begin sentences). In some cases scholars are uncertain whether pronouns in the original texts refer to God or someone else. In these cases the presence of capitalized pronouns would be misleading. Additionally, in some cases Hebrew or Greek pronouns are not ambiguous but an English pronoun would be. In those cases, GW uses the appropriate proper noun in its place.

Gender References

The Scriptures contain many passages that apply to all people. Therefore, *GOD'S WORD* strives to use gender-inclusive language in these passages so that all readers will apply these passages to themselves. For example, traditionally, Psalm 1:1 has been translated, "Blessed is the man who does not follow the advice of the wicked. . . ." As a result, many readers will understand this verse to mean that only adult males, not women or children, can receive a blessing. In GW the first psalm begins "Blessed is the person who does not follow the advice of the wicked. . . ."

If a passage focuses upon an individual, however, GW does not use plural nouns and pronouns to avoid the gender-specific pronouns *he, him,* and *his.* In these cases the translators considered the text's focus upon an individual more important than an artificial use of plural pronouns. For example, Psalm 1:2 has been translated "Rather, he delights in the teachings of the LORD. . . ." In addition, gender-accurate language is preserved in passages that apply specifically to men or specifically to women.

Word Choice

The translation team chose words that were natural in context and that were as easily understood as possible without losing accuracy and faithfulness to the Hebrew and Greek texts of the Bible.

One of the challenges faced by the translators of GW was finding words that accurately communicate the meaning of important theological concepts in the Bible. Many of these concepts have traditionally been translated by words that no longer communicate to most English speakers. Examples of these theological terms include *covenant, grace, justify, repent,* and *righteousness.* While these words continue to be used by theologians and even by many Christians, the meanings that readers assign to them in everyday use do not equate to the meanings of the Hebrew or Greek words they are intended to translate. *GOD'S WORD* avoids using these terms and substitutes words that carry the same meaning in clear, natural English. In some cases traditional theological words are contained in footnotes the first time they occur in a chapter.

Living, Active, and Life-changing

While all these features make *GOD'S WORD* Translation an accurate and readable Bible, the ultimate goal of the God's Word to the Nations Mission Society is to bring the readers of GW into a new or closer relationship with Jesus. The translation team and support staff of the Mission Society pray that your reading of GW makes the living, active, and life-changing words of our great God and Savior clear and meaningful.

For more details on the translation process and the unique features that enable GW to accurately and clearly communicate God's saving, life-changing message, visit www.godsword.org. For more information on available editions of GW, visit www.godswordtranslation.org.

Brackets

Proper names or foreign words whose meaning is significant for understanding a particular Bible passage are translated in brackets ([ ]) following the name or phrase. When reading aloud, a bracketed word may be treated as "that is."

Half-brackets (⌐ ¬) enclose words that the translation team supplied because the context contains meaning that is not explicitly stated in the original language.

Footnotes

Five types of footnotes are used in *God's Word:*

1. Explanatory footnotes clarify historical, cultural, and geographical details from the ancient world to make the text more understandable to modern readers. These footnotes also identify word play in Hebrew or Greek that would otherwise be lost to the English reader.

2. Alternate translation footnotes offer other plausible translations. They are introduced by the word *or.*

3. Footnotes that state "English equivalent difficult" mark passages where a Hebrew or Greek expression cannot be adequately translated into modern English without resorting to a long, inappropriate paraphrase.

4. Footnotes that state "Hebrew meaning uncertain" or "Greek meaning uncertain" mark passages where scholars are not sure exactly what a Hebrew or Greek expression means.

5. Textual footnotes are included wherever *God's Word* translates the meaning of some text other than the Masoretic Text printed in *Biblia Hebraica Stuttgartensia* or its footnotes (Old Testament) or the Greek text printed in the twenty-seventh edition of *Novum Testamentum Graece* (New Testament).

Terms Used in Footnotes

Aramaic	one of the languages of the Old Testament, related to Hebrew
Dead Sea Scrolls	one or more of the Qumran manuscripts
Egyptian	one or more of the ancient translations of the Bible into the ancient Egyptian or Ethiopic languages
Greek	in the Old Testament: one or more of the ancient Greek translations of the Old Testament; in the New Testament: the Greek language, the language of the New Testament
Hebrew	the primary language of the Old Testament
Latin	one or more of the ancient Latin translations of the Bible
Masoretic Text	the traditional Hebrew text of the Old Testament
manuscript	an ancient, handwritten copy of a text
Samaritan Pentateuch	Samaritan Hebrew version of the first five books of the Bible
Syriac	the ancient Syriac translation of the Bible
Targum	one of the ancient Aramaic translations of the Old Testament

INTRODUCTION TO
PRAY THE SCRIPTURES BIBLE

Most people pray. Many of us struggle. We wonder what to say to God and how to say it. We worry if we will get what we ask or if we can speak honest questions.

Pray the Scriptures Bible shows that all of God's Word teaches us how to pray. I envisioned this experiential Bible as a fresh, accurate, straightforward translation together with a stream of prayers flowing from both heart and mind, speaking back to the God who speaks to us in the Bible.

The prayers intentionally stay close to the Bible text. Prompted by Scripture, they capture an everyday conversation with God. Praying the whole Bible forces us to form prayers from both teachings and stories . . . to make sense of challenging and awkward passages . . . to find personal relevance in verses dense with history and sparse on obvious application.

Pray the Scriptures Bible is a personal response to Scripture, but I searched for themes and words that fit easily in anyone's mouth. I hope these prayers encourage your own one-on-one conversation with God—that these simple words help you process your own life circumstances and give voice to your own spiritual longings, wonderings, and worship.

Don't keep these prayers to yourself. Pray them *for* others—family, friends, neighbors, co-workers, people you struggle to love, and the world at large. Pray them *with* others—in pairs, groups, and gatherings.

Thanks to Bethany House Publishers, from David Horton and Natasha Sperling to the entire staff, for partnering to use the GOD'S WORD® Translation to make this idea real. They join me in praying that this unique Bible will inspire your quest to know and experience God.

KEVIN JOHNSON
May 2011

Introduction to Psalms

As the songbook of God's Old Testament people, the psalms breathe prayer from start to finish. These songs, poems, and prayers were composed by a variety of people over a thousand-year span. Many flowed from King David, "the singer of Israel's psalms" (2 Samuel 23:1). Others come from Asaph and Ethan, national worship leaders appointed by David. Several of the earliest psalms trace back to Moses, Solomon added others, and a priestly family named the "Son of Korah" contributed songs over a period of centuries.

Although Israel incorporated these psalms into formal group worship, many relay intensely personal cries of individuals. Praise, confusion, remorse, anger, and joy come raw and unfiltered. And throughout history this songbook of Israel has become the prayer book of all God's people. Believers find here not only comforting words and beautiful prose but also a grid for processing life's most extreme difficulties. The psalms leave no doubt God can handle your speaking out loud your most wrenching emotions. They also make obvious that God won't abandon you to despair. He aims to lead you to new calm, purpose, and trust.

A surprising number of these songs talk about God and his acts in third person. Praying this book invites you to turn these declarations *about* God into prayers *to* God. Whatever the subject of these psalms, however much their bluntness challenges you, no matter how near or far their world seems from yours, you can make these inspired words part of your everyday conversation with God.

PSALMS

BOOK ONE

(Psalms 1–41)

Psalm 1

[1] Blessed is the person who does not
    follow the advice of wicked people,
      take the path of sinners,
        or join the company of mockers.
[2] Rather, he delights in the teachings of the Lord
    and reflects on his teachings day and night.
[3] He is like a tree planted beside streams—
    a tree that produces fruit in season
      and whose leaves do not wither.
He succeeds in everything he does.[a]

[4] Wicked people are not like that.
    Instead, they are like husks that the wind blows away.
[5]   That is why wicked people will not be able to stand
      in the judgment
    and sinners will not be able to stand where
      righteous people gather.

[6] The Lord knows the way of righteous people,
    but the way of wicked people will end.

1:1–2 I would rather search your Word day and night than indulge evil opinions or sinful paths or mocking crowds. Lift me to your place of blessing.

1:3 Plant me beside life-giving streams where I can drink you deeply. Let me be and do everything you plan for me. Give me success as I live your way.

1:4–5 Don't let me dry up and blow away in the wind of your judgment. I choose to stand side by side with those who love you.

Psalm 2

[1] Why do the nations gather together?
    Why do their people devise useless plots?
[2]   Kings take their stands.
    Rulers make plans together
      against the Lord and against his Messiah[b]
        by saying,
[3]   "Let's break apart their chains
      and shake off their ropes."

[4] The one enthroned in heaven laughs.
    The Lord makes fun of them.
[5]   Then he speaks to them in his anger.
    In his burning anger he terrifies them by saying,

2:1–3 The whole world revolts against you with useless plots. The powerful and powerless alike try to shake off your reign. But I bow to you as my Lord.

2:4–5 You laugh at human rebels and burn with anger against them. You terrify them with the announcement of your rule.

---

[a] 1:3 Or "and its leaves do not wither, and whatever it produces thrives."
[b] 2:2 Or "anointed one."

2:6–8 You've enthroned your Son as the one and only King over the whole earth. Every nation belongs to him.

⁶   "I have installed my own king on Zion, my
         holy mountain."

⁷ I will announce the LORD's decree.
  He said to me:
    "You are my Son.
       Today I have become your Father.
⁸   Ask me, and I will give you the nations as
             your inheritance
          and the ends of the earth as your
             own possession.

2:9–10 You break those who war against you, shattering them like brittle clay. I grow wise when I think hard about this fact!

⁹   You will break them with an iron scepter.
          You will smash them to pieces like pottery."

¹⁰ Now, you kings, act wisely.
  Be warned, you rulers of the earth!
¹¹ Serve the LORD with fear, and rejoice with trembling.

2:11–12 I serve you with trembling joy. I give you a loyal kiss. I smile as I submit to you. And I enjoy your blessing as I take refuge in you.

¹² Kiss the Son, or he will become angry
      and you will die on your way
        because his anger will burst into flames.
  Blessed is everyone who takes refuge in him.

Psalm 3

A psalm by David when he fled from his son Absalom.

3:1–2 My enemies swarm around me. They say your help isn't enough.

¹ O LORD, look how my enemies have increased!
    Many are attacking me.
²   Many are saying about me,
       "Even with God ⌐on his side⌐,
        he won't be victorious."   *Selah*

3:3–4 But you protect me on every side. You hold my head high. You are my powerful answer from heaven.

³ But you, O LORD, are a shield that surrounds me.
    You are my glory.
    You hold my head high.

⁴ I call aloud to the LORD,
    and he answers me from his holy mountain.   *Selah*

3:5 Because you support me I can fall asleep each night and wake every morning.

⁵ I lie down and sleep.
  I wake up again because the LORD continues to
      support me.

3:6–8 The thousands who entrap me don't scare me, because I know you'll come to my rescue. Strike the jaws set hard against me. Seize your victory!

⁶ I am not afraid of the tens of thousands
    who have taken positions against me on all sides.

⁷ Arise, O LORD!
  Save me, O my God!
    You have slapped all my enemies in the face.
    You have smashed the teeth of wicked people.
⁸   Victory belongs to the LORD!
      May your blessing rest on your people.   *Selah*

Psalm 4

For the choir director; with stringed instruments; a psalm by David.

¹ Answer me when I call, O God of my righteousness.
  You have freed me from my troubles.
Have pity on me, and hear my prayer!

² You important people,
  how long are you going to insult my honor?
  How long are you going to love what is empty
    and seek what is a lie?   *Selah*

³   Know that the LORD singles out godly people
      for himself.
    The LORD hears me when I call to him.
⁴   Tremble and do not sin.
    Think about this on your bed and remain quiet. *Selah*
⁵   Offer the sacrifices of righteousness
      by trusting the LORD.

⁶ Many are saying, "Who can show us anything good?"
    Let the light of your presence shine on us, O LORD.
⁷   You put more joy in my heart
        than when their grain and new wine increase.
⁸ I fall asleep in peace the moment I lie down
    because you alone, O LORD, enable me to live securely.

19 • PSALMS 4–5

4:1–2 Answer me, O God who makes me righteous. As you've freed me in the past, hear my prayer now! Important people hurl insults at me as they chase empty and untrue things. Protect me!

4:3–4 You've singled me out and made me your own. I'll keep doing good while I wait quietly for your answer.

4:5–7 You shine on everyone who trusts you. You give me more joy than every kind of abundant possession.

Psalm 5

For the choir director; for flutes; a psalm by David.

¹ Open your ears to my words, O LORD.
  Consider my innermost thoughts.
² Pay attention to my cry for help, my king and my God,
    because I pray only to you.
³   In the morning, O LORD, hear my voice.
      In the morning I lay my needs in front of you,
        and I wait.

⁴ You are not a God who takes pleasure in wickedness.
    Evil will never be your guest.
⁵   Those who brag cannot stand in your sight.
    You hate all troublemakers.
⁶ You destroy those who tell lies.
    The LORD is disgusted with bloodthirsty and
      deceitful people.

⁷ But I will enter your house because of your
      great mercy.
  Out of reverence for you, I will bow toward your
      holy temple.
⁸ O LORD, lead me in your righteousness because of
      those who spy on me.
  Make your way in front of me smooth.

5:1–3 Help me! Hear my words and my unspoken thoughts. I count on you alone. Each morning I tell you my needs, and all day long I watch for your answers.

5:4–6 You can't stand evil. You chase it from your presence. Braggers and troublemakers and liars can't come close to you.

5:7–8 Only your mercy allows me to come near you. Only your righteousness leads my path and smooths my way.

5:9–10 Liars breathe death in my direction. Don't let these rebels stand. Trap them in their own schemes. Toss them from your presence.

5:11–12 But let me stay close to you and sing. Support those who do your will. Surround them with your favor.

⁹ Nothing in their mouths is truthful.
　　Destruction comes from their hearts.
　　　Their throats are open graves.
　　　They flatter with their tongues.

¹⁰ Condemn them, O God.
　　Let their own schemes be their downfall.
　　Throw them out for their many crimes
　　　because they have rebelled against you.
¹¹ But let all who take refuge in you rejoice.
　　Let them sing with joy forever.
　　Protect them, and let those who love your name
　　　triumph in you.
¹²　　You bless righteous people, O Lord.
　　Like a large shield, you surround them with
　　　your favor.

Psalm 6

For the choir director; with stringed instruments, on the sheminith,ᵃ a psalm by David.

6:1–2 You have every reason to rage at me. But treat me with mercy, because I'm weak. Heal me, because I shake with terror.

6:3–5 I wonder where you've gone and when you'll be back to save me. It won't do you any good to watch me die, because no one will be left to worship you.

6:6–7 I can't stop groaning and crying. My eyes overflow with tears and I can't see straight.

6:8–10 I know you've heard my cries. And now my tormenters will run scared because you're coming to help me. You'll push them away and put them to shame.

¹ O Lord, do not punish me in your anger
　　or discipline me in your rage.
² Have pity on me, O Lord, because I am weak.
　　Heal me, O Lord, because my bones shake
　　　with terror.
³　　My soul has been deeply shaken with terror.
　　But you, O Lord, how long . . . ?

⁴ Come back, O Lord.
　　Rescue me.
　　Save me because of your mercy!
⁵　　In death, no one remembers you.
　　In the grave, who praises you?

⁶ I am worn out from my groaning.
　　My eyes flood my bed every night.
　　I soak my couch with tears.
⁷ My eyes blur from grief.
　　They fail because of my enemies.

⁸ Get away from me, all you troublemakers,
　　because the Lord has heard the sound of
　　　my crying.
⁹　　The Lord has heard my plea for mercy.
　　The Lord accepts my prayer.
¹⁰ All my enemies will be put to shame and deeply
　　shaken with terror.
　　In a moment they will retreat and be put to shame.

ᵃ6:1 Unknown musical terrm

Psalm 7

*A shiggaion[a] by David; he sang it to the L*ORD *about the* ⌐slanderous⌐ *words of Cush, a descendant of Benjamin.*

[1] O LORD my God, I have taken refuge in you.
  Save me, and rescue me from all who are
    pursuing me.
[2]   Like a lion they will tear me to pieces
    and drag me off with no one to rescue me.

[3] O LORD my God,
  if I have done this—
    if my hands are stained with injustice,
[4]   if I have paid back my friend with evil
    or rescued someone who has no reason to
      attack me—[b]

[5] then let the enemy chase me and catch me.
  Let him trample my life into the ground.
  Let him lay my honor in the dust.   *Selah*

[6] Arise in anger, O LORD.
  Stand up against the fury of my attackers.
  Wake up, my God.[c]
    You have already pronounced judgment.
[7]   Let an assembly of people gather around you.
    Take your seat high above them.
[8] The LORD judges the people of the world.
  Judge me, O LORD,
    according to my righteousness,
    according to my integrity.

[9] Let the evil within wicked people come to an end,
  but make the righteous person secure,
    O righteous God who examines thoughts
      and emotions.
[10] My shield is God above,
  who saves those whose motives are decent.

[11] God is a fair judge,
  a God who is angered by injustice every day.
[12]   If a person does not change, God sharpens
      his sword.
    By bending his bow, he makes it ready
      ⌐to shoot⌐.
[13]   He prepares his deadly weapons
      and turns them into flaming arrows.
[14] See how that person conceives evil,
  is pregnant with harm,
    and gives birth to lies.

7:1–2 People hungry for my flesh hunt me. They mean to tear me apart. But you are my safe place.

7:3–5 If I've done wrong, then let my pursuers catch me and kill me. If I've acted unjustly or wronged my friends, then let them drag me to my death.

7:6–7 Wake up! You've already decided I'm right. Let the whole world hear your verdict. Let them watch you rise against my attackers.

7:8–9 You judge everybody on earth. So confirm my integrity. Examine my pure mind and heart. Consider my motives. Then shield me from sinners. Lock me in a safe place.

7:11–13 You never tolerate injustice. It angers you every time you see it. A person's failure to change for the better invites your flaming arrows.

7:14–17 You cause trouble to boomerang back at people who conceive, carry, and bear evil.

---

[a] Unknown musical term

[b] 7:4 Hebrew meaning of this line uncertain.

[c] 7:6 Greek; Masoretic Text "Wake up to me."

They suffer the pain they plan for others. I'm grateful for your righteous verdict.

¹⁵ He digs a pit and shovels it out.
Then he falls into the hole that he made ⌐for others⌐.
¹⁶ His mischief lands back on his own head.
His violence comes down on top of him.

¹⁷ I will give thanks to the LORD for his righteousness.
I will make music to praise the name of the LORD
Most High.

Psalm 8

For the choir director; on the gittith;ᵃ *a psalm by David.*

8:1–2 Your name is regal everywhere on earth. Your glory inspires worship throughout the universe. All it takes is praise on the lips of babes to hush your enemies.

¹ O LORD, our Lord, how majestic is your name
throughout the earth!

Your glory is sung above the heavens.ᵇ
² From the mouths of little children and infants,
you have built a fortress against your opponents
to silence the enemy and the avenger.

8:3–4 I'm stunned and shrunken when I compare myself to the vastness of your creation. Why do you bother with me?

³ When I look at your heavens,
the creation of your fingers,
the moon and the stars that you have set in place—
⁴ what is a mortal that you remember him
or the Son of Man that you take care of him?

8:5–9 You seat me just below your throne and invest me with honor. You share your reign and put creation under my control. Your name is matchless in majesty and authority!

⁵ You have made him a little lower than yourself.
You have crowned him with glory and honor.
⁶ You have made him rule what your hands created.
You have put everything under his control:
⁷ all the sheep and cattle, the wild animals,
⁸ the birds, the fish,
whatever swims in the currents of the seas.

⁹ O LORD, our Lord, how majestic is your name throughout
the earth!

Psalm 9

For the choir director; according to muth labben;ᶜ *a psalm by David.*ᵈ

9:1–2 My heart bursts with gratitude for your miracles. You give me joy. Praise wells up inside me, O Most High.

¹ I will give ⌐you⌐ thanks, O LORD, with all my heart.
I will tell about all the miracles you have done.
² I will find joy and be glad about you.
I will make music to praise your name, O Most High.

9:3–6 My enemies collapse when they meet you. They hear you defend me even though

³ When my enemies retreat, they will stumble and die in
your presence.
⁴ You have defended my just cause:

ᵃ 8:1 Unknown musical term.
ᵇ 8:1 Hebrew meaning of this line uncertain.
ᶜ 9:1 Or "*almuth labben*"; unknown musical term.
ᵈ 9:1 Some Hebrew manuscripts, Greek, and Latin treat Psalms 9 and 10 as one psalm.

You sat down on your throne as a fair judge.
5 You condemned nations.
   You destroyed wicked people.
   You wiped out their names forever and ever.
6 The enemy is finished—in ruins forever.
   You have uprooted their cities.
   Even the memory of them has faded.

7 Yet, the LORD is enthroned forever.
   He has set up his throne for judgment.
8 He alone judges the world with righteousness.
   He judges ⌊its⌋ people fairly.
9 The LORD is a stronghold for the oppressed,
   a stronghold in times of trouble.
10 Those who know your name trust you, O LORD,
   because you have never deserted those who seek
        your help.

11 Make music to praise the LORD, who is enthroned
        in Zion.
   Announce to the nations what he has done.
12   The one who avenges murder has remembered
        oppressed people.
   He has never forgotten their cries.
13 Have pity on me, O LORD.
   Look at what I suffer because of those who hate me.
   You take me away from the gates of death
14   so that I may recite your praises one by one
        in the gates of Zion
        and find joy in your salvation.

15 The nations have sunk into the pit they have made.
   Their feet are caught in the net they have hidden ⌊to
        trap others⌋.
16 The LORD is known by the judgment he has carried out.
   The wicked person is trapped
   by the work of his own hands.   *Higgaion Selah*
17 Wicked people, all the nations who forget God,
   will return to the grave.
18 Needy people will not always be forgotten.
   Nor will the hope of oppressed people be lost forever.
19 Arise, O LORD.
   Do not let mortals gain any power.
   Let the nations be judged in your presence.
20   Strike them with terror, O LORD.
   Let the nations know that they are
        ⌊only⌋ mortal.   *Selah*

Psalm 10

1 Why are you so distant, LORD?
   Why do you hide yourself in times of trouble?

9:7–10 Even as evildoers perish, you reign forever. You alone judge fairly and protect the oppressed. You never abandon anyone who counts on you for help.

9:11–14 I see you on your throne and sing to you. I tell the world that you avenge murder and help the oppressed. Though others hate me, you pity me. You carry me back from the brink of death. I'll praise you for every detail of how you have saved me.

9:15–16 Individuals and nations that plot evil get caught in their own traps. This is a sign of your judgment.

9:17–20 Everyone who forgets you will die, but you never forget the needy or exploited. Don't let mere human beings seize control of our world. Prove that you are boss. Warn them that they will disappear in your judgment.

10:1 Why can't I see you when I need you most? Why are you so distant and hard to find?

you condemn whole nations and peoples. You wipe them out so completely that no one remembers that they ever existed.

10:2–6 Some people think they can get away with any kind of evil. They assume you don't care. They even conclude you don't exist. Why? Because these people always succeed. They can't picture themselves facing your judgment. They can't imagine failure.

10:7–11 Do I need to remind you how the wicked act? They do evil with their words. They ambush and kill the innocent. They lure and crush the unsuspecting. And they think you don't know or care!

10:12–14 Stand up! Do something to save the oppressed! Don't give the wicked one more reason to think you don't care—especially while victims and orphans trust in your help.

10:15–16 Crush those who crush others. Punish every last bit of wickedness. Make evil nations disappear.

10:16–18 Rule over earth forever. Pay attention to the browbeaten and abandoned. Lift them out of discouragement. Give them justice so they can live free from fear.

² The wicked person arrogantly pursues oppressed people.
He will be caught in the schemes that he planned.
³ The wicked person boasts about his selfish desires.
He blesses robbers, but he curses the LORD.
⁴ He turns up his nose ⌐and says⌐, "God doesn't care."
His every thought ⌐concludes⌐, "There is no God."
⁵ He always seems to succeed.
Your judgments are beyond his understanding.
He spits at all his opponents.
⁶ He says to himself, "Nothing can shake me.
I'll never face any trouble."
⁷ His mouth is full of cursing, deception,
and oppression.
Trouble and wrongdoing are on the tip of
his tongue.
⁸ He waits in ambush in the villages.
From his hiding places he kills innocent people.
His eyes are on the lookout for victims.
⁹ He lies in his hiding place like a lion in his den.
He hides there to catch oppressed people.
He catches oppressed people when he draws them
into his net.
¹⁰ ⌐His⌐ victims are crushed.
They collapse,
and they fall under ⌐the weight of⌐ his power.
¹¹ He says to himself,
"God has forgotten.
He has hidden his face.
He will never see it!"

¹² Arise, O LORD!
Lift your hand, O God.
Do not forget oppressed people!
¹³ Why does the wicked person despise God?
Why does he say to himself, "God doesn't care"?
¹⁴ You have seen ⌐it⌐; yes, you have taken note of trouble
and grief
and placed them under your control.
The victim entrusts himself to you.
You alone have been the helper of orphans.
¹⁵ Break the arm of the wicked and evil person.
Punish his wickedness until you find no more.

¹⁶ The LORD is king forever and ever.
The nations have vanished from his land.
¹⁷ You have heard the desire of oppressed people, O LORD.
You encourage them.
You pay close attention to them
¹⁸ in order to provide justice for orphans and
oppressed people
so that no mere mortal will terrify them again.

Psalm 11

For the choir director; by David.

1 I have taken refuge in the LORD.
　　How can you say to me:
　　　"Flee to your mountain like a bird?
2　　　Wicked people bend their bows.
　　　　They set their arrows against the strings
　　　　　to shoot in the dark at people whose motives
　　　　　　are decent.
3　　　When the foundations ⌐of life⌐ are undermined,
　　　　what can a righteous person do?"

4 The LORD is in his holy temple.
　The LORD's throne is in heaven.
　　His eyes see.
　　　They examine Adam's descendants.
5 The LORD tests righteous people,
　　but he hates wicked people and the ones who
　　　love violence.
6　　　He rains down fire and burning sulfur upon
　　　　wicked people.
　　　He makes them drink from a cup filled with
　　　　scorching wind.
7 The LORD is righteous.
　　He loves a righteous way of life.
　　　Decent people will see his face.

11:1–3 People mock me for depending on you to protect me. Evildoers shoot at me and everyone decent. What are we supposed to do?

11:4–6 From your throne in heaven you see everyone and everything. You study all of us. Even good people don't escape your tests, but evil people face your stinking sulfur and scorching wind.

11:7 You are good. You love when people follow your good way. You let them see you.

Psalm 12

For the choir director; on the sheminith*; a psalm by David.*

1 Help, O LORD.
　　No godly person is left.
　　Faithful people have vanished from among
　　　Adam's descendants!
2 All people speak foolishly.
　They speak with flattering lips. They say one thing but
　　mean another.
3　May the LORD cut off every flattering lip
　　and every bragging tongue
4　　　that has said,
　　　　"We will overcome with our tongues.
　　　　With lips such as ours, who can be
　　　　　our master?"

5 "Because oppressed people are robbed and needy
　　people groan,
　　I will now arise," says the LORD.
　　"I will provide safety for those who long for it."

12:1–2 I need your help. I look around and see no one who loves you. Everyone left is a lying, flattering fool.

12:3–5 People who beat others with their words think no one can stop them. But put an end to them. Rescue the robbed and needy. Quiet their groaning and give them safety.

12:6–8 I trust your promises. I fully expect you to protect the oppressed. Don't let wicked people strut their sinfulness for everyone to see.

[6] The promises of the LORD are pure,
  like silver refined in a furnace[a] and purified
    seven times.
[7] O LORD, you will protect them.
  You will keep each one safe from those people forever.
[8]   Wicked people parade around
    when immorality increases among
      Adam's descendants.

Psalm 13

For the choir director; a psalm by David.

13:1–2 Will you ever remember me? When will I see you again? How long will I be stuck here all by myself, paralyzed with sadness and struggling to know what to do?

[1] How long, O LORD? Will you forget me forever?
  How long will you hide your face from me?
[2] How long must I make decisions alone
  with sorrow in my heart day after day?
  How long will my enemy triumph over me?

13:3–6 Look at me now! Answer me! Give me hope or I will die! I trust in your mercy and salvation. I will gladly sing of your goodness to me.

[3] Look at me! Answer me, O LORD my God!
Light up my eyes,
  or else I will die
[4]   and my enemy will say, "I have overpowered him."
    My opponents will rejoice because I have
      been shaken.

[5] But I trust your mercy.
  My heart finds joy in your salvation.
[6] I will sing to the LORD because he has been good to me.

Psalm 14[b]

For the choir director; by David.

14:1–3 Only a fool thinks you don't exist. But every human on earth acts stupidly and refuses to rely on you. We have all run from you and become rotten to the core. None of us does good.

[1] Godless fools say in their hearts,
  "There is no God."
They are corrupt.
They do disgusting things.
  There is no one who does good things.
[2] The LORD looks down from heaven on
    Adam's descendants
  to see if there is anyone who acts wisely,
    if there is anyone who seeks help from God.
[3]   Everyone has turned away.
    Together they have become rotten to the core.
      No one, not even one person, does good things.

14:4–6 Troublemakers eat your people like they gulp down food. Evildoers are so ignorant they don't pray to you. They panic when they see you help people who obey you.

[4] Are all those troublemakers,
  those who devour my people as if they were
    devouring food,
    so ignorant that they do not call on the LORD?
[5] There they are—panic-stricken

---

[a] 12:6 Hebrew meaning uncertain.
[b] 14:1 Psalm 14 is virtually identical in wording to Psalm 53.

because God is with the person who is righteous.
[6] They put the advice of oppressed people to shame
because the LORD is their refuge.

[7] If only salvation for Israel would come from Zion!
When the LORD restores the fortunes of his people,
Jacob will rejoice.
Israel will be glad.

14:7 Send help from your holy dwelling. Give us back our lives so we have reason to rejoice in you.

Psalm 15

A psalm by David.

[1] O LORD, who may stay in your tent?
Who may live on your holy mountain?

[2]   The one who walks with integrity,
      does what is righteous,
      and speaks the truth within his heart.

[3]   The one who does not slander with his tongue,
      do evil to a friend,
      or bring disgrace on his neighbor.

[4]   The one who despises those rejected by God
      but honors those who fear the LORD.

      The one who makes a promise and does not break it,
      even though he is hurt by it.

[5]   The one who does not collect interest on a loan
      or take a bribe against an innocent person.

Whoever does these things will never be shaken.

15:1–3 Who is good enough to approach you? What kind of person can truly worship you? I'll never experience your presence if my life is a lie. Or if I spend my days doing wrong. Or if I spread evil words. I commit all of myself to you—thoughts, words, and actions.

15:4 Train me to honor your people. Push me to keep my promises even when it hurts.

Psalm 16

A miktam[a] by David.

[1] Protect me, O God, because I take refuge in you.
[2]   I said to the LORD,
      "You are my Lord. Without you, I have
         nothing good."
[3] Those who lead holy lives on earth
are the noble ones who fill me with joy.[b]
[4] Those who quickly chase after other gods multiply
their sorrows.
I will not pour out their sacrificial offerings of blood
or use my lips to speak their names.

[5] The LORD is my inheritance and my cup.
You are the one who determines my destiny.
[6]   Your boundary lines mark out pleasant places
      for me.

16:1–2 Protect me because I trust in you. You are my master. Without you I have nothing.

16:3–4 I love being with your followers. Those who dedicate themselves to anything but you will encounter deep pain. I won't worship their idols.

16:5–6 You are my only real possession. You determine my future. When I live within your boundaries I find pleasure and beauty.

---

[a] 16:1 Unknown musical term.

[b] 16:3 English equivalent of this verse difficult.

Indeed, my inheritance is something beautiful.

[7] I will praise the LORD, who advises me.
My conscience warns me at night.
[8] I always keep the LORD in front of me.
When he is by my side, I cannot be moved.
[9] That is why my heart is glad and my soul rejoices.
My body rests securely
[10] because you do not abandon my soul to
the grave
or allow your holy one to decay.
[11] You make the path of life known to me.
Complete joy is in your presence.
Pleasures are by your side forever.

16:7–11 Lead me and warn me. I won't be shaken as long as I follow you. You are the reason I am happy, and because of you I rest. You won't let me rot in the grave but will lift me up to be with you forever.

Psalm 17

A prayer by David.

[1] Hear my plea for justice, O LORD.
Pay attention to my cry.
Open your ears to my prayer,
⌐which comes⌐ from lips free from deceit.
[2] Let the verdict of my innocence come directly from you.
Let your eyes observe what is fair.

17:1–3 Haven't you noticed my cries for justice? I need you, because you alone can declare me innocent. You constantly probe and confront me, so you know my heart is faultless.

[3] You have probed my heart.
You have confronted me at night.
You have tested me like silver,
but you found nothing wrong.
I have determined that my mouth will not sin.
[4] I have avoided cruelty because of your word.
In spite of what others have done,
[5] my steps have remained firmly in your paths.
My feet have not slipped.
[6] I have called on you because you answer me, O God.
Turn your ear toward me.
Hear what I have to say.
[7] Reveal your miraculous deeds of mercy,
O Savior of those who find refuge by your side
from those who attack them.
[8] Guard me as if I were the pupil in your eye.
Hide me in the shadow of your wings.
[9] Hide me from wicked people who violently attack me,
from my deadly enemies who surround me.

17:3–5 I've decided not to sin in what I say. Your Word keeps me from inflicting cruelty. Even when others stray from you, my feet grip your paths.

17:7–9 Show me your miraculous mercy. You save everyone who runs to you for protection, so guard me as carefully as you guard your own eye. Hide me from the violent swarm.

[10] They have shut out all feeling.[a]
Their mouths have spoken arrogantly.
[11] They have tracked me down.
They have surrounded me.

17:10–12 Wicked people are numb to their own evil. Their mouths spew pride. They circle me so they can toss me to the ground and tear me apart.

[a] 17:10 Hebrew meaning uncertain.

They have focused their attention on throwing me to
    the ground.
¹² Each one of them is like a lion eager to tear ⌊its
    prey⌋ apart
    and like a young lion crouching in hiding places.

¹³ Arise, O Lord; confront them!
    Bring them to their knees!
       With your sword rescue my life from wicked people.
¹⁴ With your power rescue me from mortals, O Lord,
       from mortals who enjoy their inheritance only in
       this life.
       You fill their bellies with your treasure.
       Their children are satisfied ⌊with it⌋,
          and they leave what remains to their children.

¹⁵ I will see your face when I am declared innocent.
    When I wake up, I will be satisfied ⌊with seeing⌋ you.

17:13–15 Confront these killers like you always confront me! Knock them down! For all I care they can enjoy a rich life and pass their treasures down to their children. That's all they will get. But I want more. You alone can satisfy me.

Psalm 18^a

*For the choir director; by David, the servant of the Lord.
He sang this song to the Lord when the Lord rescued
him from all his enemies, especially from Saul. He said,*

¹ I love you, O Lord, my strength.
² The Lord is my rock and my fortress and my Savior,
    my God, my rock in whom I take refuge,
       my shield, and the strength of my salvation,
       my stronghold.
³ The Lord should be praised.
    I called on him, and I was saved from my enemies.

⁴ The ropes of death had become tangled around me.
    The torrents of destruction had overwhelmed me.
⁵   The ropes of the grave had surrounded me.
       The clutches of death had confronted me.

⁶ I called on the Lord in my distress.
    I cried to my God for help.
       He heard my voice from his temple,
          and my cry for help reached his ears.

⁷ Then the earth shook and quaked.
    Even the foundations of the mountains trembled.
       They shook violently because he was angry.
⁸ Smoke went up from his nostrils,
    and a raging fire came out of his mouth.
       Glowing coals flared up from it.
⁹ He spread apart the heavens
    and came down with a dark cloud under his feet.
¹⁰ He rode on one of the angels^b as he flew,

18:1–2 My Lord, I love you. You are my strength, rock, fortress, and Savior. You are my God, shield, salvation, and stronghold.

18:3–5 I praise you because you saved me. I was tangled in death and drowning in destruction. Death held me in its clutches.

18:6–8 I cried to you and you heard. In anger you shook the earth. Smoke and fire billowed from your breath.

18:9–14 You split the heavens as you rushed to my aid. You hid in the darkness. You hurled

---

^a 18:1 Psalm 18 is virtually identical in wording to 2 Samuel 22.
^b 18:10 Or "cherubim."

hailstones and flashed lightning as your voice thundered in the heavens. You threw my enemies into confusion and scattered them.

and he soared on the wings of the wind.
¹¹ He made the darkness his hiding place,
the dark rain clouds his covering.
¹² Out of the brightness in front of him,
those rain clouds passed by with hailstones
and lightning.
¹³ The LORD thundered in the heavens.
The Most High made his voice heard with hailstones
and lightning.
¹⁴ He shot his arrows and scattered them.
He flashed streaks of lightning and threw them
into confusion.
¹⁵   Then the ocean floor could be seen.
The foundations of the earth were laid bare
at your stern warning, O LORD,
at the blast of the breath from your nostrils.

18:15–19 Your stern warning bared the ocean floor, your breath pushing back the waters. You reached down and plucked me from raging waters and rescued me from hateful enemies. You came to my defense and deposited me in a wide-open place.

¹⁶ He reached down from high above and took hold of me.
He pulled me out of the raging water.
¹⁷ He rescued me from my strong enemy
and from those who hated me,
because they were too strong for me.
¹⁸ On the day when I faced disaster, they confronted me,
but the LORD came to my defense.
¹⁹   He brought me out to a wide-open place.
He rescued me because he was pleased with me.

18:20–23 You reward me because I do right. You pay me back because I keep your ways and stay close to you. I remember your laws and keep them all. You know that I'm innocent.

²⁰ The LORD rewarded me
because of my righteousness,
because my hands are clean.
He paid me back
²¹   because I have kept the ways of the LORD
and I have not wickedly turned away from my God,
²²   because all his judgments are in front of me
and I have not turned away from his laws.
²³   I was innocent as far as he was concerned.
I have kept myself from guilt.
²⁴ The LORD paid me back
because of my righteousness,
because he can see that my hands are clean.

18:25–26 Because I'm faithful, you're faithful toward me. Because I live with integrity, I experience your integrity. Because I'm pure, I witness your purity. If I chose to be devious, you would outsmart me.

²⁵ ⌊In dealing⌋ with faithful people you are faithful,
with innocent people you are innocent,
²⁶   with pure people you are pure.
⌊In dealing⌋ with devious people you are clever.

²⁷ You save humble people,
but you bring down a conceited look.
²⁸ O LORD, you light my lamp.
My God turns my darkness into light.

18:29 With you on my side I can conquer an army. I can break through every barrier.

²⁹   With you I can attack a line of soldiers.
With my God I can break through barricades.

30 God's way is perfect!

The promise of the LORD has proven to be true.

He is a shield to all those who take refuge in him.

31   Who is God but the LORD?

Who is a rock except our God?

32 God arms me with strength

and makes my way perfect.

33   He makes my feet like those of a deer

and gives me sure footing on high places.

34   He trains my hands for battle

so that my arms can bend an ⌐archer's⌐ bow of bronze.

35 You have given me the shield of your salvation.

Your right hand supports me.

Your gentleness makes me great.

36 You make a wide path for me to walk on

so that my feet do not slip.

37 I chased my enemies and caught up with them.

I did not return until I had ended their lives.

38 I wounded them so badly that they were unable to get up.

They fell under my feet.

39 You armed me with strength for battle.

You made my opponents bow at my feet.

40 You made my enemies turn their backs to me,

and I destroyed those who hated me.

41 They cried out for help, but there was no one to save them.

They cried out to the LORD, but he did not answer them.

42   I beat them into a powder as fine as the dust blown by the wind.

I threw them out as though they were dirt on the streets.

43 You rescued me from my conflicts with the people.

You made me the leader of nations.

A people I did not know will serve me:

44   As soon as they hear of me, they will obey me.

Foreigners will cringe in front of me.

45   Foreigners will lose heart,

and they will tremble when they come out of their fortifications.

46 The LORD lives!

Thanks be to my rock!

May God my Savior be honored.

47 God gives me vengeance!

He brings people under my authority.

48   He saves me from my enemies.

You lift me up above my opponents.

You rescue me from violent people.

18:30–31 Your way is perfect and your promises always true. There is no God but you. There is no rock except my God.

18:32–35 You make me like an agile deer and give me sure footing. You train me to fight so I can bend a bow of bronze. Your salvation is like a shield. And your gentleness makes me great.

18:37–42 I chase my enemies until I catch them. I don't give up until they are gone, and you don't give in to them when they suddenly beg you for help. Because of you they become like dirt under my feet.

18:43–45 You rescue me from conflict and lift me to leadership. People obey me because you put them under my authority. Evil gets its due reward because you are my avenger.

18:46–48 I'm convinced you are real. You're my sure and solid rock! God my Savior, may my life honor you.

18:49–50 I sing you thanks so loudly that everyone on earth can hear. Victory and mercy come from you!

19:1–3 I gaze at the stars and see your glory. I study the sky and grasp your workmanship. Both day and night spell out your greatness without speaking a word.

19:4–6 Nowhere on earth is too remote to hear your message. The sun blazes your Word across the sky.

19:7–9 Your flawless teachings renew me. Your trustworthy testimony makes this fool wise. Your accurate instructions cheer my heart. Your radiant commands ignite my eyes. You inspire me with unfading awe. Your true decisions strike me as completely fair.

19:10–11 Your words are far more precious than gold. Moment by moment they warn me as I serve you. Keeping your commands gives me breathtaking rewards.

19:12–14 Forgive my faults I can't see. Keep evil habits from mastering me. Let my every word and thought please you. You are my master, my rock, and my defender.

[49] That is why I will give thanks to you, O Lord, among
the nations
and make music to praise your name.
[50] He gives great victories to his king.
He shows mercy to his anointed,
to David, and to his descendant[a] forever.

Psalm 19

For the choir director; a psalm by David.

[1] The heavens declare the glory of God,
and the sky displays what his hands have made.
[2] One day tells a story to the next.
One night shares knowledge with the next
[3]   without talking,
without words,
without their voices being heard.
[4] ⌞Yet,⌟ their sound has gone out into the entire world,
their message to the ends of the earth.
He has set up a tent in the heavens for the sun,
[5]   which comes out of its chamber like a bridegroom.
Like a champion, it is eager to run its course.
[6]   It rises from one end of the heavens.
It circles around to the other.
Nothing is hidden from its heat.

[7] The teachings of the Lord are perfect.
They renew the soul.
The testimony of the Lord is dependable.
It makes gullible people wise.
[8] The instructions of the Lord are correct.
They make the heart rejoice.
The command of the Lord is radiant.
It makes the eyes shine.
[9] The fear of the Lord is pure.
It endures forever.
The decisions of the Lord are true.
They are completely fair.
[10]   They are more desirable than gold, even the
finest gold.
They are sweeter than honey, even the drippings from
a honeycomb.
[11]   As your servant I am warned by them.
There is a great reward in following them.

[12] Who can notice every mistake?
Forgive my hidden faults.
[13]   Keep me from sinning.
Do not let anyone gain control over me.
Then I will be blameless,
and I will be free from any great offense.

---

[a] 18:50 Or "to his descendants."

¹⁴May the words from my mouth and the thoughts from
my heart
be acceptable to you, O Lord, my rock and
my defender.

Psalm 20

For the choir director; a psalm by David.

¹The Lord will answer you in times of trouble.
The name of the God of Jacob will protect you.
²He will send you help from his holy place
and support you from Zion.
³He will remember all your grain offerings
and look with favor on your burnt offerings.   *Selah*

⁴He will give you your heart's desire
and carry out all your plans.

⁵We will joyfully sing about your victory.
We will wave our flags in the name of our God.
The Lord will fulfill all your requests.

⁶Now I know that the Lord will give victory to his
anointed king.
He will answer him from his holy heaven
with mighty deeds of his powerful hand.
⁷Some ⌞rely⌟ on chariots and others on horses,
but we will boast in the name of the Lord our God.
⁸   They will sink to their knees and fall,
but we will rise and stand firm.

⁹Give victory to the king, O Lord.
Answer us when we call.

20:1–3 You answer me every time I hit trouble. You protect me when I rely on your name. You never forget my sincere worship.

20:4–5 You grant my heart's wish and carry my plans to completion. You give me abundant reasons to sing with your people.

20:7–9 Some count on their own strength and speed, but I will never rely on anything but you. Others sink to their knees and crumble, but I will rise and stand firm. Answer me when I call!

Psalm 21

For the choir director; a psalm by David.

¹The king finds joy in your strength, O Lord.
What great joy he has in your victory!
²You gave him his heart's desire.
You did not refuse the prayer from his lips.   *Selah*
³You welcomed him with the blessings of good things
and set a crown of fine gold on his head.
⁴He asked you for life.
You gave him a long life, forever and ever.
⁵Because of your victory his glory is great.
You place splendor and majesty on him.
⁶   Yes, you made him a blessing forever.
You made him glad with the joy of your presence.
⁷   Indeed, the king trusts the Lord,
and through the mercy of the Most High, he will
not be moved.

21:1 I feel joy when I think of your strength. I rejoice whenever you win!

21:2–4 You give me the longings of my heart and answer my prayers. You wrap me in blessings and crown me with gold. I ask you for long life and you give it.

21:5–7 You robe me with splendor and majesty. You make me a blessing to others and energize me with your presence. Because I trust in you I won't be moved.

21:8–13 I know you will scorch your enemies and swallow them in anger. You will end their dynasties and halt their evil schemes. When they see your judgment aimed square at their faces they will flee in terror. I will praise your power.

[8] Your hand will discover all your enemies.
Your powerful hand will find all who hate you.
[9]   When you appear, you will make them ⌐burn⌐ like a blazing furnace.
    The LORD will swallow them up in his anger.
    Fire will devour them.
[10]   You will destroy their children from the earth
     and their offspring from among
        Adam's descendants.
[11]   Although they scheme and plan evil against you,
        they will not succeed.
[12]   They turn their backs ⌐and flee⌐
        because you aim your bow at their faces.[a]

[13] Arise, O LORD, in your strength.
We will sing and make music to praise your power.

Psalm 22

For the choir director; according to ayyeleth hashachar;[b] *a psalm by David.*

22:1–2 Why have you left me? Why is your help so distant? Can't you hear my groans? I plead with you day and night, but you don't answer me.

[1] My God, my God,
   why have you abandoned me?
   Why are you so far away from helping me,
      so far away from the words of my groaning?
[2] My God,
   I cry out by day, but you do not answer—
      also at night, but I find no rest.

22:3–5 I worship your pure and perfect holiness. I trust you and you answer me. I cry to you and you save me.

[3] Yet, you are holy, enthroned on the praises of Israel.
[4] Our ancestors trusted you.
   They trusted, and you rescued them.
[5]   They cried to you and were saved.
   They trusted you and were never disappointed.

22:6–8 I don't even feel like a human being. I'm a worm. People despise me and make fun of me. They mock me for trusting myself to you. They say you won't rescue me.

[6] Yet, I am a worm and not a man.
   I am scorned by humanity and despised by people.
[7] All who see me make fun of me.
   Insults pour from their mouths.
      They shake their heads and say,
[8]   "Put yourself in the LORD's hands.
       Let the LORD save him!
       Let God rescue him since he is pleased
          with him!"
[9] Indeed, you are the one who brought me out of
   the womb,
      the one who made me feel safe at my mother's breasts.
[10] I was placed in your care from birth.
   From my mother's womb you have been my God.

22:9–11 You brought me into this world, and you've been my safety since the day of my birth. You've always been my God. So don't be so far from me. There's no one else to help me.

---

[a] 21:12 Hebrew meaning of this verse uncertain.
[b] 22:1 Unknown musical term.

¹¹ Do not be so far away from me.
Trouble is near, and there is no one to help.
¹² Many bulls have surrounded me.
Strong bulls from Bashan have encircled me.
¹³ They have opened their mouths to attack me
like ferocious, roaring lions.
¹⁴ I am poured out like water,
and all my bones are out of joint.
My heart is like wax.
It has melted within me.
¹⁵ My strength is dried up like pieces of broken pottery.
My tongue sticks to the roof of my mouth.
You lay me down in the dust of death.
¹⁶ Dogs have surrounded me.
A mob has encircled me.
They have pierced my hands and feet.
¹⁷ I can count all my bones.
People stare.
They gloat over me.
¹⁸ They divide my clothes among themselves.
They throw dice for my clothing.

¹⁹ Do not be so far away, O LORD.
Come quickly to help me, O my strength.
²⁰ Rescue my soul from the sword,
my life from vicious dogs.
²¹ Save me from the mouth of the lion
and from the horns of wild oxen.

You have answered me.

²² I will tell my people about your name.
I will praise you within the congregation.
²³ All who fear the LORD, praise him!
All you descendants of Jacob, glorify him!
Stand in awe of him, all you descendants of Israel.
²⁴ The LORD has not despised or been disgusted
with the plight of the oppressed one.
He has not hidden his face from that person.
The LORD heard when that oppressed person
cried out to him for help.
²⁵ My praise comes from you while I am among those
assembled for worship.
I will fulfill my vows in the presence of those who fear
the LORD.
²⁶ Oppressed people will eat until they are full.
Those who look to the LORD will praise him.
May you live forever.
²⁷ All the ends of the earth will remember and return to
the LORD.
All the families from all the nations will worship you

22:12–15 Powerful enemies surround me. They spread their jaws to maul me. My insides melt and my life spills like water on dirt. I'm weak and can't speak. Do you like watching me die in the dust?

22:16–18 Vicious and unfaithful people surround me. A mob pierces my hands and feet. They strip me naked. They can't stop staring at this starving sack of bones.

22:19–24 Don't be so far from me. Come quickly to my side. Save me from the hideous death my enemies plan for me. Then I will praise you for all your people to hear.

22:23–24 I praise you because you are awesome. I worship you because I belong to you. I'm confident you don't despise me. I'm sure you don't run from me in disgust. I'm certain you hear me.

22:26 You'll feed the starving until they're full. Everyone who looks to you will praise you.

22:27–31 One day the whole world will realize you rule all humankind. The thriving and the dying alike will kneel and worship you. Children not yet born will learn about you.

²⁸ because the kingdom belongs to the LORD
and he rules the nations.
²⁹ All prosperous people on earth will eat and worship.
All those who go down to the dust will kneel in front of him,
even those who are barely alive.
³⁰ There will be descendants who serve him,
a generation that will be told about the Lord.
³¹ They will tell people yet to be born about
his righteousness—
that he has finished it.

Psalm 23

A psalm by David.

23:1–3 Because you are my shepherd, I will never lack. You let me stretch out in peace. You fill my soul. You guide my life so your name receives glory.

¹ The LORD is my shepherd.
I am never in need.
² He makes me lie down in green pastures.
He leads me beside peaceful waters.
³ He renews my soul.
He guides me along the paths of righteousness
for the sake of his name.

23:4–5 I won't fear even when I face death, because you are with me. You replace my cowardice with courage. You invite me to feast while my enemies watch. My life overflows.

⁴ Even though I walk through the dark valley of death,
because you are with me, I fear no harm.
Your rod and your staff give me courage.

⁵ You prepare a banquet for me while my enemies watch.
You anoint my head with oil.
My cup overflows.

23:6 Your goodness and mercy will never go away, and I will never leave your presence.

⁶ Certainly, goodness and mercy will stay close to me
all the days of my life,
and I will remain in the LORD's house for days
without end.

Psalm 24

A psalm by David.

24:1–2 There's not a thing on earth you didn't make. Everything and everyone belongs to you.

¹ The earth and everything it contains are the LORD's.
The world and all who live in it are his.
² He laid its foundation on the seas
and set it firmly on the rivers.

24:3–6 Who can draw close to you? People who are pure inside and out. If I seek your face and rely on your righteousness, I know I'll receive your blessing.

³ Who may go up the LORD's mountain?
Who may stand in his holy place?
⁴ ⌊The one who⌋ has clean hands and a pure heart
and does not long for what is false[a]
or lie when he is under oath.
⁵ ⌊This person⌋ will receive a blessing from the LORD
and righteousness from God, his savior.

---

[a] 24:4 Hebrew meaning uncertain.

⁶ This is the person who seeks him,
  who searches for the face of the God of Jacob.ᵃ *Selah*

⁷ Lift your heads, you gates.
 Be lifted, you ancient doors,
  so that the king of glory may come in.

⁸ Who is this king of glory?
  The LORD, strong and mighty!
  The LORD, heroic in battle!

⁹ Lift your heads, you gates.
 Be lifted, you ancient doors,
  so that the king of glory may come in.

¹⁰ Who, then, is this king of glory?
  The LORD of Armies is the king of glory!   *Selah*

24:7–9 I open my heart to you. You're as welcome in me as you are in your own holy city. You're the King of Glory—strong and mighty, heroic in battle. I open my life to you. Please enter in!

Psalm 25ᵇ

By David.

¹ To you, O LORD, I lift my soul.
² I trust you, O my God.
  Do not let me be put to shame.
  Do not let my enemies triumph over me.
³ No one who waits for you will ever be put to shame,
  but all who are unfaithful will be put to shame.
⁴ Make your ways known to me, O LORD,
  and teach me your paths.
⁵ Lead me in your truth and teach me
  because you are God, my savior.
  I wait all day long for you.
⁶ Remember, O LORD, your compassionate and
    merciful deeds.
  They have existed from eternity.
⁷ Do not remember the sins of my youth or my
    rebellious ways.
  Remember me, O LORD, in keeping with your mercy
    and your goodness.

⁸ The LORD is good and decent.
  That is why he teaches sinners the way they
    should live.
⁹ He leads humble people to do what is right,
  and he teaches them his way.
¹⁰ Every path of the LORD is ˻one of˼ mercy and truth
  for those who cling to his promiseᶜ and
    written instructions.

25:1–2 I offer you my whole being. I trust in you with my whole heart. Don't let my enemies shame me or beat me.

25:4–5 Show me how you want me to live. Instruct me in the real facts of life. You alone can do this for me, because you alone are my Savior.

25:6–7 Be merciful to me today just as you have been merciful from all eternity. Forgive and forget my youthful rebellion.

25:8–10 You're always good and fair. You give your commands to give us life. You teach everyone who bows to you. And when I cling to your promises and instructions, I always discover your mercy and truth.

ᵃ 24:6 A few Hebrew manuscripts, Greek, Syriac; Masoretic Text "your face, Jacob."
ᵇ 25:1 Psalm 25 is a poem in Hebrew alphabetical order.
ᶜ 25:10 Or "covenant."

25:11 Forgive my great guilt, for your name is even greater.

25:12–14 When I choose your path, I enjoy life's best things. I see my children experience your presence and provision. And I comprehend your promises.

25:16–18 Turn to me and meet me in my loneliness. Lift my burdens and release me from my distress. Don't ignore my misery. Forgive my sins.

25:19–22 My enemies and their hatred for me never stop multiplying. Protect me and rescue me, because I hide in you and no one else. I'm waiting for help. Save me! Save all your followers!

26:1–3 Rule in my favor, because you know my integrity and unwavering trust. Examine me up close, because you can peer into my heart and mind. Lead me with your mercy, and light my path with your truth.

26:4–6 I don't partner with liars or hypocrites. You won't find me joining a mob of evildoers or plotting with the wicked. I'll keep myself pure.

26:7–8 I boldly sing you thanks and tell of the miracles you have worked on my behalf. I love to be in your presence.

26:9–12 Don't sweep me away with people committed to sinning, because I live with integrity. Keep

---

¹¹ For the sake of your name, O LORD,
  remove my guilt, because it is great.
¹² Who, then, is this person that fears the LORD?
  He is the one whom the LORD will teach which path to choose.
¹³ He will enjoy good things in life,
  and his descendants will inherit the land.
¹⁴ The LORD advises those who fear him.
  He reveals to them the intent of his promise.

¹⁵ My eyes are always on the LORD.
  He removes my feet from traps.
¹⁶ Turn to me, and have pity on me.
  I am lonely and oppressed.
¹⁷ Relieve my troubled heart,
  and bring me out of my distress.
¹⁸ Look at my misery and suffering,
  and forgive all my sins.
¹⁹ See how my enemies have increased in number,
  how they have hated me with vicious hatred!
²⁰ Protect my life, and rescue me!
  Do not let me be put to shame.
  I have taken refuge in you.
²¹ Integrity and honesty will protect me because I wait for you.
²² Rescue Israel, O God, from all its troubles!

Psalm 26

By David.

¹ Judge me favorably, O LORD,
  because I have walked with integrity
  and I have trusted you without wavering.
² Examine me, O LORD, and test me.
  Look closely into my heart and mind.
³ I see your mercy in front of me.
  I walk in the light of your truth.
⁴ I did not sit with liars,
  and I will not be found among hypocrites.
⁵ I have hated the mob of evildoers
  and will not sit with wicked people.
⁶ I will wash my hands in innocence.
  I will walk around your altar, O LORD,
⁷ so that I may loudly sing a hymn of thanksgiving
  and tell about all your miracles.

⁸ O LORD, I love the house where you live,
  the place where your glory dwells.

⁹ Do not sweep away my soul along with hardened sinners
  or my life along with bloodthirsty people.

10   Evil schemes are in their hands.
        Their right hands are full of bribes.
11 But I walk with integrity.
        Rescue me, and have pity on me.
12 My feet stand on level ground.
    I will praise the LORD with the choirs in worship.

Psalm 27

By David.

1 The LORD is my light and my salvation.
        Who is there to fear?
    The LORD is my life's fortress.
        Who is there to be afraid of?

2 Evildoers closed in on me to tear me to pieces.
        My opponents and enemies stumbled and fell.
3   Even though an army sets up camp against me,
            my heart will not be afraid.
        Even though a war breaks out against me,
            I will still have confidence ⌐in the LORD⌐.

4 I have asked one thing from the LORD.
    This I will seek:
        to remain in the LORD's house all the days of my life
            in order to gaze at the LORD's beauty
                and to search for an answer in his temple.
5 He hides me in his shelter when there is trouble.
    He keeps me hidden in his tent.
    He sets me high on a rock.
6 Now my head will be raised above my enemies who
        surround me.
    I will offer sacrifices with shouts of joy in his tent.
    I will sing and make music to praise the LORD.
7 Hear, O LORD, when I cry aloud.
    Have pity on me, and answer me.
8 ⌐When you said,⌐
    "Seek my face,"
        my heart said to you,
            "O LORD, I will seek your face."[a]
9   Do not hide your face from me.
            Do not angrily turn me away.
        You have been my help.
            Do not leave me!
            Do not abandon me, O God, my savior!
10   Even if my father and mother abandon me,
                the LORD will take care of me.
11 Teach me your way, O LORD.
    Lead me on a level path

my feet firmly planted, and I'll
worship you along with
your people.

27:1 You're my light and my
salvation, so I have nothing to
fear. With you as my fortress, I'm
scared by no one.

27:2–3 Evildoers surrounded
me to tear me apart, but they
tripped and fell. Even if an army
declared war on me, I would
count on you.

27:4 There's only one thing I
want from you—to live each day
so close to you that I can gaze on
your beauty and get the answers
I need.

27:5–6 You shelter me from my
troubles. You raise me above my
enemies. I shout joyfully to you!

27:8–9 You invite me to seek
you—and so my heart searches
high and low for more of you. Let
me see your face. Don't push me
away in anger.

27:9–10 Savior, don't abandon
me! I will trust you to care for me
even when I'm discarded by the
people who should love me most.

27:11–12 Teach me to know
and do your will. Don't hand me

---

[a] 27:8 Hebrew meaning uncertain; Greek "My heart said to you, 'I have
sought your face. O LORD, I will seek your face.'"

over to people who want to
do me in.

27:13–14 I'm convinced I'll
live to see your goodness, so I'll
keep hoping in you. Fill me with
strength and courage as
I await you!

because I have enemies who spy on me.
[12] Do not surrender me to the will of my opponents.
False witnesses have risen against me.
They breathe out violence.
[13] I believe that I will see the goodness of the LORD
in this world of the living.

[14] Wait with hope for the LORD.
Be strong, and let your heart be courageous.
Yes, wait with hope for the LORD.

Psalm 28

By David.

28:1–3 I've built my life on you,
O my rock, so answer me before I
die. I'm begging for mercy. Don't
punish me along with two-faced
troublemakers, people who hate
and harm their neighbors.

[1] O LORD, I call to you.
O my rock, do not turn a deaf ear to me.
If you remain silent,
I will be like those who go into the pit.
[2] Hear my prayer for mercy when I call to you for help,
when I lift my hands toward your most holy place.
[3] Do not drag me away with wicked people,
with troublemakers who speak of peace with
their neighbors
but have evil in their hearts.

28:4–5 Pay back evildoers for
their evil deeds. Give them what
they deserve. Demolish them
and leave them broken. Why?
Because they don't acknowledge
a single thing you have done.

[4] Pay them back for what they have done,
for their evil deeds.
Pay them back for what their hands have done,
and give them what they deserve.
[5] The LORD will tear them down and never build them
up again,
because they never consider what he has done
or what his hands have made.

28:6–7 Thank you for hearing
my plea for mercy! I trusted you
and got help, so my heart
sings in triumph.

[6] Thank the LORD!
He has heard my prayer for mercy!
[7] The LORD is my strength and my shield.
My heart trusted him, so I received help.
My heart is triumphant; I give thanks to him with
my song.

28:8–9 You are strong for
your people. You ensure your
Messiah's victory. Save us.
Shepherd us. Carry us forever.

[8] The LORD is the strength of his people
and a fortress for the victory of his Messiah.[a]
[9] Save your people, and bless those who belong to you.
Be their shepherd, and carry them forever.

Psalm 29

A psalm by David.

29:1–2 Let every heavenly
being praise your glory and
power. Let them recognize the
worthiness of your name. Let

[1] Give to the LORD, you heavenly beings.
Give to the LORD glory and power.
[2] Give to the LORD the glory his name deserves.

[a] 28:8 Or "anointed one."

Worship the LORD in ⌊his⌋ holy splendor.

³The voice of the LORD rolls over the water.
  The God of glory thunders.
  The LORD shouts over raging water.
⁴The voice of the LORD is powerful.
  The voice of the LORD is majestic.
⁵The voice of the LORD breaks the cedars.
  The LORD splinters the cedars of Lebanon.
⁶ He makes Lebanon skip along like a calf
    and Mount Sirion like a wild ox.
⁷The voice of the LORD strikes with flashes of lightning.
⁸The voice of the LORD makes the wilderness tremble.
  The LORD makes the wilderness of
    Kadesh tremble.
⁹The voice of the LORD splits the oaksᵃ
  and strips ⌊the trees of⌋ the forests bare.
  Everyone in his temple is saying, "Glory!"

¹⁰The LORD sat enthroned over the flood.
  The LORD sits enthroned as king forever.
¹¹The LORD will give power to his people.
  The LORD will bless his people with peace.

Psalm 30

A psalm by David sung at the dedication of the temple.

¹I will honor you highly, O LORD,
  because you have pulled me out ⌊of the pit⌋
    and have not let my enemies rejoice over me.
²O LORD my God,
  I cried out to you for help,
    and you healed me.
³O LORD, you brought me up from the grave.
  You called me back to life
    from among those who had gone into the pit.
⁴Make music to praise the LORD, you faithful people
    who belong to him.
  Remember his holiness by giving thanks.
⁵His anger lasts only a moment.
  His favor lasts a lifetime.
    Weeping may last for the night,
    but there is a song of joy in the morning.

⁶When all was well with me, I said,
  "I will never be shaken."
⁷O LORD, by your favor you have made my mountain
    stand firm.
  When you hid your face, I was terrified.
⁸I will cry out to you, O LORD.

them bow whenever they see
your magnificence.

29:3–6 Your voice thunders
over the ocean, powerful and
majestic. It splits towering trees.
It makes the nation skip like
a calf.

29:7–9 Your voice strikes like
lightning. Its thunder strips the
forests bare. Everyone who sees
you shouts "Glory!"

29:10–11 You ruled mightily
over the flood, and you will reign
as King forever. Give your people
power, and bless us with your
peace.

30:1–3 Nothing and no one
deserves more honor than you,
because you plucked me from
the pit. You kept my enemies
from dancing on my grave. You
healed me and rescued me from
death itself.

30:4 Because I belong to you I
make music to praise you. I think
about your holiness and give you
thanks.

30:5 Your anger lasts only a
moment, but your favor lasts a
lifetime. Even if I weep all night, I
will sing for joy in the morning.

30:6–9 When my life went well,
I was sure nothing could shake
me. But when you hid, I feared
my own bloody death. I wondered
how that would help your cause.

ᵃ 29:9 Hebrew meaning of "splits the oaks" uncertain.

Can my dead body thank you?
Can it tell anyone your truth?

30:10–12 Your help turned my sobbing into dancing. You stripped off my mourning clothes and wrapped me with joy. I'll sing to you forever. I'll never be silent.

I will plead to the Lord for mercy:
⁹ "How will you profit if my blood is shed,
if I go into the pit?
Will the dust ˪of my body˩ give thanks to you?
Will it tell about your truth?"
¹⁰ Hear, O Lord, and have pity on me!
O Lord, be my helper!
¹¹ You have changed my sobbing into dancing.
You have removed my sackcloth and clothed me
with joy
¹² so that my soul[a] may praise you with music and not
be silent.
O Lord my God, I will give thanks to you forever.

Psalm 31

For the choir director; a psalm by David.

31:1–2 I look to you for help. Don't make me feel stupid for counting on you. Come help me quickly and be the strength I need.

¹ I have taken refuge in you, O Lord.
Never let me be put to shame.
Save me because of your righteousness.
² Turn your ear toward me.
Rescue me quickly.
Be a rock of refuge for me,
a strong fortress to save me.

31:3–6 Lead me and bring honor to your name. Break me free from my enemies' secret traps. You save me and speak honestly with me, so I trust my innermost self to you. I won't trust strange gods.

³ Indeed, you are my rock and my fortress.
For the sake of your name, lead me and guide me.
⁴ You are my refuge,
so pull me out of the net that they have secretly
laid for me.
⁵ Into your hands I entrust my spirit.
You have rescued me, O Lord, God of truth.

⁶ I hate those who cling to false gods, but I trust the Lord.

31:7–8 You noticed my misery inside and out. You didn't hand me over to my enemies. You put my feet on free land.

⁷ I will rejoice and be glad because of your mercy.
You have seen my misery.
You have known the troubles in my soul.
⁸ You have not handed me over to the enemy.
You have set my feet in a place where I can
move freely.

31:9–10 Years of agony have laid waste to my entire being. I stagger under the guilty burden I've piled on my own shoulders.

⁹ Have pity on me, O Lord, because I am in distress.
My eyes, my soul, and my body waste away
from grief.
¹⁰ My life is exhausted from sorrow,
my years from groaning.
My strength staggers under ˪the weight of˩ my guilt,
and my bones waste away.

31:11–13 My opponents have made me such a disgrace that

¹¹ I have become a disgrace because of all
my opponents.

ᵃ 30:12 Or "glory."

I have become someone dreaded by my friends,
even by my neighbors.
Those who see me on the street run away
from me.
¹² I have faded from memory as if I were dead
and have become like a piece of broken pottery.
¹³ I have heard the whispering of many people—
terror on every side—
while they made plans together against me.
They were plotting to take my life.

¹⁴I trust you, O Lord.
I said, "You are my God."

¹⁵My future is in your hands.
Rescue me from my enemies, from those who
persecute me.
¹⁶ Smile on me.
Save me with your mercy.
¹⁷O Lord, I have called on you, so do not let me be put
to shame.
Let wicked people be put to shame.
Let them be silent in the grave.
¹⁸Let ⌊their⌋ lying lips be speechless,
since they speak against righteous people with
arrogance and contempt.

¹⁹Your kindness is so great!
You reserve it for those who fear you.
Adam's descendants watch
as you show it to those who take refuge in you.
²⁰ You hide them in the secret place of your presence
from those who scheme against them.
You keep them in a shelter,
safe from quarrelsome tongues.
²¹Thank the Lord!
He has shown me the miracle of his mercy
in a city under attack.
²²When I was panic-stricken, I said,
"I have been cut off from your sight."
But you heard my pleas for mercy when I cried out to
you for help.
²³Love the Lord, all you godly ones!
The Lord protects faithful people,
but he pays back in full those who act arrogantly.
²⁴Be strong, all who wait with hope for the Lord,
and let your heart be courageous.

even my friends and neighbors dread me. They treat me like trash, a tossed-out piece of shattered pottery. They whisper plans to destroy me.

31:14–16 In the midst of all my troubles I still trust in you. I forever call you my God. My future belongs to you, so smile on me.

31:17–18 I've prayed to you, so don't let me be put to shame. Let it be evildoers who experience disgrace. Stop their arrogant lies against good people.

31:19–20 You burst with kindness toward those who respect you. All humankind can see how you shower love on those who count on you, protecting them with your presence and sparing them from quarrels.

31:22 I panicked when I thought I'd lost you. But you heard my cries and came to help.

31:23–24 Help me persist in my love for you. Protect your followers and pay back the arrogant. Give courageous hearts to everyone who counts on you.

Psalm 32

A psalm by David; a maskil.[a]

32:1–2 Your forgiveness is proof that I'm blessed. My happiness returns when you pardon my guilt.

[1] Blessed is the person whose disobedience is forgiven
  and whose sin is pardoned.
[2] Blessed is the person whom the Lord no longer accuses of sin
  and who has no deceitful thoughts.

32:3–5 My bones shook when I hid my sins from you. Your judgment weighed on me day and night. Your heat baked away all my strength. But you forgave my sins when I quit hiding my guilt.

[3] When I kept silent ⌐about my sins⌐,
  my bones began to weaken because of my groaning all day long.
[4] Day and night your hand laid heavily on me.
  My strength shriveled in the summer heat.   *Selah*

[5] I made my sins known to you, and I did not cover up my guilt.
  I decided to confess them to you, O Lord.
  Then you forgave all my sins.   *Selah*

32:6 Use my pain to teach others to pray to you quickly— before floods overwhelm them.

[6] For this reason let all godly people pray to you
  when you may be found.
    Then raging floodwater will not reach them.

32:7 You're my hiding place, my protection from every trouble. You joyfully sing me songs to remind me that you save me.

[7] You are my hiding place.
  You protect me from trouble.
  You surround me with joyous songs of salvation. *Selah*

32:8–9 You promise you'll watch me and teach me how to live. I promise I'll hear your instructions and quickly obey. You won't have to bridle me like a beast to make me listen.

[8] ⌐The Lord says,⌐
  "I will instruct you.
  I will teach you the way that you should go.
  I will advise you as my eyes watch over you.
[9] Don't be stubborn like a horse or mule.
    ⌐They need⌐ a bit and bridle in their mouth to
      restrain them,
    or they will not come near you."

32:10–11 Take me far away from the heartaches of sin. Surround me with mercy as I trust you. You are my joy!

[10] Many heartaches await wicked people,
  but mercy surrounds those who trust the Lord.

[11] Be glad and find joy in the Lord, you righteous people.
  Sing with joy, all whose motives are decent.

Psalm 33

33:1–3 I'll sing joyfully to you. I'll sing thanks to you. I refuse to sing tired old words to you. I'll find beautiful new songs.

[1] Joyfully sing to the Lord, you righteous people.
  Praising ⌐the Lord⌐ is proper for decent people.
[2] Give thanks with a lyre to the Lord.
  Make music for him on a ten-stringed harp.
[3] Sing a new song to him.
  Play beautifully and joyfully on stringed instruments.

33:4–5 Your every word is true. Your every deed is dependable.

[4] The word of the Lord is correct,

---

[a] 32:1 Unknown musical term.

and everything he does is trustworthy.
⁵The LORD loves righteousness and justice.
His mercy fills the earth.
⁶The heavens were made by the word of the LORD
and all the stars by the breath of his mouth.
⁷He gathers the water in the sea like a dam
and puts the oceans in his storehouses.
⁸Let all the earth fear the LORD.
Let all who live in the world stand in awe of him.
⁹He spoke, and it came into being.
He gave the order, and there it stood.

¹⁰The LORD blocks the plans of the nations.
He frustrates the schemes of the people of the world.
¹¹ The LORD's plan stands firm forever.
His thoughts stand firm in every generation.
¹²Blessed is the nation whose God is the LORD.
Blessed are the people he has chosen as his own.

¹³The LORD looks down from heaven.
He sees all of Adam's descendants.
¹⁴From the place where he sits enthroned,
he looks down upon all who live on earth.
¹⁵The one who formed their hearts
understands everything they do.

¹⁶No king achieves a victory with a large army.
No warrior rescues himself by his own great strength.
¹⁷Horses are not a guarantee for victory.
Their great strength cannot help someone escape.
¹⁸The LORD's eyes are on those who fear him,
on those who wait with hope for his mercy
¹⁹ to rescue their souls from death
and keep them alive during a famine.

²⁰We wait for the LORD.
He is our help and our shield.
²¹ In him our hearts find joy.
In his holy name we trust.
²²Let your mercy rest on us, O LORD,
since we wait with hope for you.

You love doing right and acting justly. Your mercy spills over on the whole earth.

33:6–9 Your Word lit up the heavens. Your hands stretched the ocean shores. I stand in awe of you. A command from your mouth brought everything into existence.

33:10–12 You frustrate evildoers' goals but your own plans always succeed. Your chosen people live in your blessing.

33:13–15 From your throne you watch all humankind. Because you made our hearts, you understand everything we do.

33:16–20 There's not a single battle I can win in my own strength. There's no mighty thing or powerful person who can help me like you do. You watch out for me because I live in awe of you. I look to you to save me from hunger and death. I wait for you.

33:21–22 In you I find joy. In your perfect holiness I discover calm. Show mercy to me and everyone who relies on you.

Psalm 34^a

By David when he pretended to be insane in the presence of Abimelech; Abimelech threw him out, so David left.

¹I will thank the LORD at all times.
My mouth will always praise him.
²My soul will boast about the LORD.
Those who are oppressed will hear it and rejoice.
³Praise the LORD's greatness with me.

34:1–2 I won't stop thanking you or praising you or boasting about you. Oppressed people will be glad to hear of your greatness.

---

^a 34:1 Psalm 34 is a poem in Hebrew alphabetical order.

34:5 I shine because of you. Shame never covers my face.

34:6–7 Even at my poorest I can count on you to answer. You stand watch over all who respect you.

34:8–10 I test you in real life and you prove your goodness. Because I hide in you, I'm blessed. Because I belong to you, I never lack. You promise to meet my every real need.

34:11 I come to you like a trusting child. Teach me to live in awe of you.

34:12–14 I can't expect a long and full life if I don't quit evil. Help me do good and find peace.

34:15–16 Moment by moment you keep watch over me, but you erase every sign that evildoers even existed.

34:18–20 You feel nearest when I bow to you. You save me when I'm crushed. You rescue me when I'm in trouble. You keep me whole.

Let us highly honor his name together.
⁴ I went to the LORD for help.
   He answered me and rescued me from all my fears.
⁵ All who look to him will be radiant.ᵃ
   Their faces will never be covered with shame.
⁶ Here is a poor man who called out.
   The LORD heard him and saved him from all
      his troubles.
⁷ The Messenger of the LORD camps around those who
      fear him,
   and he rescues them.
⁸ Taste and see that the LORD is good.
   Blessed is the person who takes refuge in him.
⁹ Fear the LORD, you holy people who belong to him.
   Those who fear him are never in need.
¹⁰ Young lions go hungry and may starve,
   but those who seek the LORD's help have all the good
      things they need.
¹¹ Come, children, listen to me.
   I will teach you the fear of the LORD.
¹² Which of you wants a full life?
   Who would like to live long enough to enjoy
      good things?
¹³   Keep your tongue from saying evil things
      and your lips from speaking deceitful things.
¹⁴   Turn away from evil, and do good.
      Seek peace, and pursue it!
¹⁵ The LORD's eyes are on righteous people.
   His ears hear their cry for help.
¹⁶ The LORD confronts those who do evil
   in order to wipe out all memory of them from
      the earth.
¹⁷ ⌐Righteous people⌐ cry out.
   The LORD hears and rescues them from all
      their troubles.
¹⁸ The LORD is near to those whose hearts are humble.
   He saves those whose spirits are crushed.
¹⁹ The righteous person has many troubles,
   but the LORD rescues him from all of them.
²⁰   The LORD guards all of his bones.
      Not one of them is broken.
²¹ Evil will kill wicked people,
   and those who hate righteous people will
      be condemned.
²² The LORD protects the souls of his servants.
   All who take refuge in him will never be condemned.

ᵃ 34:5 Hebrew meaning uncertain.

Psalm 35

By David.

¹ O Lᴏʀᴅ, attack those who attack me.
 Fight against those who fight against me.
² Use your shields, ⌐both⌐ small and large.
 Arise to help me.
³ Hold your spear to block the way of those who
 pursue me.
 Say to my soul, "I am your savior."

⁴ Let those who seek my life be put to shame
 and disgraced.
 Let those who plan my downfall be turned back
 in confusion.
⁵ Let them be like husks blown by the wind
 as the Messenger of the Lᴏʀᴅ chases them.
⁶ Let their path be dark and slippery
 as the Messenger of the Lᴏʀᴅ pursues them.
⁷ For no reason they hid their net in a pit.
 For no reason they dug the pit ⌐to trap me⌐.
⁸ Let destruction surprise them.
 Let the net that they hid catch them.
 Let them fall into their own pit and be destroyed.
⁹ My soul will find joy in the Lᴏʀᴅ
 and be joyful about his salvation.
¹⁰ All my bones will say, "O Lᴏʀᴅ, who can compare
 with you?
 You rescue the weak person from the one who is too
 strong for him
 and weak and needy people from the one who
 robs them."

¹¹ Malicious people bring charges against me.
 They ask me things I know nothing about.
¹² I am devastated
 because they pay me back with evil instead of good.
¹³ But when they were sick, I wore sackcloth.
 I humbled myself with fasting.
 When my prayer returned unanswered,
¹⁴ I walked around as if I were mourning for my
 friend or my brother.
 I was bent over as if I were mourning for
 my mother.

¹⁵ Yet, when I stumbled,
 they rejoiced and gathered together.
 They gathered together against me.
 Unknown attackers tore me apart without stopping.
¹⁶ With crude and abusive mockers,
 they grit their teeth at me.
¹⁷ O Lord, how long will you look on?

35:1–3 Fight those who fight me. Raise your shields and block my pursuers. Convince my quaking heart that you will save me.

35:4–6 Disgrace the people aiming to do me in. Confuse their plans. Scatter them. Chase them down a dark and slippery path.

35:7–8 My enemies turned on me for no reason. Catch them when they won't see you coming. Push them into the same pit they dug for me.

35:9–10 My soul thrills at the thought of you and your salvation. In the core of my bones I know that nothing compares with you. You rescue me from enemies too strong for me.

35:11–15 Hateful people accuse me of things I know nothing about. Even when I do them good they pay me back with evil. I see them hurting and respond by mourning for their pain. I fast and pray for them. Yet they attack me and won't stop.

35:16–18 Can't you see how these crude mockers threaten me? How long will you watch and do nothing? Lions pounce on me. Rescue me now! Then I will praise you for all your people to hear.

35:19–22 My enemies pretend to talk peace at the same time they plot to destroy me. They drum up false charges against me, but you have seen the truth. Stop their gloating. End their laughter.

35:22–24 Don't be silent. Don't wander from me. Wake up and defend me. Measure me by your perfect standard.

35:25–28 My enemies assume they've beat me. They think they've swallowed me alive. Disgrace those gloaters. Warm the hearts of everyone who believes in my innocence. Give them reason to praise your greatness.

36:1–4 You've convinced me: Rebellion flows from a heart that forgets to fear you. So don't let me flatter myself or overlook my guilt. Make my words true and my actions wise. When I map out my life, I'll choose to go your direction.

36:5–6 Your mercy and faithfulness stretch to the skies. Your righteousness looms as

Rescue me from their attacks.
Rescue my precious life from the lions.
18 I will give you thanks in a large gathering.
I will praise you in a crowd ⌐of worshipers⌐.

19 Do not let my treacherous enemies gloat over me.
Do not let those who hate me for no reason wink
⌐at me⌐.
20 They do not talk about peace.
Instead, they scheme against the peaceful people in the land.
21 They open their big mouths and say about me,
"Aha! Aha! Our own eyes have seen it."
22 You have seen it, O LORD.
Do not remain silent.
O Lord, do not be so far away from me.
23 Wake up, and rise to my defense.
Plead my case, O my God and my Lord.
24 Judge me by your righteousness, O LORD my God.
Do not let them gloat over me
25 or think, "Aha, just what we wanted!"
Do not let them say, "We have swallowed him up."
26 Let those who gloat over my downfall
be thoroughly put to shame and confused.
Let those who promote themselves at my expense
be clothed with shame and disgrace.
27 Let those who are happy when I am declared innocent
joyfully sing and rejoice.
Let them continually say, "The LORD is great.
He is happy when his servant has peace."
28 Then my tongue will tell about your righteousness,
about your praise all day long.

Psalm 36

For the choir director; by David, the LORD's servant.

1 There is an inspired truth about the wicked person
who has rebellion in the depths of his heart:
He is not terrified of God.
2 He flatters himself and does not hate or ⌐even⌐
recognize his guilt.
3 The words from his mouth are ⌐nothing but⌐ trouble
and deception.
He has stopped doing what is wise and good.
4 He invents trouble while lying on his bed
and chooses to go the wrong direction.
He does not reject evil.

5 O LORD, your mercy reaches to the heavens,
your faithfulness to the skies.
6 Your righteousness is like the mountains of God,

your judgments like the deep ocean.
You save people and animals, O Lord.
[7] Your mercy is so precious, O God,
that Adam's descendants take refuge
in the shadow of your wings.
[8] They are refreshed with the rich foods in your house,
and you make them drink from the river of
your pleasure.
[9] Indeed, the fountain of life is with you.
In your light we see light.
[10] Continue to show your mercy to those who know you
and your righteousness to those whose motives
are decent.
[11] Do not let the feet of arrogant people step on me
or the hands of wicked people push me away.
[12] Look at the troublemakers who have fallen.
They have been pushed down and are unable to
stand up again.

large as the mountains. Your wisdom runs as deep as the sea.

36:7–9 Your mercy reaches everyone who hides in your shadow. Refresh me with your richness. Let me drink full of everything you delight in. Light my life.

36:10–11 Keep showing me mercy, and let me see your righteousness one more time. Don't let arrogant people walk all over me.

Psalm 37[a]

By David.

[1] Do not be preoccupied with evildoers.
Do not envy those who do wicked things.
[2] They will quickly dry up like grass
and wither away like green plants.
[3] Trust the Lord, and do good things.
Live in the land, and practice being faithful.
[4] Be happy with the Lord,
and he will give you the desires of your heart.
[5] Entrust your ways to the Lord.
Trust him, and he will act ⌐on your behalf⌐.
[6] He will make your righteousness shine like a light,
your just cause like the noonday sun.
[7] Surrender yourself to the Lord, and wait patiently
for him.
Do not be preoccupied with ⌐an evildoer⌐ who
succeeds in his way
when he carries out his schemes.
[8] Let go of anger, and leave rage behind.
Do not be preoccupied.
It only leads to evil.
[9] Evildoers will be cut off ⌐from their inheritance⌐,
but those who wait with hope for the Lord will
inherit the land.
[10] In a little while a wicked person will vanish.
Then you can carefully examine where he was,
but there will be no trace of him.

37:1–2 I refuse to let evildoers cloud my mind for even a minute. They're just like grass that quickly dries and withers.

37:3–5 I'll trust in you and do good. I'll live close to you and practice being faithful. When I make you my greatest happiness, you'll grant me my heart's desire. When I trust my life to you, you'll act on my behalf.

37:7–11 I'll let go of my rage. I won't allow myself to envy the prosperity of evildoers. I'll quit pondering their supposed success before I'm tempted to join them in sin. Evildoers will vanish, but if I count on you I'll endure and enjoy peace.

a 37:1 Psalm 37 is a poem in Hebrew alphabetical order.

37:12–15 The wicked plot my ruin because I do good. But you laugh at them, knowing their end is near. They'll be destroyed by their own weapons.

37:16–18 I would rather do good and have a little than sin and have a lot. I trust you to support me in my everyday struggles.

37:19 Don't let me be put to shame. Feed me even when I'm surrounded by famine.

37:21–22 I'll repay my debts and be generous with all I have.

37:23–24 You direct my steps. You like the path you plan for me. If I stumble you'll catch me, because you hold on to my hand.

37:25–27 You'll never abandon me or let me go hungry. You provide for me so I can give and lend freely. I'll do good with eternity in mind.

37:28–29 You love justice. You won't abandon people committed to you. I'll live close to you forever.

37:31–33 Your teachings fill my heart, and I follow them wherever I go. Evildoers want to kill me, but you protect me from their power.

---

¹¹ Oppressed people will inherit the land
   and will enjoy unlimited peace.
¹² The wicked person plots against a righteous one
   and grits his teeth at him.
¹³ The Lord laughs at him
   because he has seen that his time is coming.
¹⁴ Wicked people pull out their swords and bend their bows
   to kill oppressed and needy people,
   to slaughter those who are decent.
¹⁵ ⌊But⌋ their own swords will pierce their hearts,
   and their bows will be broken.
¹⁶ The little that the righteous person has is better
   than the wealth of many wicked people.
¹⁷ The arms of wicked people will be broken,
   but the Lord continues to support righteous people.
¹⁸ The Lord knows the daily ⌊struggles⌋ of
   innocent people.
   Their inheritance will last forever.
¹⁹ They will not be put to shame in trying times.
   Even in times of famine they will be satisfied.
²⁰ But wicked people will disappear.
   The Lord's enemies will vanish like the best part of
   a meadow.
   They will vanish like smoke.
²¹ A wicked person borrows, but he does not repay.
   A righteous person is generous and giving.
²²   Those who are blessed by him will inherit the land.
   Those who are cursed by him will be cut off.
²³ A person's steps are directed by the Lord,
   and the Lord delights in his way.
²⁴ When he falls, he will not be thrown down headfirst
   because the Lord holds on to his hand.
²⁵ I have been young, and now I am old,
   but I have never seen a righteous person abandoned
   or his descendants begging for food.
²⁶   He is always generous and lends freely.
      His descendants are a blessing.
²⁷ Avoid evil, do good, and live forever.
²⁸ The Lord loves justice,
   and he will not abandon his godly ones.
   They will be kept safe forever,
   but the descendants of wicked people will be cut off.
²⁹ Righteous people will inherit the land
   and live there permanently.
³⁰ The mouth of the righteous person reflects on wisdom.
   His tongue speaks what is fair.
³¹ The teachings of his God are in his heart.
   His feet do not slip.
³² The wicked person watches the righteous person
   and seeks to kill him.

³³ But the Lord will not abandon him to the wicked
    person's power
  or condemn him when he is brought to trial.
³⁴ Wait with hope for the Lord, and follow his path,
  and he will honor you by giving you the land.
    When wicked people are cut off, you will see it.

³⁵ I have seen a wicked person ⌐acting like⌐ a tyrant,
  spreading himself out like a large cedar tree.
³⁶ But he moved on, and now there is no trace of him.
  I searched for him, but he could not be found.
³⁷ Notice the innocent person,
  and look at the decent person,
    because the peacemaker has a future.
³⁸   But rebels will be completely destroyed.
      The future of wicked people will be cut off.
³⁹ The victory for righteous people comes from the Lord.
  He is their fortress in times of trouble.
⁴⁰ The Lord helps them and rescues them.
  He rescues them from wicked people.
  He saves them because they have taken refuge in him.

37:34–36 When I follow your path, I encounter blessings of every kind. Though the wicked seem strong and healthy, they die and vanish.

37:37–40 Innocent people have hope and a future, but rebels will be utterly destroyed. I depend on you as my fortress and victory, my help and my rescuer. I'll always take refuge in you.

Psalm 38

*A psalm by David; to be kept in mind.*ᵃ

¹ O Lord, do not angrily punish me
  or discipline me in your wrath.
²   Your arrows have struck me.
    Your hand has struck me hard.
³ No healthy spot is left on my body
  because of your rage.
  There is no peace in my bones
  because of my sin.

⁴ My guilt has overwhelmed me.
  Like a heavy load, it is more than I can bear.
⁵ My wounds smell rotten.
  They fester because of my stupidity.
⁶ I am bent over and bowed down very low.
  All day I walk around in mourning.
⁷ My insides are filled with burning pain,
  and no healthy spot is left on my body.
⁸ I am numb and completely devastated.
  I roar because my heart's in turmoil.
⁹ You know all my desires, O Lord,
  and my groaning has not been hidden from you.
¹⁰ My heart is pounding.
  I have lost my strength.
    Even the light of my eyes has left me.

38:1–4 Quit punishing me! Your hand has already struck me hard and bruised my whole body. My bones shake because of my sin. My guilt crushes me.

38:5–8 My wounds stink because my sins were so stupid. My shoulders sag as I walk around in mourning. My insides burn. I'm numb. My heart reels with such turmoil I do nothing but groan.

38:10–12 My heart pounds and my strength has vanished. I can't even see straight. People

ᵃ 38:1 Hebrew meaning of "to be kept in mind" uncertain.

who love me stay away because
I'm diseased, and my enemies
plot ways to ruin me.

38:13–16 I'm deaf, mute,
defenseless. But I'm sure you'll
answer me. You'll keep my
enemies from gloating and
gaining an edge over me.

38:17–18 I'm ready to fall
over. Pain constantly nags me. I
confess my guilt to you because
my sin troubles me.

38:19–22 My enemies keep
getting stronger, many who hate
me for no reason. They punish
me for doing good. So don't be
distant from me. Come quickly to
help me, my Savior!

39:1–3 I tried hard not to sin
with my words, but keeping silent
did me no good. My mind raced
and my pain grew worse. My
heart burned until I spoke up.

39:4–5 I need you to remind
me that my days are short.
The span of my life is nothing
compared to your eternal
existence. I'm just a whisper in
the wind.

[11] My loved ones and my friends keep their distance
and my relatives stand far away because of
my sickness.
[12] Those who seek my life lay traps for me.
Those who are out to harm me talk about ruining me.
All day long they think of ways to deceive me.
[13] But I am like a person who cannot hear
and like a person who cannot speak.
[14] I am like one who cannot hear
and who can offer no arguments.

[15] But I wait with hope for you, O LORD.
You will answer, O Lord, my God.
[16] I said, "Do not let them gloat over me.
When my foot slips,
do not let them promote themselves at
my expense."

[17] I am ready to fall.
I am continually aware of my pain.
[18] I confess my guilt.
My sin troubles me.

[19] My mortal enemies are growing stronger.
Many hate me for no reason.
[20] They pay me back with evil instead of good,
and they accuse me because I try to do what is good.

[21] Do not abandon me, O LORD.
O my God, do not be so distant from me.
[22] Come quickly to help me, O Lord, my savior.

Psalm 39

For the choir director; for Jeduthun; a psalm by David.

[1] I said,
"I will watch my ways so that I do not sin with
my tongue.
I will bridle my mouth while wicked people are in
my presence."
[2] I remained totally speechless.
I kept silent, although it did me no good.
While I was deep in thought, my pain grew worse.
[3] My heart burned like a fire flaring up within me.
Then I spoke with my tongue:
[4] "Teach me, O LORD, about the end of my life.
Teach me about the number of days I have left
so that I may know how temporary my life is.
[5] Indeed, you have made the length of my days ⌊only⌋
a few inches.
My life span is nothing compared to yours.
Certainly, everyone alive is like a whisper in
the wind. *Selah*

⁶ Each person who walks around is like a shadow.
    They are busy for no reason.
        They accumulate riches without knowing who
            will get them."

⁷ And now, Lord, what am I waiting for?
    My hope is in you!
⁸ Rescue me from all my rebellious acts.
    Do not disgrace me in front of godless fools.
⁹ I remained speechless.
    I did not open my mouth
        because you are the one who has done this.
¹⁰ Remove the sickness you laid upon me.
        My life is over because you struck me with
           your hand.
¹¹ With stern warnings you discipline people for
        their crimes.
    Like a moth you eat away at what is dear to them.
    Certainly, everyone is like a whisper in the wind. *Selah*

¹² Listen to my prayer, O LORD.
    Open your ear to my cry for help.
    Do not be deaf to my tears,
        for I am a foreign resident with you,
           a stranger like all my ancestors.
¹³ Look away from me so that I may smile again
        before I go away and am no more.

Psalm 40

For the choir director; a psalm by David.

¹ I waited patiently for the LORD.
    He turned to me and heard my cry for help.
² He pulled me out of a horrible pit,
        out of the mud and clay.
    He set my feet on a rock
        and made my steps secure.
³ He placed a new song in my mouth,
        a song of praise to our God.
           Many will see this and worship.
           They will trust the LORD.
⁴ Blessed is the person
        who places his confidence in the LORD
           and does not rely on arrogant people
           or those who follow lies.
⁵ You have done many miraculous things, O LORD
    my God.
    You have made many wonderful plans for us.
        No one compares to you!
    I will tell others about your miracles,
        which are more than I can count.

39:6 People are just shadows. They act busy but accomplish nothing, because someone else always gets what they accumulate.

39:7–8 I'm waiting for you to help me! Rescue me from my rebellion. Don't disgrace me in front of fools who don't believe in you.

39:9–11 I've kept silent because you're the one who makes me suffer. Remove my sickness and save me before I die. You have disciplined me for my crimes.

39:12–13 Hear my prayers. I feel like a stranger to you. Turn away your wrath so I can live.

40:1–2 I waited for you and you helped me. You pulled me out of a muddy pit, then set my feet on solid rock.

40:3 You filled me with a new song of praise to you. Many will see how you rescued me. They'll worship and trust you.

40:4 I'm completely satisfied when I count on you instead of trusting proud people.

40:5 You do more miracles than I can count. You have wonderful plans for me. No one compares to you!

40:6–8 You don't want my sacrifices. You want my obedience. I'm happy to do your will. Your words live deep inside me.

40:9–10 You know I can't keep quiet about you. I won't keep silent about your righteousness and faithfulness and salvation. I promise to tell others about your mercy and truth.

40:11–12 Don't hold back your kindness. Protect me with your mercy and truth. I'm surrounded by countless evils and my own wrongdoing blinds me.

40:12–15 My sins outnumber the hairs on my head—and I am discouraged. Rescue me quickly. Confuse those who want to kill me. Disgrace those who want my downfall. Stun them with their own shame.

40:16–17 I will rejoice and be glad because of you. Because I love your salvation, I will continually speak of your greatness. You are my Savior. Help me now!

41:1–3 Because I worry about the helpless, you'll rescue me from my own troubles. You'll protect me and keep me alive.

⁶ You were not pleased with sacrifices and offerings.
　You have dug out two ears for me.[a]
　You did not ask for burnt offerings or sacrifices for sin.
⁷　Then I said, "I have come!
　　　(It is written about me in the scroll of the book.)
⁸　　I am happy to do your will, O my God."
　Your teachings are deep within me.
⁹ I will announce the good news of righteousness
　　among those assembled for worship.
　　I will not close my lips.
　　　You know that, O Lord.
¹⁰ I have not buried your righteousness deep in my heart.
　I have been outspoken about your faithfulness and
　　your salvation.
　I have not hidden your mercy and your truth
　　from those assembled for worship.

¹¹ Do not withhold your compassion from me, O Lord.
　May your mercy and your truth always protect me.
¹²　Countless evils have surrounded me.
　　My sins have caught up with me so that I can no
　　　longer see.
　　They outnumber the hairs on my head.
　　I have lost heart.

¹³ O Lord, please rescue me!
　Come quickly to help me, O Lord![b]
¹⁴ Let all those who seek to end my life
　　be confused and put to shame.
　Let those who want my downfall
　　be turned back and disgraced.
¹⁵ Let those who say to me, "Aha! Aha!"
　　be stunned by their own shame.
¹⁶ Let all who seek you rejoice and be glad because of you.
　Let those who love your salvation continually say,
　　"The Lord is great!"

¹⁷ But I am oppressed and needy.
　May the Lord think of me.
　　You are my help and my savior.
　　O my God, do not delay!

Psalm 41

For the choir director; a psalm by David.

¹ Blessed is the one who has concern for helpless people.
　　The Lord will rescue him in times of trouble.
²　The Lord will protect him and keep him alive.
　　He will be blessed in the land.

---

[a] 40:6 Hebrew meaning of this line uncertain.
[b] 40:13 Verses 13–17 are virtually identical in wording to Psalm 70.

Do not place him at the mercy of his enemies.
³ The LORD will support him on his sickbed.
You will restore this person to health when he is ill.

⁴I said, "O LORD, have pity on me!
Heal my soul because I have sinned against you."
⁵My enemies say terrible things about me:
"When will he die, and when will his family
name disappear?"
⁶When one of them comes to visit me, he
speaks foolishly.
His heart collects gossip.
⌐Then⌐ he leaves to tell others.
⁷Everyone who hates me whispers about me.
They think evil things about me and say,
⁸ "A devilish disease has attached itself to him.
He will never leave his sickbed."
⁹Even my closest friend whom I trusted,
the one who ate my bread,
has lifted his heel against me.
¹⁰Have pity on me, O LORD!
Raise me up so that I can pay them back
¹¹ and my enemy cannot shout in triumph over me.
When you do this, I know that you are pleased
with me.
¹²You defend my integrity,
and you set me in your presence forever.

¹³ Thank the LORD God of Israel through
all eternity!
Amen and amen!

You'll shower me with your blessings and restore my health.

41:4–6 I cry to you for pity because I've sinned against you. My enemies can't wait for me to die and disappear. The only reason they visit me is to see my suffering and gossip about me.

41:7–9 People who hate me are whispering about me. They say I'm too sick to recover. Even my most trusted friend has turned on me.

41:10–11 Pity me! Heal me so I can pay back my enemies and silence their shouts of victory. Then I will know that I please you.

41:12–13 Defend my integrity. Let me live close to you forever. I'll thank you now and forever!

BOOK TWO

(Psalms 42–72)

Psalm 42

For the choir director; a maskil[a] *by Korah's descendants.*

¹As a deer longs for flowing streams,
so my soul longs for you, O God.
²My soul thirsts for God, for the living God.
When may I come to see God's face?
³My tears are my food day and night.
People ask me all day long, "Where is your God?"
⁴I will remember these things as I pour out my soul:
how I used to walk with the crowd
and lead it in a procession to God's house.
⌐I sang⌐ songs of joy and thanksgiving
while crowds of people celebrated a festival.

42:1–2 I long for you like a deer thirsts for fresh streams. I want more and more of the living God. When can I see your face?

42:3–4 Everyone hears my crying and wonders why you've deserted me. I used to lead crowds in jubilant worship.

a 42:1 Unknown musical term.

42:5–6 Why am I so discouraged and agitated when I have you as my Savior? When sadness takes me down, I'll purposely focus on you.

42:7–9 My soul's despair runs as deep as the sea. Your judgment sweeps over me like waves. All day and night you send me mercy, but still I wonder why you've forgotten me.

42:10–11 My enemies keep asking where you are. Their taunts shatter my bones. I keep telling myself to trust you. I praise you, my Savior and God.

43:1–2 Examine me, O God, then plead my case against liars. I've run to you for protection. So why do you reject me and force me to mourn and suffer?

43:3–4 Send your light and truth to guide me home to you. Welcome me close and I'll sing thanks to you. You are God, my highest joy.

⁵ Why are you discouraged, my soul?
  Why are you so restless?
    Put your hope in God,
      because I will still praise him.
        He is my savior and my God.

⁶ My soul is discouraged.
    That is why I will remember you
      in the land of Jordan, on the peaks of Hermon,
        on Mount Mizar.
⁷ One deep sea calls to another at the roar of
      your waterspouts.
  All the whitecaps on your waves have swept
      over me.ᵃ
⁸ The LORD commands his mercy during the day,
    and at night his song is with me—
      a prayer to the God of my life.
⁹   I will ask God, my rock,
        "Why have you forgotten me?
        Why must I walk around in mourning
          while the enemy oppresses me?"
¹⁰   With a shattering blow to my bones,
        my enemies taunt me.
          They ask me all day long, "Where is
            your God?"

¹¹   Why are you discouraged, my soul?
      Why are you so restless?
        Put your hope in God,
          because I will still praise him.
            He is my savior and my God.

Psalm 43

¹ Judge me, O God,
    and plead my case against an ungodly nation.
  Rescue me from deceitful and unjust people.
² You are my fortress, O God!
      Why have you rejected me?
      Why must I walk around in mourning
        while the enemy oppresses me?
³ Send your light and your truth.
    Let them guide me.
    Let them bring me to your holy mountain
      and to your dwelling place.
⁴ Then let me go to the altar of God, to God my
      ⌐highest⌐ joy,
        and I will give thanks to you on the lyre, O God,
          my God.

⁵   Why are you discouraged, my soul?

ᵃ 42:7 Hebrew meaning of this verse uncertain.

Why are you so restless?
Put your hope in God,
    because I will still praise him.
        He is my savior and my God.

Psalm 44

For the choir director; a maskil *by Korah's descendants.*

¹O God,
    we have heard it with our own ears.
Our ancestors have told us
    about the miracle you performed in their day,
        in days long ago.
²By your power you forced nations ˌout of the landˌ,
    but you planted our ancestors ˌthereˌ.
You shattered many groups of people,
    but you set our ancestors free.ᵃ
³It was not with their swords that they took possession
        of the land.
    They did not gain victory with their own strength.
It was your right hand, your arm,
    and the light of your presence ˌthat did itˌ,
        because you were pleased with them.

⁴You alone are my king, O God.
    You won those victories for Jacob.
⁵ With you we can walk over our enemies.
    With your name we can trample those who attack us.
⁶   I do not rely on my bow,
        and my sword will never save me.
⁷But you saved us from our enemies.
    You put to shame those who hate us.
⁸All day long we praise our God.
    We give thanks to you forever.   *Selah*

⁹But now you have rejected and disgraced us.
    You do not even go along with our armies.
¹⁰ You make us retreat from the enemy.
        Those who hate us rob us at will.
¹¹ You hand us over to be butchered like sheep
        and scatter us among the nations.
¹² You sell your people for almost nothing,
        and at that price you have gained nothing.
¹³ You made us a disgrace to our neighbors
        and an object of ridicule and contempt to those
            around us.
¹⁴ You made our ˌdefeatˌ a proverb among the nations
        so that people shake their heads at us.
¹⁵All day long my disgrace is in front of me.
    Shame covers my face

43:5 I'm discouraged and restless. But I keep reminding myself to trust and praise you. You'll always be my Savior and God.

44:1–2 I've heard the story of the miracle you did long ago. With brute strength you pushed out nations and planted your followers in a good land. You shattered others but set us free.

44:3 No human power gave your people victory. Only you did. Your might and your presence accomplished your purpose.

44:4–6 You alone are my King and God. You're my victory. You give me power to walk over my enemies. Human weapons can't save me.

44:7–8 You save me, putting people who hate me to shame. All day long I praise and thank you.

44:9–12 Long ago you did a miracle. But now you've rejected me and left me to fight my battles alone. I'm forced to retreat. I'm feeling robbed, butchered, and lost. You're selling me out.

44:13–16 My neighbors ridicule me. In fact, the story of my defeat has become legend. People shake their heads at me. Shame smears my face. My enemies spare no insult.

ᵃ 44:2 Or "and you sent them away."

16   because of the words of those who insult and
                slander us,
        because of the presence of the enemy and
                the avenger.

44:17–19 Despite my suffering I never gave up on your promises. I never stopped loving or obeying you. Yet you crushed me and shrouded me in death.

17 Although all of this happened to us,
        we never forgot you.
        We never ignored your promise.[a]
18   Our hearts never turned away.
        Our feet never left your path.
19 Yet, you crushed us in a place for jackals
        and covered us with the shadow of death.

44:20–22 You'd know if I forgot you. You'd overhear if I prayed to another god. But I'm dying because of you. I'm nothing but a sheep ready for slaughter.

20 If we forgot the name of our God
        or stretched out our hands to pray to another god,
21   wouldn't God find out,
                since he knows the secrets in our hearts?
22 Indeed, we are being killed all day long because of you.
        We are thought of as sheep to be slaughtered.

44:23–26 Wake up! Why are you sleeping? Why are you hiding from me and forgetting my misery? My body lies in the dirt. Be merciful and help me!

23 Wake up! Why are you sleeping, O Lord?
        Awake! Do not reject us forever!
24   Why do you hide your face?
        Why do you forget our suffering and misery?
25   Our souls are bowing in the dust.
                Our bodies cling to the ground.
26   Arise! Help us!
                Rescue us because of your mercy!

Psalm 45

For the choir director; according to shoshannim;[b] *a* maskil
by Korah's descendants; a love song.

45:1–2 My heart overflows with good news. You, O King, inspire my song. You are the most handsome of all human beings. Grace fills your lips.

1 My heart is overflowing with good news.
        I will direct my song to the king.
        My tongue is a pen for a skillful writer.

2 You are the most handsome of Adam's descendants.
        Grace is poured on your lips.
                That is why God has blessed you forever.

45:3–4 Mount your steed for the cause of truth, humility, and goodness. Show off your splendor and majesty.

3 O warrior, strap your sword to your side
        with your splendor and majesty.
4 Ride on victoriously in your majesty
        for the cause of truth, humility, and righteousness.
        Let your right hand teach you awe-inspiring things.
5 Your arrows are sharp in the heart of the king's enemies.
        Nations fall beneath you.

45:6–7 Your throne, O God, endures forever. Your reign

6 Your throne, O God, is forever and ever.
        The scepter in your kingdom is a scepter for justice.
7 You have loved what is right and hated what is wrong.

---

[a] 44:17 Or "covenant."
[b] 45:1 Unknown musical term.

That is why God, your God, has anointed you,
    rather than your companions, with the oil of joy.
[8] All your robes are ⌐fragrant⌐ with myrrh, aloes,
    and cassia.
From ivory palaces the music of stringed instruments
    delights you.
[9] The daughters of kings are among your noble ladies.
The queen takes her place at your right hand
    and wears gold from Ophir.

[10] Listen, daughter! Look closely!
Turn your ear ⌐toward me⌐.
Forget your people, and forget your father's house.
[11] The king longs for your beauty.
      He is your Lord.
      Worship him.

[12] The people of Tyre, the richest people,
    want to win your favor with a gift.
[13] The daughter of the king is glorious inside ⌐the palace⌐.
Her dress is embroidered with gold.
[14] Wearing a colorful gown, she is brought to the king.
Her bridesmaids follow her.
    They will be brought to you.
[15]   With joy and delight they are brought in.
      They enter the palace of the king.

[16] Your sons will take the place of your father.
You will make them princes over the whole earth.

[17] I will cause your name to be remembered throughout
    every generation.
That is why the nations will give thanks to you forever
    and ever.

Psalm 46

For the choir director; a song by the descendants of Korah; according to alamoth.[a]

[1] God is our refuge and strength,
    an ever-present help in times of trouble.
[2] That is why we are not afraid
    even when the earth quakes
      or the mountains topple into the depths of the sea.
[3]   Water roars and foams,
        and mountains shake at the
            surging waves.   *Selah*

[4] There is a river
    whose streams bring joy to the city of God,
      the holy place where the Most High lives.

45:9–11 Your bride is at your right hand. Her beauty is all for you. She worships you.

45:12–15 Outsiders will honor your bride. She is dazzling as she enters your presence.

45:17 Every generation will recall your majestic name. Every nation will thank you forever and ever.

46:1–3 You're my refuge and strength, my always-present help in trouble. So I won't fear when the ground shakes or mountains tumble, when waters roar or waves surge against the mountains.

46:4–5 Your presence brings joy to your people. Nothing can

---

[a] 46:1 Unknown musical term.

stands for justice. You love what's right and hate what's wrong.

topple your holy city, because you are there.

46:6–7 Turmoil engulfs the world and kingdoms tumble. The earth melts when it hears your voice. But you're my strength.

46:8–9 I can see your works, the judgments you pour out on earth. You end wars and halt violence.

46:10–11 When I let go of my concerns, I find rest in you, ruler of the whole earth. Your strength is with me. You're my stronghold.

⁵ God is in that city.
　　It cannot fall.
　　　God will help it at the break of dawn.
⁶ Nations are in turmoil, and kingdoms topple.
　　The earth melts at the sound of ⌐God's⌐ voice.

⁷ The Lord of Armies is with us.
　　The God of Jacob is our stronghold.　　　*Selah*

⁸ Come, see the works of the Lord,
　　the devastation he has brought to the earth.
⁹ 　　He puts an end to wars all over the earth.
　　　He breaks an archer's bow.
　　　He cuts spears in two.
　　　He burns chariots.
¹⁰ Let go ⌐of your concerns⌐!
　　Then you will know that I am God.
　　　I rule the nations.
　　　I rule the earth.

¹¹ The Lord of Armies is with us.
　　The God of Jacob is our stronghold.　　　*Selah*

Psalm 47

For the choir director; a psalm by Korah's descendants.

47:1–4 I'll clap and shout a joyful song to you. I live in awe of you, Lord Most High. You're the great King of the whole world. You're the source of my power. You're the gift-giver of everything I have.

¹ Clap your hands, all you people.
　　Shout to God with a loud, joyful song.
² We must fear the Lord, the Most High.
　　He is the great king of the whole earth.
³ 　　He brings people under our authority
　　　　and ⌐puts⌐ nations under our feet.
⁴ 　　He chooses our inheritance for us,
　　　　the pride of Jacob, whom he loved.　　*Selah*

47:6–7 I'll make music to praise my King. You rule the whole earth, so I'll bring you my very best.

⁵ God has gone up with a joyful shout.
　　The Lord has gone up with the sound of a ram's horn.
⁶ 　　Make music to praise God.
　　　　Play music for him!
　　　Make music to praise our king.
　　　　Play music for him!
⁷ God is the king of the whole earth.
　　Make your best music for him!
⁸ God rules the nations.
　　He sits upon his holy throne.

47:8–9 From your holy throne you rule the world. Powerful people from every nation gather as your own. Every human ruler belongs to you. You rule it all!

⁹ The influential people from the nations gather together
　　as the people of the God of Abraham.
　　The rulers of the earth belong to God.
　　　He rules everything.

Psalm 48

A song; a psalm by Korah's descendants.

[1] The LORD is great.
He should be highly praised.
His holy mountain is in the city of our God.
[2] Its beautiful peak is the joy of the whole earth.
Mount Zion is on the northern ridge.
It is the city of the great king.
[3] God is in its palaces.
He has proved that he is a stronghold.

[4] The kings have gathered.
They marched together.
[5] ⌐When⌐ they saw ⌐Mount Zion⌐,
they were astonished.
They were terrified and ran away in fear.
[6] Trembling seized them
like the trembling that a woman experiences
during labor.
[7] With the east wind you smash the ships of Tarshish.

[8] The things we had only heard about, we have now seen
in the city of the LORD of Armies,
in the city of our God.
God makes Zion stand firm forever.   *Selah*
[9] Inside your temple we carefully reflect on your mercy,
O God.
[10] Like your name, O God,
your praise ⌐reaches⌐ to the ends of the earth.
Your right hand is filled with righteousness.
[11] Let Mount Zion be glad
and the cities of Judah rejoice
because of your judgments.

[12] Walk around Zion.
Go around it.
Count its towers.
[13] Examine its embankments.
Walk through its palaces.
Then you can tell the next generation,
[14] "This God is our God forever and ever.
He will lead us beyond death."

48:1–3 You're great—and you deserve the highest praise. You dwell among your people on your holy mountain. Your presence graces your palace.

48:4–6 Kings march against you only to flee in fear when they see your dwelling. They tremble like women in labor.

48:8 I'd only heard of your power, but now I've seen it with my own eyes.

48:9–10 As I come near you I'll reflect on your mercy. Praise for you reaches to the ends of the earth.

48:11–14 I'm glad because of your wise judgments. I'll tell everyone who comes after me that you are God forever and ever. You'll guide us to death and beyond.

Psalm 49

For the choir director; a psalm by Korah's descendants.

[1] Listen to this, all you people.
Open your ears, all who live in the world—
[2] common people and important ones,
rich people and poor ones.
[3] My mouth will speak wise sayings,

49:1–3 Let everyone in the world hear my words—everyday people and powerful people, the poor and the rich. Let them hear the wisdom you've taught me.

the insights I have carefully considered.
[4] I will turn my attention to a proverb.
I will explain my riddle with the ⌊music of⌋ a lyre.

49:5–9 Why should I fear when slanderers surround me with evil? They think money means everything and brag about their abundance. But money can't buy a life. Wealth won't save a soul from death.

[5]   Why should I be afraid in times of trouble,
when slanderers surround me with evil?
[6]   They trust their riches
and brag about their abundant wealth.

[7] No one can ever buy back another person
or pay God a ransom for his life.
[8]   The price to be paid for his soul is too costly.
He must always give up
[9]   in order to live forever and never see the pit.

49:10–12 Everyone dies. Both the smart and the stupid die and leave their wealth behind. No mortal can enjoy earthly treasures forever.

[10] Indeed, one can see that wise people die,
that foolish and stupid people meet the same end.
They leave their riches to others.
[11] Although they named their lands after themselves,
their graves[a] have become their homes for ages
to come,
their dwelling places throughout
every generation.

[12] But mortals will not continue here with what
they treasure.
They are like animals that die.

[13] This is the final outcome for fools and their followers
who are delighted by what they say: *Selah*

49:14–15 Death pushes fools and their followers to the grave as if they were sheep. But you will buy my freedom from hell and welcome me to yourself.

[14]   Like sheep, they are driven to hell
with death as their shepherd.
(Decent people will rule them in the morning.)
Their forms will decay in the grave,
far away from their comfortable homes.
[15] But God will buy me back from the power of hell
because he will take me.   *Selah*

49:16–20 I won't fear when people pile up wealth or build big houses. They can't take anything with them, and their greatness will end when they die. The wealthy congratulate themselves and others who do well at making money, but they don't understand they will die like animals.

[16] Do not be afraid when someone becomes rich,
when the greatness of his house increases.
[17]   He will not take anything with him when he dies.
His greatness cannot follow him.
[18] Even though he blesses himself while he is alive
(and they praise you when you do well for yourself),
[19]   he must join the generation of his ancestors,
who will never see light ⌊again⌋.

[20] Mortals, with what they treasure, still don't
have understanding.
They are like animals that die.

---

[a] 49:11 Greek, Syriac, Targum; Masoretic Text "their insides."

Psalm 50

A psalm by Asaph.

[1] The LORD, the only true God, has spoken.
He has summoned the earth
from where the sun rises to where it sets.
[2] God shines from Zion,
the perfection of beauty.
[3] Our God will come and will not remain silent.
A devouring fire is in front of him
and a raging storm around him.
[4] He summons heaven and earth to judge his people:
[5] "Gather around me, my godly people
who have made a pledge to me through sacrifices."

[6] The heavens announce his righteousness
because God is the judge.   *Selah*

[7] "Listen, my people, and I will speak.
Listen, Israel, and I will testify against you:
I am God, your God!
[8] I am not criticizing you for your sacrifices or
burnt offerings,
which are always in front of me.
[9] ⌐But⌐ I will not accept ⌐another⌐ young bull from
your household
or a single male goat from your pens.
[10] Every creature in the forest,
⌐even⌐ the cattle on a thousand hills, is mine.
[11] I know every bird in the mountains.
Everything that moves in the fields is mine.
[12] If I were hungry, I would not tell you,
because the world and all that it contains are mine.
[13] Do I eat the meat of bulls or drink the blood of goats?
[14] Bring ⌐your⌐ thanks to God as a sacrifice,
and keep your vows to the Most High.
[15] Call on me in times of trouble.
I will rescue you, and you will honor me."

[16] But God says to wicked people,
"How dare you quote my decrees
and mouth my promises![a]
[17] You hate discipline.
You toss my words behind you.
[18] When you see a thief, you want to make friends
with him.
You keep company with people who
commit adultery.
[19] You let your mouth say anything evil.
Your tongue plans deceit.

50:1–2 You're the one true God, shining with beauty on your throne.

50:1–6 You've gathered your people and won't keep your thoughts to yourself. A devouring fire warns your judgment is near. The heavens announce your righteousness.

50:7–9 You're God, deserving every kind of worship. Yet you don't want another sacrifice. You don't need any more offerings.

50:10–13 Everything in the world is yours. If you were hungry you wouldn't ask people for something to eat, because everything in the world is yours.

50:14–15 You don't need sacrifices and offerings. What you really long for is gratitude and obedience and worship.

50:16–17 You hate when I mouth your commands but don't keep them. I need your discipline. I want to hold tight to your words.

50:18–20 Don't let me partner with thieves or sexual sinners. Stop me when I lie and spread gossip.

---

[a] 50:16 Or "covenant."

20 You sit and talk against your own brother.
You slander your own mother's son.
21 When you did these things, I remained silent.
ᴸThatᴶ made you think I was like you.
I will argue my point with you
and lay it all out for you to see.
22 Consider this, you people who forget God.
Otherwise, I will tear you to pieces,
and there will be no one left to rescue you.
23 Whoever offers thanks as a sacrifice honors me.
I will let everyone who continues in my way
see the salvation that comes from God."

50:21–22 If you don't confront me when I sin, I'll think you don't care. Speak to me now! Tear me to pieces if I ever forget you.

50:23 Thanksgiving is the sacrifice that truly honors you. I want to obey you fully and see your salvation.

Psalm 51

For the choir director; a psalm by David when the prophet Nathan came to him after David's adultery with Bathsheba.

51:1–2 Pity me because of your mercy. With your unlimited compassion wipe away my rebellion. Cleanse every bit of my sin.

1 Have pity on me, O God, in keeping with your mercy.
In keeping with your unlimited compassion, wipe out
my rebellious acts.
2 Wash me thoroughly from my guilt,
and cleanse me from my sin.

51:3–5 I admit I'm rebellious. I've sinned against many but against none more than you. You're right to judge me. I've been sinful my whole life.

3 I admit that I am rebellious.
My sin is always in front of me.
4 I have sinned against you, especially you.
I have done what you consider evil.
So you hand down justice when you speak,
and you are blameless when you judge.

5 Indeed, I was born guilty.
I was a sinner when my mother conceived me.

51:6–8 You desire genuine truth and sincerity, so teach me wisdom deep inside. Scour me thoroughly, and I'll finally be clean. Give me joy and fix my broken places.

6 Yet, you desire truth and sincerity.[a]
Deep down inside me you teach me wisdom.
7 Purify me from sin with hyssop,[b] and I will be clean.[c]
Wash me, and I will be whiter than snow.
8 Let me hear ᴸsounds ofᴶ joy and gladness.
Let the bones that you have broken dance.
9 Hide your face from my sins,
and wipe out all that I have done wrong.

51:9–12 Wipe away my guilt and give me a clean and faithful heart. Don't push me away or take back your Spirit. Make me glad to be saved and eager to obey.

10 Create a clean heart in me, O God,
and renew a faithful spirit within me.
11 Do not force me away from your presence,
and do not take your Holy Spirit from me.
12 Restore the joy of your salvation to me,
and provide me with a spirit of willing obedience.

---

[a] 51:6 Hebrew meaning uncertain.
[b] 51:7 Branches from the hyssop plant were used in purification rites.
[c] 51:7 "Clean" refers to anything that Moses' Teachings say is presentable to God.

¹³ ⌐Then⌐ I will teach your ways to those who
are rebellious,
and sinners will return to you.
¹⁴ Rescue me from the guilt of murder,
O God, my savior.
Let my tongue sing joyfully about your righteousness!
¹⁵ O Lord, open my lips,
and my mouth will tell about your praise.
¹⁶ You are not happy with any sacrifice.
Otherwise, I would offer one ⌐to you⌐.
You are not pleased with burnt offerings.
¹⁷ The sacrifice pleasing to God is a broken spirit.
O God, you do not despise a broken and
sorrowful heart.
¹⁸ Favor Zion with your goodness.
Rebuild the walls of Jerusalem.
¹⁹ Then you will be pleased with sacrifices offered in the
right spirit—
with burnt offerings and whole burnt offerings.
Young bulls will be offered on your altar.

51:13 Give me the chance to teach rebels and lead sinners back to you.

51:14–15 Rescue me from the worst of my sins. I'll let my tongue praise your righteousness.

51:16–19 If a sacrifice could satisfy you I'd give it. But I'll bring the broken heart you desire. Favor me with your goodness. Rebuild me and the people I've hurt. Then you'll be pleased.

Psalm 52

For the choir director; a maskil; *a psalm by David when Doeg (who was from Edom) told Saul that David had come to Ahimelech's home.*

¹ Why do you brag about the evil you've done, you hero?
The mercy of God lasts all day long!
² Your tongue makes up threats.
It's like a sharp razor, you master of deceit.
³ You prefer evil to good.
You prefer lying to speaking the truth.   *Selah*
⁴ You love every destructive accusation, you
deceitful tongue!

⁵ But God will ruin you forever.
He will grab you and drag you out of your tent.
He will pull your roots out of this world of
the living.   *Selah*
⁶ Righteous people will see ⌐this⌐ and be struck
with fear.
They will laugh at you and say,
⁷ "Look at this person who refused to make God
his fortress!
Instead, he trusted his great wealth
and became strong through his greed."

⁸ But I am like a large olive tree in God's house.
I trust the mercy of God forever and ever.
⁹ I will give thanks to you forever
for what you have done.

52:1–3 Why do evildoers brag about their sins? These masters of deceit speak razor-sharp lies. They prefer evil to good.

52:4–5 Evildoers love to hurt others. But you'll ruin the wicked. You'll drag them out of this world of the living.

52:6–7 I'll be filled with awe when I see you act. Show me the foolishness of trusting money instead of you.

52:8–9 Make me flourish as I'm planted close to you. I'll forever trust in your mercy. I'll always give you thanks. Together with your people I'll continue to count on you.

In the presence of your godly people,
  I will wait with hope in your good name.

Psalm 53[a]

For the choir director; according to mahalath,[b] *a maskil by David.*

53:1 Fools think you don't exist. They sin and do nothing good.

[1] Godless fools say in their hearts,
  "There is no God."
They are corrupt.
They do disgusting things.
  There is no one who does good things.

53:2–3 You study all humankind to see if anyone acts wisely or seeks your help. But all of us have sinned and become rotten to the core. I don't do good. Nor does anyone else.

[2] God looks down from heaven on Adam's descendants
  to see if there is anyone who acts wisely,
    if there is anyone who seeks help from God.
[3] Everyone has fallen away.
    Together they have become rotten to the core.
      No one, not even one person, does good things.

53:4 Troublemakers swallow up your people. Are evildoers completely ignorant of you?

[4] Are all those troublemakers,
  those who devour my people as if they were
    devouring food,
  so ignorant that they do not call on God?

53:5 Give our enemies reason to panic. Scatter their bones. Shame and reject them.

[5] There they are—panic-stricken—
  ⌊but⌋ there was no reason to panic,
    because God has scattered the bones
      of those who set up camp against you.[c]
You put them to shame.
  After all, God has rejected them.

53:6 Send victory from your throne! Restore the fortunes of your people and give us reason to be glad.

[6] If only salvation for Israel would come from Zion!
When God restores the fortunes of his people,
  Jacob will rejoice.
  Israel will be glad.

Psalm 54

For the choir director; on stringed instruments; a maskil by David when people from the city of Ziph told Saul that David was hiding among them.

54:1–3 Save me because of your character. Defend me with your power. I'm under attack by people who ignore you, so don't ignore my pleas.

[1] O God, save me by your name,
  and defend me with your might.
[2] O God, hear my prayer,
  and open your ears to the words from my mouth.

[3] Strangers have attacked me.
Ruthless people seek my life.
  They do not think about God.[d]   *Selah*

---

[a] 53:1 Psalm 53 is virtually identical in wording to Psalm 14.
[b] 53:1 Unknown musical term.
[c] 53:5 Hebrew meaning uncertain.
[d] 54:3 Hebrew meaning of this line uncertain.

⁴God is my helper!
The Lord is the provider for my life.
⁵ My enemies spy on me.
Pay them back with evil.
Destroy them with your truth!

⁶I will make a sacrifice to you along with a
freewill offering.
I will give thanks to your good name, O LORD.
⁷ Your name rescues me from every trouble.
My eyes will gloat over my enemies.

54:4–5 You help me and provide for my life. Pay back evil to people who spy on me. Destroy them with your truth!

54:6–7 I offer everything to you because you're good. When you rescue me I'll watch my enemies go down in defeat.

Psalm 55

For the choir director; on stringed instruments; a maskil
by David.

¹Open your ears to my prayer, O God.
Do not hide from my plea for mercy.
²Pay attention to me, and answer me.
My thoughts are restless, and I am confused
³ because my enemy shouts at me
and a wicked person persecutes me.
They bring misery crashing down on me,
and they attack me out of anger.
⁴My heart is in turmoil.
The terrors of death have seized me.
⁵ Fear and trembling have overcome me.
Horror has overwhelmed me.
⁶I said, "If only I had wings like a dove—
I would fly away and find rest.
⁷ Indeed, I would run far away.
I would stay in the desert.   *Selah*
⁸ I would hurry to find shelter
from the raging wind and storm."

⁹Completely confuse their language, O Lord,
because I see violence and conflict in the city.
¹⁰Day and night they go around on ⌞top of⌟ the city walls.
Trouble and misery are everywhere.
¹¹ Destruction is everywhere.
Oppression and fraud never leave the streets.[a]

¹²If an enemy had insulted me,
then I could bear it.
If someone who hated me had attacked me,
then I could hide from him.
¹³But it is you, my equal,
my best friend,
one I knew so well!

55:1–2 Pay attention to me! Hear my prayers and don't hide when I plead for mercy.

55:2–3 I can't think straight with my enemy shouting so loudly. Protect me from the misery crashing down on me.

55:4–8 Trembling overwhelms me. Deathly terrors seize me. Horrors bury me. I wish I could fly away to find rest or run away to the desert. I need shelter from the raging storm.

55:9–11 Confuse my enemies, the violent ones who creep around spreading misery.

55:12–14 I wouldn't be so grief-stricken if an enemy had attacked me. But it was my best friend who turned on me, someone I trusted and considered an equal in faith.

[a] 55:11 Or "its marketplace."

14 We used to talk to each other in
    complete confidence
    and walk into God's house with the
    festival crowds.

15 Let death suddenly take ⌐wicked people⌐!
    Let them go into the grave while they are still alive,
        because evil lives in their homes as well as in
        their hearts.
16 But I call on God,
    and the LORD saves me.
17 Morning, noon, and night I complain and groan,
    and he listens to my voice.
18 With ⌐his⌐ peace, he will rescue my soul
    from the war waged against me,
        because there are many ⌐soldiers fighting⌐
        against me.
19 God will listen.
    The one who has sat enthroned from the beginning
        will deal with them.   *Selah*
            They never change. They never fear God.
20 ⌐My best friend⌐ has betrayed his friends.
    He has broken his solemn promise.
21   His speech is smoother than butter,
        but there is war in his heart.
    His words are more soothing than oil,
        but they are like swords ready to attack.
22 Turn your burdens over to the LORD,
    and he will take care of you.
        He will never let the righteous person stumble.
23 But you, O God, will throw ⌐wicked people⌐ into the
    deepest pit.
        Bloodthirsty and deceitful people will not live out
        half their days.
        But I will trust you.

55:16–18 I call on you and you save me. I groan day and night and you hear me. Your peace will rescue my soul. You'll deal with my enemies from your eternal throne.

55:19–21 Evildoers never change. I'm not the only one my best friend has betrayed. Over and over he's broken his promises then smoothed things over with slippery words.

55:22–23 I give you my burdens and trust myself to your care. Keep me from stumbling. I'll always keep trusting you.

Psalm 56

For the choir director; according to yonath elem rechokim;[a] *a* miktam *by David when the Philistines captured him in Gath.*

1 Have pity on me, O God, because people are
    harassing me.
    All day long warriors oppress me.
2   All day long my enemies spy on me.
    They harass me.
        There are so many fighting against me.
3 Even when I am afraid, I still trust you.

4   I praise the word of God.

56:1–2 Pity me! I'm harassed and oppressed, the target of spies watching me without a break. I'm surrounded by enemies.

56:3–4 Even when fear grips me I keep trusting you. You quiet my fears. How can mere people hurt me?

---

a 56:1 Unknown musical term.

I trust God.
I am not afraid.
What can mere flesh ⌐and blood⌐ do to me?

[5] All day long my enemies twist my words.
Their every thought is an evil plan against me.
[6] They attack, and then they hide.
They watch my every step as they wait to take my life.
[7] With the wrong they do, can they escape?
O God, angrily make the nations fall.
[8] (You have kept a record of my wanderings.
Put my tears in your bottle.
They are already in your book.)
[9] Then my enemies will retreat when I call ⌐to you⌐.
This I know: God is on my side.

[10] I praise the word of God.
I praise the word of the LORD.
[11] I trust God.
I am not afraid.
What can mortals do to me?

[12] I am bound by my vows to you, O God.
I will keep my vows by offering songs of thanksgiving
to you.
[13] You have rescued me from death.
You have kept my feet from stumbling
so that I could walk in your presence, in the light
of life.

Psalm 57

For the choir director; al tashcheth;[a] *a miktam by David
when he fled from Saul into the cave.*

[1] Have pity on me, O God. Have pity on me,
because my soul takes refuge in you.
I will take refuge in the shadow of your wings
until destructive storms pass by.
[2] I call to God Most High,
to the God who does everything for me.
[3] He sends his help from heaven and saves me.
He disgraces the one who is harassing me.   *Selah*
God sends his mercy and his truth!
[4] My soul is surrounded by lions.
I must lie down with man-eating lions.
Their teeth are spears and arrows.
Their tongues are sharp swords.
[5]   May you be honored above the heavens, O God.
Let your glory extend over the whole earth.

[6] ⌐My enemies⌐ spread out a net to catch me.

---
[a] 57:1 Unknown musical term.

56:5–7 My enemies never stop twisting my words. They attack me, then retreat to prepare another attack. Are you really going to let them escape?

56:8 You remember the times I've wandered from you. You keep all my tears in a bottle.

56:9–11 My enemies flee when I pray to you. My fears fade when I trust in you. Nothing any humans do can hurt me.

56:13 You've rescued me from death. Now keep me walking in the light of your presence.

57:1 Take pity on me, because I hide my whole being in you. I tuck under your wings while life's storms pass by.

57:2–3 I cry to you, God Most High. You do everything for me, sending help from heaven.

57:4 I feel trapped by man-eating lions with mouths like swords.

57:5 You deserve honor higher than the heavens. Your glory reaches to the whole earth.

57:6 When my enemies try to trap me, let them fall into their own pit.

57:7–10 Because of you I'm confident. I'll sing and make music to you. I'll wake up at dawn to say thanks. I'll praise you so everyone realizes that your mercy and truth reach to the skies.

57:11 You deserve honor higher than the heavens. Your glory reaches to the whole earth.

58:1–3 Rulers judge unjustly, while they themselves commit violent crimes. Evildoers are strangers to you from the time they're conceived.

58:4–8 The wicked bite with deadly venom, so knock out their teeth! Make them like water draining away. Let their arrows miss their targets. Make them nothing more than snails leaving slimy trails.

58:9–11 Sweep evildoers away! Good people will be glad when they see you take your revenge. Show us that you're real—and that you're fair.

(My soul is bowed down.)[a]
They dug a pit to trap me,
  but then they fell into it.   *Selah*
[7] My heart is confident, O God.
My heart is confident.
I want to sing and make music.[b]
[8]   Wake up, my soul![c]
  Wake up, harp and lyre!
I want to wake up at dawn.
[9] I want to give thanks to you among the people, O Lord.
I want to make music to praise you among the nations
[10]   because your mercy is as high as the heavens.
    Your truth reaches the skies.

[11]   May you be honored above the heavens, O God.
    Let your glory extend over the whole earth.

Psalm 58

For the choir director; al tashcheth*; a miktam by David.*

[1] Do you rulers really give fair verdicts?
Do you judge Adam's descendants fairly?
[2]   No, you invent new crimes on earth,
    and your hands spread violence.

[3] ⌊Even⌋ inside the womb wicked people are strangers
    ⌊to God⌋.
From their birth liars go astray.
[4]   They have poisonous venom like snakes.
    They are like a deaf cobra that shuts its ears
[5]   so that it cannot hear the voice of a snake charmer
    or of anyone trained to cast spells.

[6] O God, knock the teeth out of their mouths.
  Break the young lions' teeth, O LORD.
[7]   Let them disappear like water that drains away.
    When they aim their bows, let their arrows miss
      the target.[d]
[8]   Let them become like a snail that leaves behind a
      slimy trail
    or like a stillborn child who never sees the sun.
[9]   Let ⌊God⌋ sweep them away
      faster than a cooking pot is heated by
        burning twigs.[e]

[10] Righteous people will rejoice when they see ⌊God⌋
    take revenge.

---

[a] 57:6 Hebrew meaning of this line uncertain.
[b] 57:7 Verses 7–11 are virtually identical in wording to Psalm 108:1–5.
[c] 57:8 Or "my glory."
[d] 58:7 Hebrew meaning of this sentence uncertain.
[e] 58:9 Hebrew meaning uncertain.

They will wash their feet in the blood of
  wicked people.
[11] Then people will say,
  "Righteous people certainly have a reward.
  There is a God who judges on earth."

Psalm 59

*For the choir director; al tashcheth; a miktam by David
when Saul sent men to watch David's home and kill him.*

[1] Rescue me from my enemies, O my God.
  Protect me from those who attack me.
[2] Rescue me from troublemakers.
  Save me from bloodthirsty people.
[3]   They lie in ambush for me right here!
  Fierce men attack me, O LORD,
    but not because of any disobedience,
[4]   or any sin, or any guilt on my part.
  They hurry to take positions against me.
  Wake up, and help me; see ⌞for yourself⌟.
[5] O LORD God of Armies, God of Israel,
  arise to punish all the nations.
  Have no pity on any traitors.   *Selah*

[6]   They return in the evening.
  They howl like dogs.
  They prowl the city.

[7] See what pours out of their mouths—
  swords from their lips!
  ⌞They think,⌟ "Who will hear us?"
[8] O LORD, you laugh at them.
  You make fun of all the nations.

[9]   O my strength, I watch for you!
    God is my stronghold, my merciful God!

[10] God will come to meet me.
  He will let me gloat over those who spy on me.
[11] Do not kill them.
  Otherwise, my people may forget.
  Make them wander aimlessly by your power.
  Bring them down, O Lord, our shield,
[12]   ⌞because of⌟ the sins from their mouths
    and the words on their lips.
  Let them be trapped by their own arrogance
    because they speak curses and lies.
[13] Destroy them in your rage.
  Destroy them until not one of them is left.
    Then they will know that God rules Jacob
      to the ends of the earth.   *Selah*

59:1–3 Rescue me. Protect me. Save me from bloodthirsty troublemakers. Can't you see my enemies waiting in ambush?

59:4–5 My enemies attack me for no reason. See for yourself, then rise up and stop them.

59:6–8 My enemies howl at me like dogs. They speak deadly words, thinking you won't hear them. But you do—and you laugh at them.

59:9–11 Because you're my strength, I'll watch for your help. You'll meet me with mercy and make me victorious over my foes. Keep my enemies alive so others can see how aimlessly they wander.

59:12–13 Trap my enemies with their own arrogant words. Don't let a single one escape. Bring an end to their evil.

59:14–15 My foes prowl the city hunting for something to eat. They stay up all night until they fill their stomachs with kills.

59:16–17 I sing about your strength. I joyfully hum of your mercy. You're my safe place when trouble strikes. I'll always make music to you, my strong and merciful God!

[14] They return in the evening.
They howl like dogs.
They prowl the city.

[15] They wander around to find something to eat.
If they are not full enough,
they will stay all night.

[16] But I will sing about your strength.
In the morning I will joyfully sing about your mercy.
You have been my stronghold
and a place of safety in times of trouble.

[17] O my strength, I will make music to praise you!
God is my stronghold, my merciful God!

Psalm 60

For the choir director; according to shushan eduth;[a] *a* miktam *by David; for teaching. When David fought Aram Naharaim and Aram Zobah, and ⌐when⌐ Joab came back and killed 12,000 men from Edom in the Dead Sea region.*

60:1–2 You've rejected your people and left us defenseless. You shook the land and split it wide open. Heal the land, because it's falling apart.

60:3–4 You're the reason we endure hardship and stagger in confusion. So pull us to safety. Gather us to yourself.

60:6–8 You've spoken and said you're in charge, ruler of all of us. Every place and people belong to you. You're Lord over every enemy.

[1] O God, you have rejected us.
You have broken down our defenses.
You have been angry.
Restore us!

[2] You made the land quake.
You split it wide open.
Heal the cracks in it
because it is falling apart.

[3] You have made your people experience hardships.
You have given us wine that makes us stagger.

[4] Yet, you have raised a flag for those who fear you
so that they can rally to it
when attacked by bows ⌐and arrows⌐.   *Selah*

[5] Save ⌐us⌐ with your powerful hand, and answer us
so that those who are dear to you may be rescued.[b]

[6] God has promised the following through his holiness:
"I will triumph!
I will divide Shechem.
I will measure the valley of Succoth.

[7] Gilead is mine.
Manasseh is mine.
Ephraim is the helmet on my head.
Judah is my scepter.

[8] Moab is my washtub.
I will throw my shoe over Edom.
I will shout in triumph over Philistia."

[9] Who will bring me into the fortified city?

[a] 60:1 Unknown musical term.
[b] 60:5 Verses 5–12 are virtually identical in wording to Psalm 108:6–13.

Who will lead me to Edom?
¹⁰ Isn't it you, O God, who rejected us?
Isn't it you, O God, who refused to accompany
our armies?

¹¹ Give us help against the enemy
because human assistance is worthless.
¹² With God we will display great strength.
He will trample our enemies.

60:10–12 How can we count on you for help when you've rejected your people? Isn't it true that you've refused to stand with us? Human assistance is worthless, so help us now. You alone make us strong.

Psalm 61

For the choir director; on a stringed instrument; by David.

¹ Listen to my cry for help, O God.
Pay attention to my prayer.
² From the ends of the earth, I call to you
when I begin to lose heart.
Lead me to the rock that is high above me.
³ You have been my refuge,
a tower of strength against the enemy.
⁴ I would like to be a guest in your tent forever
and to take refuge under the protection of
your wings.   *Selah*
⁵ O God, you have heard my vows.
You have given me the inheritance
that belongs to those who fear your name.
⁶ Add days upon days to the life of the king.
May his years endure throughout every generation.
⁷ May he sit enthroned in the presence of God forever.
May mercy and truth protect him.
⁸ Then I will make music to praise your name forever,
as I keep my vows day after day.

61:1–2 Hear my cry for help. Pay attention to the words I pray from far-off places. Carry me to a safe and solid place.

61:3–4 You're the place that I run, my safe place. I want to stay and enjoy your protection forever.

61:5–7 You hear everything I promise you—and you give me every gift you promise your people. Give me a long life and let me enjoy your presence forever. Protect me with your mercy and truth.

Psalm 62

For the choir director; according to Jeduthun; a psalm by David.

¹ My soul waits calmly for God alone.
My salvation comes from him.
² He alone is my rock and my savior—my stronghold.
I cannot be severely shaken.

³ How long will all of you attack a person?
How long will you try to murder him,
as though he were a leaning wall or a sagging fence?
⁴ They plan to force him out of his high position.
They are happy to lie.
They bless with their mouths,
but in their hearts they curse.   *Selah*

⁵ Wait calmly for God alone, my soul,

62:1–2 My soul waits calmly for you alone, because only you can save me. You're my rock and Savior. Nothing can shake me.

62:3–4 How long do I have to endure these attacks? People try to topple me like a sagging fence. They'll do anything to take me down.

62:5–7 I wait calmly for you

alone, because my hope comes from you. You're my rock and my fortress.

62:8 Show your people that they can always trust you. Invite them to come close and pour out their hearts to you.

62:9 Common people and powerful people all amount to nothing. Like them I'm less than a whisper in the wind.

62:10–12 I won't turn to extortion or robbery to get rich, and even if you make me wealthy I'll still cling to you. Power and mercy belong to you alone.

because my hope comes from him.
⁶ He alone is my rock and my savior—my stronghold.
    I cannot be shaken.

⁷ My salvation and my glory depend on God.
    God is the rock of my strength, my refuge.
⁸ Trust him at all times, you people.
    Pour out your hearts in his presence.
        God is our refuge.   *Selah*

⁹ Common people are only a whisper in the wind.
    Important people are only a delusion.
        When all of them are weighed on a scale, they amount
            to nothing.
        They are less than a whisper in the wind.
¹⁰ Do not count on extortion ⌊to make you rich⌋.
    Do not hope to gain anything through robbery.
        When riches increase, do not depend on them.

¹¹ God has spoken once.
    I have heard it ⌊said⌋ twice:
        "Power belongs to God.
¹²   Mercy belongs to you, O Lord.
            You reward a person based on what he
                has done."

Psalm 63

A psalm by David when he was in the wilderness of Judah.

63:1 You are my God. I start searching for you at dawn, because my whole being wants more of you. I thirst for you like a desert wanderer.

63:2–4 I look for you to see your power and glory. I'll praise you because your mercy is better than life. I'll thank you forever and lift my hands to you in prayer.

63:5–8 You fill me up like rich food. I remember you all night long. I sing to you from the shadow of your protection. I cling to you and you hold me up.

63:9–11 Those who try to destroy me are done for. Others

¹ O God, you are my God.
    At dawn I search for you.
        My soul thirsts for you.
        My body longs for you
            in a dry, parched land where there is no water.
² So I look for you in the holy place
    to see your power and your glory.
³ My lips will praise you
    because your mercy is better than life ⌊itself⌋.
⁴ So I will thank you as long as I live.
    I will lift up my hands ⌊to pray⌋ in your name.
⁵ You satisfy my soul with the richest foods.
    My mouth will sing ⌊your⌋ praise with joyful lips.
⁶ As I lie on my bed, I remember you.
    Through the long hours of the night, I think about you.
⁷ You have been my help.
    In the shadow of your wings, I sing joyfully.
⁸ My soul clings to you.
    Your right hand supports me.

⁹ But those who try to destroy my life
    will go into the depths of the earth.

10 They will be cut down by swords.
    Their dead bodies will be left as food for jackals.
11 But the king will find joy in God.
    Everyone who takes an oath by God will brag,
        but the mouths of liars will be shut.

Psalm 64

For the choir director; a psalm by David.

1 Hear my voice, O God, when I complain.
    Protect my life from a terrifying enemy.
2 Hide me from the secret plots of criminals,
    from the mob of troublemakers.
3   They sharpen their tongues like swords.
    They aim bitter words like arrows
4   to shoot at innocent people from their
            hiding places.
    They shoot at them suddenly, without any fear.
5   They encourage one another in their evil plans.
    They talk about setting traps and say,
        "Who can see them?"
6   They search for the perfect crime and say,
        "We have perfected a foolproof scheme!"
        Human nature and the human heart are
        a mystery!

7 But God will shoot them with an arrow.
    Suddenly, they will be struck dead.
8 They will trip over their own tongues.
    Everyone who sees them will shake his head.
9 Everyone will be afraid and conclude,
    "This is an act of God!"
    They will learn from what he has done.

10 Righteous people will find joy in the LORD and take
    refuge in him.
    Everyone whose motives are decent will be able to brag.

Psalm 65

For the choir director; a psalm by David; a song.

1 You are praised with silence in Zion, O God,
    and vows ⌐made⌐ to you must be kept.
2 You are the one who hears prayers.
    Everyone will come to you.
3 Various sins overwhelm me.
    You are the one who forgives our rebellious acts.
4 Blessed is the person you choose
    and invite to live with you in your courtyards.
        We will be filled with good food from your house,
        from your holy temple.

---

will finish them off and devour them. I'll find joy in you.

64:1–4 Hear my worried prayers, because I need your protection from terrifying enemies. They take aim at innocent people from safe hideouts.

64:4–6 Evildoers don't worry about getting caught. They think no one is looking. They cook up foolproof schemes.

64:7–10 But you will put an end to evil people and their plans. Their own words will give them away. Everyone will know you caught them and will learn a lesson. You'll make good people happy.

65:1–2 I worship you in silent awe. You hear our prayers. We all look to you.

65:3 My sins overwhelm me, but you forgive all my rebellion.

65:4–5 There's nothing greater than living close to you. You fill me with good food. You do awesome acts of goodness.

You're the hope of everyone
on earth.

65:6–7 You built the mountains. Your power calms the chaos of the oceans and the uproar of humankind.

65:8–9 Everyone on earth lives in awe of you. They know you make the sun rise and set. You care for the earth and make it a good place to live.

65:9–11 You prepare the earth and water our fields. You soften hard soil and bless our crops. The rich harvest shouts your goodness.

65:12–13 You fill the hills with joy. You cover the pastures with flocks and carpet the valleys with grain. Your whole creation shouts to you.

66:1–4 I shout with happiness to you! I praise your bright shining greatness! I can't stop repeating to you all the amazing things you do. The whole earth will join me in worship.

66:5–6 I want others to notice the awe-inspiring things you've done for humankind. You dried up the sea so your people could

5 You answer us with awe-inspiring acts ⌊done⌋
        in righteousness,
    O God, our savior,
        the hope of all the ends of the earth and of the
            most distant sea,
6   the one who set the mountains in place with
            his strength,
        the one who is clothed with power,
7   the one who calms the roar of the seas,
            their crashing waves,
            and the uproar of the nations.
8 Those who live at the ends of the earth are in awe of
        your miraculous signs.
    The lands of the morning sunrise and evening sunset
        sing joyfully.

9 You take care of the earth, and you water it.
    You make it much richer than it was.
        (The river of God is filled with water.)
    You provide grain for them.
        Indeed, you even prepare the ground.
10 You drench plowed fields ⌊with rain⌋
        and level their clumps of soil.
    You soften them with showers
        and bless what grows in them.
11 You crown the year with your goodness,
        and richness overflows wherever you are.
12   The pastures in the desert overflow ⌊with richness⌋.
        The hills are surrounded with joy.
13   The pastures are covered with flocks.
        The valleys are carpeted with grain.
            All of them shout triumphantly. Indeed,
                they sing.

Psalm 66

For the choir director; a song; a psalm.

1 Shout happily to God, all the earth!
2 Make music to praise the glory of his name.
    Make his praise glorious.
3 Say to God,
    "How awe-inspiring are your deeds!
    Your power is so great that your enemies will cringe
            in front of you.
4   The whole earth will worship you.
        It will make music to praise you.
        It will make music to praise your name."   *Selah*
5 Come and see what God has done—
        his awe-inspiring deeds for Adam's descendants.
6   He turned the sea into dry land.
        They crossed the river on foot.

We rejoiced because of what he did there.
7 He rules forever with his might.
His eyes watch the nations.
Rebels will not be able to oppose him.   *Selah*

8 Thank our God, you nations.
Make the sound of his praise heard.
9 He has kept us alive
and has not allowed us to fall.
10 You have tested us, O God.
You have refined us in the same way silver is refined.
11 You have trapped us in a net.
You have laid burdens on our backs.
12 You let people ride over our heads.
We went through fire and water,
but then you brought us out and refreshed us.

13 I will come into your temple with burnt offerings.
I will keep my vows to you,
14 the vows made by my lips and spoken by my
⌐own⌐ mouth
when I was in trouble.
15 I will offer you a sacrifice of fattened livestock for
burnt offerings
with the smoke from rams.
I will offer cattle and goats.   *Selah*

16 Come and listen, all who fear God,
and I will tell you what he has done for me.
17 With my mouth I cried out to him.
High praise was on my tongue.
18 If I had thought about doing anything sinful,
the Lord would not have listened ⌐to me⌐.
19 But God has heard me.
He has paid attention to my prayer.

20 Thanks be to God,
who has not rejected my prayer
or taken away his mercy from me.

Psalm 67

For the choir director; on stringed instruments; a psalm;
a song.

1 May God have pity on us and bless us!
May he smile on us.   *Selah*
2 Then your ways will be known on earth,
your salvation throughout all nations.

3 Let everyone give thanks to you, O God.
Let everyone give thanks to you.
4 Let the nations be glad and sing joyfully

escape from slavery in Egypt.
66:7 You rule the whole world. Anyone who picks a fight with you won't win.

66:8–9 Let the whole world thank you, because you keep us alive. You never let us fall.

66:10–12 You test and refine your people. You put burdens on our backs. We face fire and water. But then you rescue and refresh us.

66:13–15 I'll draw close to you to worship. I'll keep the promises I made when I was in trouble. I'll always offer you my very best.

66:16–19 I want the God-fearers to hear what you've done for me. I cried to you. I praised you as best I know how. If my mind had been set on sinning, you wouldn't have heard me. But you paid attention to my prayers.

67:1–2 Pity us. Bless us. Smile on us. Then everyone will know your ways. The whole world will see your salvation.

67:3–4 We thank you. We sing to you with joy because you're just and guide every nation on earth.

because you judge everyone with justice
and guide the nations on the earth. *Selah*
[5] Let the people give thanks to you, O God.
Let all the people give thanks to you.
[6] The earth has yielded its harvest.
May God, our God, bless us.
[7] May God bless us,
and may all the ends of the earth worship him.

Psalm 68

For the choir director; a psalm by David; a song.

67:5–7 May all humankind experience your blessing. May all of us say thanks for the food the earth produces. May the whole world worship you.

68:1–2 You scatter people who hate you. You blow them away like smoke. You melt them like wax next to a flame.

[1] God will arise.
His enemies will be scattered.
Those who hate him will flee from him.
[2] Blow them away like smoke.
Let wicked people melt in God's presence like wax
next to a fire.

68:3–4 Let good people celebrate in your presence. Let them spill over with joy as they sing to you. They'll clear a wide path for you in the deserts.

[3] But let righteous people rejoice.
Let them celebrate in God's presence.
Let them overflow with joy.
[4] Sing to God; make music to praise his name.
Make a highway for him to ride through the deserts.[a]
The LORD is his name.
Celebrate in his presence.

68:5–6 You act as Father to the fatherless. You defend widows and put the lonely in families. You make prisoners whole.

[5] The God who is in his holy dwelling place
is the father of the fatherless and the defender
of widows.
[6] God places lonely people in families.
He leads prisoners out of prison into productive lives,
but rebellious people must live in an
unproductive land.

68:7–10 The earth shook and the sky poured rain when you marched your people through the desert. You refreshed the land and gave your flock a home.

[7] O God, when you went in front of your people,
when you marched through the desert, *Selah*
[8] the earth quaked and the sky poured
in the presence of the God of Sinai,
in the presence of the God of Israel.

[9] You watered the land with plenty of rain, O God.
You refreshed it when your land was exhausted.
[10] Your flock settled there.
Out of your goodness, O God,
you provided for oppressed people.

[11] The Lord gives instructions.
The women who announce the good news are a
large army.

[a] 68:4 Or "Lift a song to him who rides upon the clouds."

12   ⌊They say,⌋ "The kings of the armies flee; they
            run away.
        The women who remained at home will divide
            the goods.
13   Though you stayed among the sheep pens,
            ⌊you will be like⌋ the wings of a dove
                covered with silver,
                its feathers with yellow gold.
14   Meanwhile, the Almighty was still scattering
            kings there
            like snow falling on Mount Zalmon."

15 The mountain of Bashan is the mountain of God.
    The mountain of Bashan is the mountain with
        many peaks.
16   Why do you look with envy, you mountains with
        many peaks,
        at the mountain where God has chosen to live?
        Certainly, the LORD will live there forever.

68:15–16 Though the mountains are high, none measure up to the mountain where you dwell. You'll live there forever.

17 The chariots of God are twenty thousand in number,
    thousands upon thousands.
        The Lord is among them.
        ⌊The God of⌋ Sinai is in his holy place.
18 You went to the highest place.
    You took prisoners captive.
    You received gifts from people,
        even from rebellious people, so that the LORD God
            may live there.

68:17–18 Your power is beyond imagination. You live on a high holy mountain. Even rebellious people bring you gifts.

19 Thanks be to the Lord,
    who daily carries our burdens for us.
        God is our salvation.   *Selah*
20 Our God is the God of victories.
    The Almighty LORD is our escape from death.

68:19–20 Thanks for carrying our burdens day by day. You're the one who saves us. You're the God of victories.

21 Certainly, God will crush the heads of his enemies
    ⌊and destroy even⌋ the hair on the heads
        of those who continue to be guilty.
22 The Lord said, "I will bring them back from Bashan.
    I will bring them back from the depths of the sea
23   so that you, ⌊my people,⌋ may bathe[a] your feet
            in blood
            and the tongues of your dogs
                may lick the blood of your enemies."

68:21–23 You crush people who continue in sin, bringing them from near and far so your people can see your justice.

24 Your festival processions, O God, can be seen
        by everyone.
    They are the processions for my God, my king, into
        the holy place.
25   The singers are in front.

68:24–27 Everyone can see the festive parades that usher you to your throne. Singers lead. Musicians follow. The young women beat tambourines. All

---

a 68:23 Greek, Targum, Syriac; Masoretic Text "shatter."

your people honor you with
songs and noisy cheer.

The musicians are behind them.
The young women beating tambourines are
between them.
[26] Thank God, the Lord, the source of Israel, with
the choirs.
[27] Benjamin, the youngest, is leading them,
⌐next⌐ the leaders of Judah with their
noisy crowds,
⌐then⌐ the leaders of Zebulun,
⌐then⌐ the leaders of Naphtali.

68:28–29 You are strong. Show
your strength as you have before.
Kings will honor you because of
your greatness.

[28] Your God has decided you will be strong.
Display your strength, O God,
as you have for us before.
[29] Kings will bring you gifts
because of your temple high above Jerusalem.

68:30–32 Humble the powerful
of this world and scatter the
people who love war. Let every
kingdom on earth sing to you.

[30] Threaten the beast who is among the cattails,
the herd of bulls with the calves of the nations,
until it humbles itself with pieces of silver.
Scatter the people who find joy in war.[a]
[31] Ambassadors will come from Egypt.
Sudan will stretch out its hands to God ⌐in prayer⌐.

[32] You kingdoms of the world, sing to God.
Make music to praise the Lord.   *Selah*
[33] God rides through the ancient heaven, the
highest heaven.
Listen! He makes his voice heard, his
powerful voice.

68:33–35 You ride through
the heavens and speak with a
booming voice. We acknowledge
your power. We bow in awe to
you. Give us strength!

[34] Acknowledge the power of God.
His majesty is over Israel, and his power is in
the skies.

[35] God, the God of Israel, is awe-inspiring in his
holy place.
He gives strength and power to his people.
Thanks be to God!

Psalm 69

For the choir director; according to shoshannim; *by David.*

69:1–2 Save me before I
drown! I'm sinking in muck and
can't touch bottom. I'm being
swept away by a flood.

[1] Save me, O God!
The water is already up to my neck!
[2] I am sinking in deep mud.
There is nothing to stand on.
I am in deep water.
A flood is sweeping me away.

69:3–4 My throat is hoarse
from crying. My eyes hurt from
looking for you. People who hate

[3] I am exhausted from crying for help.
My throat is hoarse.
My eyes are strained ⌐from⌐ looking for my God.

---
[a] 68:30 Hebrew meaning of this verse uncertain.

⁴ Those who hate me for no reason
      outnumber the hairs on my head.
    Those who want to destroy me are mighty.
      They have no reason to be my enemies.
I am forced to pay back what I did not steal.

⁵ O God, you know my stupidity,
    and the things of which I am guilty are not hidden
      from you.
⁶ Do not let those who wait with hope for you
    be put to shame because of me, O Almighty LORD
      of Armies.
Do not let those who come to you for help
    be humiliated because of me, O God of Israel.

⁷ Indeed, for your sake I have endured insults.
    Humiliation has covered my face.
⁸ I have become a stranger to my ⌐own⌐ brothers,
    a foreigner to my mother's sons.
⁹ Indeed, devotion for your house has consumed me,
    and the insults of those who insult you have fallen
      on me.
¹⁰ I cried and fasted, but I was insulted for it.
¹¹ I dressed myself in sackcloth, but I became the object
    of ridicule.
¹² Those who sit at the gate gossip about me,
    and drunkards make up songs about me.

¹³ May my prayer come to you at an acceptable time,
    O LORD.
    O God, out of the greatness of your mercy,
      answer me with the truth of your salvation.
¹⁴ Rescue me from the mud.
    Do not let me sink ⌐into it⌐.
I want to be rescued from those who hate me
    and from the deep water.
¹⁵ Do not let floodwaters sweep me away.
    Do not let the ocean swallow me up,
      or the pit close its mouth over me.
¹⁶ Answer me, O LORD, because your mercy is good.
    Out of your unlimited compassion, turn to me.
¹⁷ I am in trouble, so do not hide your face from me.
    Answer me quickly!
¹⁸ Come close, and defend my soul.
    Set me free because of my enemies.

¹⁹ You know that I have been insulted, put to shame,
    and humiliated.
    All my opponents are in front of you.
²⁰ Insults have broken my heart, and I am sick.
    I looked for sympathy, but there was none.

me for no reason outnumber the hairs on my head.

69:5–6 You know I've been stupid. You and I both know I sin. Don't let my failures humiliate your faithful people.

69:7 People insult me because of you. My humiliation feels like a bag over my head.

69:8–12 My own family treats me like a stranger. My devotion to you draws insults. My godly mourning makes me a joke. Even drunks make up songs about me.

69:13–15 I hope my prayer reaches you at the right time. Answer me because of your great love. Rescue me from this muddy pit. Don't let the floods sweep me away.

69:16–17 Answer my prayers because your compassion is unlimited. Don't hide from me. Answer me quickly!

69:19–21 You have heard all the insults and seen my shame. You know who my opponents are—how their insults break my heart and make me sick. They

poison my food and pour vinegar
in my cup.

I looked for people to comfort me, but I found
no one.
²¹   They poisoned my food,
    and when I was thirsty, they gave me vinegar
        to drink.

69:22–24 Trap these enemies. Ensnare their friends. Cloud their vision. Make their thighs shake. Pour your rage on them. Don't let them outrun your anger.

²²Let the table set for them become a trap
    and a snare for their friends.
²³Let their vision become clouded so that they
        cannot see.
    Let their thighs continually shake.

²⁴Pour your rage on them.
    Let your burning anger catch up with them.
²⁵   Let their camp be deserted
        and their tents empty.

69:26–28 You struck me, and they mock my pain. Charge them and find them guilty. Erase their names from your book.

²⁶They persecute the one you have struck,
    and they talk about the pain of those you
        have wounded.
²⁷Charge them with one crime after another.
    Do not let them be found innocent.
²⁸Let their ⌐names¬ be erased from the Book of Life.
    Do not let them be listed with righteous people.

²⁹I am suffering and in pain.
    Let your saving power protect me, O God.
³⁰I want to praise the name of God with a song.
    I want to praise its greatness with a song
        of thanksgiving.

69:30–32 My praise means more to you than burning sacrifices. Let hurting people see my worship and be refreshed.

³¹   This will please the LORD more than ⌐sacrificing¬
        an ox
    or a bull with horns and hoofs.
³²Oppressed people will see ⌐this¬ and rejoice.
    May the hearts of those who look to God for help
        be refreshed.

69:33–36 You listen to the needy and cherish the captives. Let all heaven and earth praise you. Give your servants a safe and holy home.

³³The LORD listens to needy people.
    He does not despise his own who are in prison.
³⁴Let heaven and earth, the seas, and everything that moves
        in them, praise him.
³⁵When God saves Zion, he will rebuild the cities
        of Judah.
    His servants will live there and take possession of it.
³⁶   The descendants of his servants will inherit it.
        Those who love him will live there.

Psalm 70[a]

For the choir director; by David; to be kept in mind.

70:1–3 Help me now! Confuse everyone who wants to kill me. Chase them away in disgrace!

¹Come quickly to rescue me, O God!
    Come quickly to help me, O LORD!

---

[a] 70:1 Psalm 70 is virtually identical in wording to Psalm 40:13–17.

²Let those who seek my life
    be confused and put to shame.
Let those who want my downfall
    be turned back and disgraced.
³Let those who say, "Aha! Aha!"
    be turned back because of their own shame.
⁴Let all who seek you rejoice and be glad because
      of you.
Let those who love your salvation continually say,
    "God is great!"

⁵But I am oppressed and needy.
O God, come to me quickly.
    You are my help and my savior.
    O Lord, do not delay!

70:4–5 I'll always seek you and smile because of you. I love your salvation. It makes me shout about your greatness. But help me quickly. You're my help and my Savior. Don't delay!

Psalm 71

¹I have taken refuge in you, O Lord.
    Never let me be put to shame.
²Rescue me and free me because of your righteousness.
Turn your ear toward me, and save me.
³ Be a rock on which I may live,
      a place where I may always go.
        You gave the order to save me!
Indeed, you are my rock and my fortress.
⁴My God, free me from the hands of a wicked person,
    from the grasp of one who is cruel and unjust.
⁵You are my hope, O Almighty Lord.
You have been my confidence ever since I was young.
⁶I depended on you before I was born
    You took me from my mother's womb.
      My songs of praise constantly speak about you.
⁷I have become an example to many people,
    but you are my strong refuge.
⁸My mouth is filled with your praise,
    with your glory all day long.

⁹Do not reject me when I am old
    or abandon me when I lose my strength.
¹⁰My enemies talk about me.
    They watch me as they plot to take my life.
¹¹They say, "God has abandoned him.
    Pursue him and grab him because there is no one to
      rescue him."
¹²O God, do not be so distant from me.
    O my God, come quickly to help me.
¹³Let those who accuse me come to a shameful end.
Let those who want my downfall be covered
    with disgrace and humiliation.
¹⁴But I will always have hope.
    I will praise you more and more.

71:1–2 I count on your protection from people who want to shame me. Set me free because of your goodness.

71:3–4 Be my solid home, the place I run for safety. Set me loose from wicked hands.

71:5–6 You're my hope, the one I've depended on since before I was born. You brought me safely from my mother's womb.

71:6–8 I constantly sing about you. All day long my mouth is full of your glory.

71:9–11 Don't reject me when I'm old and weak, because my enemies already plot to kill me. They think you've abandoned me. They scheme to hunt me down because they assume no one will help me.

71:12–14 Don't be so far from me. Come quickly to help me. You're my only hope!

71:15–16 I won't stop talking about your goodness and deliverance, even though they're greater than I'll ever understand. I'll tell everyone you alone do right.

71:17–18 You've taught me since I was young, so don't desert me when I'm gray. Let me grow old and tell people what your power has done.

71:19 Your righteousness reaches the skies. You do awesome things. No one is like you.

71:20–21 You've made me face terrible troubles, yet you bring me back from death. You comfort me and make me stronger than ever.

71:22–24 Because you're faithful, I'll always sing you thanks. I'll sing with a heart full of joy and my tongue won't stop recounting your goodness.

¹⁵ My mouth will tell about your righteousness,
    about your salvation all day long.
        Even then, it is more than I can understand.
¹⁶ I will come with the mighty deeds of the
    Almighty LORD.
    I will praise your righteousness, yours alone.

¹⁷ O God, you have taught me ever since I was young,
    and I still talk about the miracles you have done.
¹⁸ Even when I am old and gray, do not abandon me,
    O God.
    Let me live to tell the people of this age
        what your strength has accomplished,
            to tell about your power to all who will come.

¹⁹ Your righteousness reaches to the heavens, O God.
    You have done great things.
        O God, who is like you?
²⁰   You have made me endure many terrible troubles.
    You restore me to life again.
    You bring me back from the depths of the earth.
²¹   You comfort me and make me greater than ever.

²² Because of your faithfulness, O my God,
    even I will give thanks to you as I play on a lyre.
    I will make music with a harp to praise you, O Holy
        One of Israel.
²³ My lips will sing with joy when I make music to
    praise you.
    My soul, which you have rescued, also will
        sing joyfully.
²⁴ My tongue will tell about your righteousness all
    day long,
    because those who wanted my downfall
        have been disgraced and put to shame.

Psalm 72

By Solomon.

72:1–2 Be just and good, my King, and judge the oppressed with justice.

¹ O God, give the king your justice
    and the king's son[a] your righteousness
²   so that he may judge your people
        with righteousness
        and your oppressed ⌊people⌋ with justice.

³ May the mountains bring peace to the people
    and the hills bring righteousness.
⁴ May he grant justice to the people who are oppressed.
    May he save the children of needy people

72:4–5 Bring justice to the broken. Save the children of the

---

[a] 72:1 According to ancient Jewish and Christian tradition, "king" and "king's son" refer to the Messiah.

and crush their oppressor.
⁵ May they fear you as long as the sun and
  moon ˺shine˹—
throughout every generation.
⁶ May he be like rain that falls on ˺freshly˹ cut grass,
  like showers that water the land.
⁷ May righteous people blossom in his day.
  May there be unlimited peace until the moon no
    longer ˺shines˹.

⁸ May he rule from sea to sea,
  from the Euphrates River to the ends of the earth.
⁹ May the people of the desert kneel in front of him.
  May his enemies lick the dust.
¹⁰ May the kings from Tarshish and the islands
    bring presents.
  May the kings from Sheba and Seba bring gifts.
¹¹ May all kings worship him.
  May all nations serve him.

¹² He will rescue the needy person who cries for help
    and the oppressed person who has no one's help.
¹³ He will have pity on the poor and needy
    and will save the lives of the needy.
¹⁴ He will rescue them from oppression and violence.
    Their blood will be precious in his sight.

¹⁵ May he live long.
  May the gold from Sheba be given to him.
  May ˺the people˹ pray for him continually.
  May ˺they˹ praise him all day long.
¹⁶ May there be plenty of grain in the land.
  May it wave ˺in the breeze˹ on the mountaintops,
    its fruit like ˺the treetops of˹ Lebanon.
  May those from the city flourish like the grass on
    the ground.
¹⁷ May his name endure forever.
  May his name continue as long as the sun ˺shines˹.
  May all nations be blessed through him and call
    him blessed.

¹⁸ Thank the Lord God, the God of Israel,
  who alone does miracles.
¹⁹ Thanks be to his glorious name forever.
  May the whole earth be filled with his glory.

Amen and amen!

²⁰ The prayers by David, son of Jesse, end here.

needy. Fend off every oppressor.
May you receive the utter respect
you deserve.

72:6–7 You are like rain
watering my soul. You make me
blossom and bring peace to my
world.

72:8–11 You reign over the
whole world. May every person
on earth bow to worship you. I
want rulers and everyday people
alike to serve you.

72:12–14 You rescue the
impoverished and powerless who
call on you. Save their lives and
spare them from violence.

72:16–17 Feed our world.
Cause our cities to flourish. Make
your name famous for all time.
You bless every nation.

72:18–19 You alone do
miracles. I won't stop telling you
thanks. Show your splendor to
the whole earth. Amen!

BOOK THREE
(Psalms 73–89)

Psalm 73

A psalm by Asaph.

73:1–5 I know you're good to people who are pure. But I don't understand why you let evildoers prosper. They feel no pain. They enjoy good health. They're never bored or troubled.

1 God is truly good to Israel,
to those whose lives are pure.

2 But my feet had almost stumbled.
They had almost slipped
3   because I was envious of arrogant people
when I saw the prosperity that wicked
people enjoy.

4 They suffer no pain.
Their bodies are healthy.
5 They have no drudgery in their lives like
ordinary people.
They are not plagued ⌐with problems⌐ like others.

73:6–10 The wicked strut and do violence. They mock and speak maliciously. Their eyes study the world from well-fed faces, dreaming up new ways to hurt others. They boast against you in heaven and bark at people here on earth. All of this is why your people turn to wickedness.

6 That is why they wear arrogance like a necklace
and acts of violence like clothing.
7 Their eyes peer out from their fat faces,[a]
and their imaginations run wild.
8 They ridicule.
They speak maliciously.
They speak arrogantly about oppression.
9 They verbally attack heaven,
and they order people around on earth.
10 That is why God's people turn to wickedness[b]
and swallow their words.

73:11–14 The wicked think you don't see their sins. Do you? They continually prosper while I get nothing for living for you. I face nonstop problems. Every day I take another beating.

11 Then wicked people ask, "What does God know?"
"Does the Most High know anything?"
12 Look how wicked they are!
They never have a worry.
They grow more and more wealthy.

13 I've received no reward for keeping my life pure
and washing my hands of any blame.
14 I'm plagued ⌐with problems⌐ all day long,
and every morning my punishment ⌐begins again⌐.

73:15–16 If I tell others my struggles, I will lead them astray. All of this is too difficult for me to understand.

15 If I had said, "I will continue to talk like that,"
I would have betrayed God's people.
16 But when I tried to understand this,
it was too difficult for me.

73:17–20 Only when I bow to you do I see the truth. You put evil people in slippery places, then

17 Only when I came into God's holy place
did I ⌐finally⌐ understand what would happen
to them.

---
[a] 73:7 Hebrew meaning uncertain.
[b] 73:10 Hebrew meaning uncertain.

22

¹⁸ You put them in slippery places
  and make them fall into ruin.
¹⁹ They are suddenly destroyed.
  They are completely swept away by terror!
²⁰ As ⌐someone⌐ gets rid of a dream when he wakes up,
  so you, O Lord, get rid of the thought of them
    when you wake up.

²¹ When my heart was filled with bitterness
  and my mind was seized ⌐with envy⌐,
²²   I was stupid, and I did not understand.
    I was like a dumb animal in your presence.
²³ Yet, I am always with you.
  You hold on to my right hand.
²⁴   With your advice you guide me,
      and in the end you will take me to glory.
²⁵ As long as I have you,
  I don't need anyone else in heaven or on earth.
²⁶ My body and mind may waste away,
  but God remains the foundation of my life
    and my inheritance forever.
²⁷ Without a doubt, those who are far from you will die.
  You destroy all who are unfaithful to you.

²⁸ Being united with God is my highest good.
  I have made the Almighty Lord my refuge
    so that I may report everything that he has done.

Psalm 74

A maskil[a] *by Asaph.*

¹ Why, O God, have you rejected us forever?
  Why does your anger
    smolder against the sheep in your care?

² Remember your congregation.
    Long ago you made it your own.
    You bought this tribe to be your possession.
      This tribe is Mount Zion, where you have
        made your home.
³ Turn your steps toward[b] these pathetic ruins.
    The enemy has destroyed everything in the
      holy temple.

⁴ Your opponents have roared inside your meeting place.
    They have set up their own emblems as symbols.
⁵   Starting from its entrance, they hacked away
      like a woodcutter in a forest.[c]

push them to destruction. You
shake them off like a bad dream.

73:21–24 I was stupid to feel
bitter and envious. I realize now
that I'm always with you. You hold
my hand and guide me in every
step of life. When I die you'll
welcome me home.

73:25–26 As long as I have you
I don't need anything else. Even
if my body and mind waste away,
you'll always be my strength.

73:27–28 People who live far
from you will die. But living close
to you is better than my biggest
dreams.

74:1–2 Why do you reject
your people? Why does your
anger smoke against your flock?
Remember that you called us to
be your people. You made our
hearts your home.

74:3–4 Look at us—we're
pathetic ruins! Your enemies have
destroyed your holy house and
claimed it as their own.

74:5–8 Your enemies have
hacked and burned your house.

---

a 74:1 Unknown musical term.
b 74:3 Hebrew meaning uncertain.
c 74:5 Hebrew meaning of this verse uncertain.

They want to crush us by burning the places we meet to honor you.

74:9–11 There are no more miracles, no more prophets. We don't know when we'll hear from you again or see you act. Get your hands out of your pockets and help us!

74:12–17 Despite my grief you've always been my King. You rule earth and sea. You make streams start and stop. All of nature marches to your orders— day and night, sun and moon, summer and winter.

74:18–19 Godless fools hate you. Don't forget how they insult you. Don't hand over your treasured people to be mauled and eaten.

74:20–22 In these dark days remember your promises to us. The weak and needy praise you. Stand up and fight for your people!

⁶ They smashed all its carved paneling with axes
and hatchets.
⁷ They burned your holy place to the ground.
They dishonored the place where you live among us.
⁸ They said to themselves, "We will crush them."
They burned every meeting place of God in the land.

⁹ We no longer see miraculous signs.
There are no prophets anymore.
No one knows how long this will last.
¹⁰ How long, O God, will the enemy insult us?
Will the enemy despise you forever?
¹¹ Why do you hold back your hand, especially your
right hand?
Take your hands out of your pockets.
Destroy your enemies!ᵃ

¹² And yet, from long ago God has been my king,
the one who has been victorious throughout the earth.
¹³ You stirred up the sea with your own strength.
You smashed the heads of sea monsters in
the water.
¹⁴ You crushed the heads of Leviathanᵇ
and gave them to the creatures of the desert
for food.
¹⁵ You opened the springs and brooks.
You dried up the ever-flowing rivers.
¹⁶ The day and the night are yours.
You set the moon and the sun in their places.
¹⁷ You determined all the boundaries of the earth.
You created summer and winter.

¹⁸ Remember how the enemy insulted you, O LORD.
Remember how an entire nation of godless fools
despised your name.
¹⁹ Do not hand over the soul of your dove to wild animals.
Do not forget the life of your oppressed people forever.
²⁰ Consider your promiseᶜ
because every dark corner of the land is filled
with violence.
²¹ Do not let oppressed people come back in disgrace.
Let weak and needy people praise your name.
²² Arise, O God!
Fight for your own cause!
Remember how godless fools insult you all day long.
²³ Do not forget the shouting of your opponents.
Do not forget the uproar made by those who attack you.

ᵃ 74:11 Hebrew meaning of this verse uncertain.
ᵇ 74:14 Hebrew meaning uncertain.
ᶜ 74:20 Or "covenant."

Psalm 75

For the choir director; al tashcheth; a psalm by Asaph; a song.

1 We give thanks to you, O God; we give thanks.
You are present, and your miracles confirm that.

2 When I choose the right time,
I will judge fairly.
3 When the earth and everyone who lives on it begin
to melt,
I will make its foundations as solid as rock.   *Selah*
4 I said to those who brag, "Don't brag,"
and to wicked people,
"Don't raise your weapons.
5   Don't raise your weapons so proudly
or speak so defiantly."

6 The ˪authority˩ to reward someone does not ˪come˩
from the east,
from the west,
or ˪even˩ from the wilderness.
7 God alone is the judge.
He punishes one person and rewards another.
8 A cup is in the LORD's hand.
(Its foaming wine is thoroughly mixed with spices.)
He will empty it,
˪and˩ all the wicked people on earth
will have to drink every last drop.

9 But I will speak ˪about your miracles˩ forever
I will make music to praise the God of Jacob.
10   I will destroy all the weapons of wicked people,
but the weapons of righteous people will be
raised proudly.

75:1 Thank you. And thank you again. Your miracles prove your presence with us.

75:2–5 You set the perfect time for judgment. When the earth melts, you alone make it solid. I keep telling the proud not to brag. I warn them not to shake their weapons and words at you.

75:6–8 You alone have real authority. Only you can judge, punish, and reward. You pour your cup of wrath and make the wicked drink every last drop.

75:9–10 I'll always talk about your miracles. I'll always praise you. You destroy the weapons of evildoers, but you empower your followers.

Psalm 76

For the choir director; on stringed instruments; a psalm by Asaph; a song.

1 God is known in Judah.
His name is great in Israel.
2 His tent is in Salem.
His home is in Zion.
3   There he destroyed flaming arrows,
shields, swords, and weapons of war.   *Selah*

4 You are the radiant one.
You are more majestic than the ancient mountains.[a]
5   Brave people were robbed.
They died.

76:1–2 Your people know you. You make your home with us.

76:4 No person shines brighter than you. No mountain rises more majestic than you.

---

[a] 76:4 Greek, Syriac; Masoretic Text "mountains of prey."

76:5–7 No power can stand against you. You strike down armies. You prove that you alone must be feared. No one can stand in your anger.

76:8–9 From heaven you announce your verdicts. You rise to judge evildoers and save the oppressed.

76:11–12 I'll keep my promises to you. I'll bring you gifts because you fill me with awe. You put an end to influential people. Even kings fear you.

None of the warriors were able to lift a hand.
6   At your stern warning, O God of Jacob,
        chariot riders and horses were put to sleep.

7 You alone must be feared!
Who can stand in your presence when you
        become angry?
8   From heaven you announced a verdict.
    The earth was fearful and silent
9   when you rose to judge, O God,
        when you rose to save every oppressed person
            on earth.   *Selah*

10 Even angry mortals will praise you.
You will wear the remainder of ˻their˼ anger.[a]
11   Make vows to the LORD your God, and keep them.
    Let everyone around him bring gifts to the one who
        must be feared.
12   He cuts short the lives of influential people.
    He terrifies the kings of the earth.

Psalm 77

For the choir director; according to Jeduthun; a psalm by Asaph.

77:1–3 I cried loudly so you would hear me. I was in trouble so I ran to you for help. I even prayed all night long. Yet I found no comfort. I'm starting to lose hope in you.

77:4–9 Now I'm too upset even to pray. I keep thinking of the songs I used to sing. Will you ever accept me? Have you run out of mercy? Have you quit keeping your promises? Are you too angry to show me compassion?

1 Loudly, I cried to God.
Loudly, I cried to God
    so that he would open his ears to ˻hear˼ me.
2 On the day I was in trouble, I went to the Lord for help.
At night I stretched out my hands in prayer without
        growing tired.
    Yet, my soul refused to be comforted.

3 I sigh as I remember God.
I begin to lose hope as I think about him.   *Selah*
4   (You keep my eyelids open.)
I am so upset that I cannot speak.
5 I have considered the days of old,
    the years long ago.
6 I remember my song in the night
    and reflect ˻on it˼.
My spirit searches ˻for an answer˼:
7   Will the LORD reject ˻me˼ for all time?
    Will he ever accept me?
8   Has his mercy come to an end forever?
    Has his promise been canceled throughout
        every generation?
9   Has God forgotten to be merciful?
    Has he locked up his compassion because of
        his anger?   *Selah*
10   Then I said, "It makes me feel sick

---

a 76:10 Hebrew meaning of this line uncertain.

that the power of the Most High is no longer
the same."[a]

[11] I will remember the deeds of the LORD.
I will remember your ancient miracles.
[12] I will reflect on all your actions
and think about what you have done.

77:10–12 I feel sick that your
infinite power seems to have
faded. I force myself to think
back to your ancient miracles. I
ponder what you've done.

[13] O God, your ways are holy!
What god is as great as our God?
[14] You are the God who performs miracles.
You have made your strength known among
the nations.
[15] With your might you have defended your people,
the descendants of Jacob and Joseph. *Selah*

77:13–15 Your ways are holy!
No god is as mighty as you. You
did miracles and demonstrated
your strength to the world. With
your might you defended
your people.

[16] The water saw you, O God.
The water saw you and shook.
Even the depths of the sea trembled.
[17] The clouds poured out water.
The sky thundered.
Even your arrows flashed in every direction.
[18] The sound of your thunder rumbled in the sky.[b]
Streaks of lightning lit up the world.
The earth trembled and shook.

77:16–20 The sea shook with
fear when it saw you coming. The
clouds burst, the sky thundered,
and lightning lit the earth. You
made a path through the sea for
your people. You led your people
like a shepherd, telling Moses
and Aaron to take them by
the hand.

[19] Your road went through the sea.
Your path went through raging water,
but your footprints could not be seen.
[20] Like a shepherd, you led your people.
You had Moses and Aaron take them by the hand.

Psalm 78

A maskil *by Asaph.*

[1] Open your ears to my teachings, my people.
Turn your ears to the words from my mouth.
[2] I will open my mouth to illustrate points.
I will explain what has been hidden long ago,
[3] things that we have heard and known about,
things that our parents have told us.
[4] We will not hide them from our children.
We will tell the next generation
about the LORD's power and great deeds
and the miraculous things he has done.

78:1–4 I want everyone to
hear my words because I have
something important to say. I'll
explain what you did long ago.
I'll tell the stories passed down
from our parents. I won't hide the
powerful deeds you've done.

[5] He established written instructions for Jacob's people.
He gave his teachings to Israel.
He commanded our ancestors to make them known to
their children
[6] so that the next generation would know them.

78:5 You wrote down your
commands so no one could miss
them. You made them easy for
children to learn.

---

[a] 77:10 Hebrew meaning of this line uncertain.
[b] 77:18 Hebrew meaning of this line uncertain.

78:6–10 You want each generation to teach their children to trust you, to remember your deeds, and to obey your commands. Then they won't rebel like their unfaithful ancestors, those well-equipped warriors who fled when they should have stood on your promises.

Children yet to be born ⌊would learn them⌋.
They will grow up and tell their children
7   to trust God, to remember what he has done,
and to obey his commands.
8   Then they will not be like their ancestors,
a stubborn and rebellious generation.
Their hearts were not loyal.
Their spirits were not faithful to God.

9 The men of Ephraim, well-equipped with bows
⌊and arrows⌋,
turned ⌊and ran⌋ on the day of battle.
10   They had not been faithful to God's promise.[a]
They refused to follow his teachings.
11   They forgot what he had done—
the miracles that he had shown them.

78:11–16 Never let me forget your miracles. You split the sea and led your people to freedom, with a cloud by day and a fiery light by night. You split rocks in the desert and gave them plenty to drink.

12 In front of their ancestors he performed miracles
in the land of Egypt, in the fields of Zoan.
13   He divided the sea and led them through it.
He made the waters stand up like a wall.
14   He guided them by a cloud during the day
and by a fiery light throughout the night.
15   He split rocks in the desert.
He gave them plenty to drink, an ocean of water.
16   He made streams come out of a rock.
He made the water flow like rivers.

78:17–20 Your people saw these miracles yet continued to rebel against you. They demanded you fill their cravings for bread and meat. They questioned your ability to provide. Show me when I treat you with such disrespect.

17 They continued to sin against him,
to rebel in the desert against the Most High.
18 They deliberately tested God by demanding the food
they craved.
19 They spoke against God by saying,
"Can God prepare a banquet in the desert?
20   True, he did strike a rock,
and water did gush out,
and the streams did overflow.
But can he also give us bread or provide us, his
people, with meat?"

78:21–28 You were furious when you overheard their doubts. They didn't believe your promises. They didn't trust you to save them. Yet you kindly dropped manna from heaven. You rained meat in the middle of their camp.

21 When the LORD heard this, he became furious.
His fire burned against Jacob
and his anger flared up at Israel
22   because they did not believe God
or trust him to save them.

23 In spite of that, he commanded the clouds above
and opened the doors of heaven.
24   He rained manna down on them to eat
and gave them grain from heaven.
25   Humans ate the bread of the mighty ones,

---

a 78:10 Or "covenant."

and God sent them plenty of food.

²⁶ He made the east wind blow in the heavens
and guided the south wind with his might.
²⁷   He rained meat down on them like dust,
birds like the sand on the seashore.
²⁸   He made the birds fall in the middle of
his camp,
all around his dwelling place.

²⁹ They ate more than enough.
He gave them what they wanted,
³⁰   but they still wanted more.
While the food was still in their mouths,
³¹   the anger of God flared up against them.
He killed their strongest men
and slaughtered the best young men
in Israel.

78:29–32 Your people ate until they were stuffed but still they wanted more. Their mouths were full but they moaned about their hunger. In your anger you killed the strong and the young. And still they continued to sin.

³² In spite of all this, they continued to sin,
and they no longer believed in his miracles.
³³   He brought their days to an end like a whisper in
the wind.
He brought their years to an end in terror.
³⁴   When he killed ⌞some of⌟ them, ⌞the rest⌟
searched for him.
They turned from their sins and eagerly looked
for God.
³⁵   They remembered that God was their rock,
that the Most High was their defender.
³⁶   They flattered him with their mouths
and lied to him with their tongues.
³⁷   Their hearts were not loyal to him.
They were not faithful to his promise.

78:34–37 Some searched for you. They turned from their sins and looked for you. They called you their rock and defender. But it was all an act. Their hearts weren't with you.

³⁸ But he is compassionate.
He forgave their sin.
He did not destroy them.
He restrained his anger many times.
He did not display all of his fury.
³⁹   He remembered that they were only flesh and blood,
a breeze that blows and does not return.

78:38–39 You are merciful and forgiving. You hold back your anger and remember that people are weak. We are but a breeze that blows once and disappears.

⁴⁰ How often they rebelled against him in the wilderness!
How often they caused him grief in the desert!
⁴¹ Again and again they tested God,
and they pushed the Holy One of Israel to the limit.
⁴² They did not remember his power—
the day he freed them from their oppressor,
⁴³   when he performed his miraculous signs in Egypt,
his wonders in the fields of Zoan.

78:40–43 I don't want to push you to the limit like they did. Help me remember your power—how you used miraculous signs and wonders to free your people from slavery.

⁴⁴ He turned their rivers into blood

78:44–48 You turned rivers

bloody and undrinkable. You sent biting flies and hopping frogs. You served the slave masters' crops to grasshoppers and destroyed their cattle with hail and lightning.

so that they could not drink from their streams.
⁴⁵ He sent a swarm of flies that bit them
and frogs that ruined them.
⁴⁶ He gave their crops to grasshoppers
and their produce to locusts.
⁴⁷ He killed their vines with hail
and their fig trees with frost.
⁴⁸ He let the hail strike their cattle
and bolts of lightning strike their livestock.

78:49–52 Anger. Rage. Fury. Hostility. You burned against the slave masters and killed their firstborn in barns and tents and homes. But like a shepherd leading his flock to safe pasture, you led your people to freedom.

⁴⁹ He sent his burning anger, rage, fury, and hostility
against them.
He sent an army of destroying angels.
⁵⁰ He cleared a path for his anger.
He did not spare them.
He let the plague take their lives.
⁵¹ He slaughtered every firstborn in Egypt,
the ones born in the tents of Ham when their fathers
were young.

78:53–55 Your people watched from dry land while the sea piled onto their enemies. You brought your people to your holy land. You forced nations out of their way and gave your people a place to live.

³² But he led his own people out like sheep
and guided them like a flock through
the wilderness.
⁵³   He led them safely.
They had no fear while the sea covered
their enemies.
⁵⁴ He brought them into his holy land,
to this mountain that his power had won.
⁵⁵   He forced nations out of their way
and gave them the land of the nations as
their inheritance.
He settled the tribes of Israel in their
own tents.

78:56–58 Your people saw all this and still rebelled against you. They disobeyed your written instructions. You fumed when they built altars to other gods.

⁵⁶ They tested God Most High and rebelled against him.
They did not obey his written instructions.
⁵⁷ They were disloyal and treacherous like their ancestors.
They were like arrows shot from a defective bow.
⁵⁸ They made him angry because of their illegal
worship sites.
They made him furious because they worshiped idols.

78:59–63 In your fury you rejected your people. You allowed the ark of your power to be captured by enemies. You let your people die in battle and sent fire to consume young men.

⁵⁹ When God heard, he became furious.
He completely rejected Israel.
⁶⁰   He abandoned his dwelling place in Shiloh,
the tent where he had lived among humans.
⁶¹   He allowed his power to be taken captive
and handed his glory over to an oppressor.
⁶²   He let swords kill his people.
He was furious with those who belonged to him.
⁶³   Fire consumed his best young men,
so his virgins heard no wedding songs.

64 His priests were cut down with swords.
The widows ˪of his priests˩ could not even
weep ˪for them˩.
65 Then the Lord woke up like one who had
been sleeping,
like a warrior sobering up from ˪too much˩ wine.
66 He struck his enemies from behind
and disgraced them forever.

67 He rejected the tent of Joseph.
He did not choose the tribe of Ephraim,
68 but he chose the tribe of Judah,
Mount Zion which he loved.
69 He built his holy place to be like the high heavens,
like the earth which he made to last for a long time.

70 He chose his servant David.
He took him from the sheep pens.
71 He brought him from tending the ewes that had lambs
so that David could be the shepherd of the people
of Jacob,
of Israel, the people who belonged to the LORD.
72 With unselfish devotion David became their shepherd.
With skill he guided them.

78:65–72 Let me never give you reason to wake up angry, nor strike me from behind, nor disgrace me forever. Let me live as one of your chosen children. Give me the heart of David. Lift me from my mundane tasks to lead your people. Give me unselfish devotion and skill.

Psalm 79

A psalm by Asaph.

1 O God, the nations have invaded the land that belongs
to you.
They have dishonored your holy temple.
They have left Jerusalem in ruins.
2 They have given the dead bodies of your servants
to the birds for food.
They have given the flesh of your godly ones
to the animals.
3 They have shed the blood of your people
around Jerusalem
as though it were water.
There is no one to bury your people.

4 We have become a disgrace to our neighbors,
an object of ridicule and contempt to those
around us.
5 How long, O LORD?
Will you remain angry forever?
Will your fury continue to burn like fire?
6 Pour your fury on the nations that do not know you,
on the kingdoms that have not called you.
7 They have devoured Jacob.
They have destroyed his home.
8 Do not hold the crimes of our ancestors against us.

79:1–4 The nations have invaded your land and dishonored your holy house. They serve our bodies to birds and animals, spilling our blood like water. There's no one left to bury the dead. Our neighbors mock us.

79:5–7 Will you always be angry with us? Turn your fury on the people who don't worship you, those intent on destroying your people.

79:8–9 Don't hold us guilty for

the sins of our ancestors. Touch us with compassion. Be our help so your name is honored. Rescue and forgive us.

79:10–11 Why do you let everyone think you've left us? Teach the nations a lesson for killing your servants. Hear the groans of your imprisoned people. Rescue us from death row.

79:12–13 Pay back our persecutors for their insults. Give us reason to thank you forever.

80:1–2 Open your ears to your people. Be the Shepherd that you are. Stand high above the angels. Show yourself and save us.

80:3–5 Restore us. Smile on us. Save us. Stop smoldering in anger when you hear our prayers. Our tears are the only thing left to drink.

80:6–7 People fight over us and make fun of us. Restore us. Smile on us. Save us.

80:8–13 You brought your people out of Egypt and planted us like a vine. You cleared the land around us so we could take root. We grew and spread our shade far and wide.

Reach out to us soon with your compassion,
  because we are helpless.
⁹ Help us, O God, our savior, for the glory of your name.
  Rescue us, and forgive our sins for the honor of
    your name.
¹⁰ Why should the nations ˻be allowed to˼ say,
  "Where is their God?"
Let us watch as the nations learn
  that there is punishment for shedding the blood of
    your servants.
¹¹ Let the groans of prisoners come into your presence.
  With your powerful arm rescue those who are condemned
    to death.
¹² Pay each one of our neighbors back
  with seven times the number of insults they used to
    insult you, O Lord.
¹³ Then we, your people, the flock in your pasture,
  will give thanks to you forever.
  We will praise you throughout every generation.

Psalm 80

For the choir director; according to shoshannim eduth;
by Asaph; a psalm.

¹ Open your ears, O Shepherd of Israel,
  the one who leads ˻the descendants of˼ Joseph
    like sheep,
  the one who is enthroned over the angels.ᵃ
² Appear in front of Ephraim, Benjamin, and Manasseh.
  Wake up your power, and come to save us.

³ O God, restore us and smile on us
  so that we may be saved.

⁴ O Lᴏʀᴅ God, commander of armies, how long will you
    smolder in anger
  against the prayer of your people?
⁵ You made them eat tears as food.
  You often made them drink ˻their own˼ tears.
⁶ You made us a source of conflict to our neighbors,
  and our enemies made fun of us.

⁷ O God, commander of armies, restore us and smile
    on us
  so that we may be saved.

⁸ You brought a vine from Egypt.
  You forced out the nations and planted it.
⁹ You cleared the ground for it
  so that it took root and filled the land.
¹⁰   Its shade covered the mountains.
  Its branches covered the mighty cedars.

ᵃ 80:1 Or "cherubim."

11   It reached out with its branches to the
           Mediterranean Sea.
       Its shoots reached the Euphrates River.

12 Why did you break down the stone fences around
       this vine?
    All who pass by are picking its fruit.
13   Wild boars from the forest graze on it.
       Wild animals devour it.
14 O God, commander of armies, come back!
    Look from heaven and see!
    Come to help this vine.
15 Take care of what your right hand planted,
    the son you strengthened for yourself.
16   The vine has been cut down and burned.
           Let them be destroyed by the threatening look
               on your face.

17 Let your power rest on the man you have chosen,
    the son of man you strengthened for yourself.
18   Then we will never turn away from you.
           Give us life again, and we will call on you.

19 O LORD God, commander of armies, restore us, and
    smile on us
    so that we may be saved.

Why have you quit protecting us?
People are picking us clean. Wild
animals graze on us.

80:14–16 God of armies, come
help! Protect what you yourself
planted. Just throw your enemies
a threatening glance and they will
be destroyed.

80:17–19 Give power to our
leaders. Give life to our souls.
Then we'll stay faithful to you.
Restore us. Smile on us. Then we
will be saved.

Psalm 81

For the choir director; on the gittith;[a] *by Asaph.*

1 Sing joyfully to God, our strength.
    Shout happily to the God of Jacob.
2 Begin a psalm, and strike a tambourine.
    Play lyres and harps with their pleasant music.
3 Blow the ram's horn on the day of the new moon,
    on the day of the full moon,
    on our festival days.
4 This is a law for Israel,
    a legal decision from the God of Jacob.
5   These are the instructions God set in place
           for Joseph
               when Joseph rose to power over Egypt.

I heard a message I did not understand:
6   "I removed the burden from his shoulder.
           His hands were freed from the basket.
7   When you were in trouble, you called out ⌐to me⌐,
           and I rescued you.
       I was hidden in thunder, but I answered you.
       I tested your ⌐loyalty⌐ at the oasis of Meribah. *Selah*

81:1–3 I sing joyfully to you,
my strength, and shout happily
to you. I sing and strike a
tambourine. I dedicate days to
celebrating you.

81:4–7 You give clear
instructions to your people. You
set us free to live for you with
total loyalty.

---

a 81:1 Unknown musical term.

81:8–12 You warn us never to worship other gods. You're the one who saved us from slavery. You fulfill our every need. Yet we refuse to listen to you. We turn from you and you let us walk away.

81:13–16 You grieve when we don't listen to you or answer your invitation to follow. Only when we come back to you will you defeat people who hate you. Only then will you feed and satisfy us.

8 Listen, my people, and I will warn you.
 Israel, if you would only listen to me!
9 Never keep any strange god among you.
 Never worship a foreign god.
10 I am the LORD your God, the one who brought you
 out of Egypt.
 Open your mouth wide, and I will fill it.

11 "But my people did not listen to me.
 Israel wanted nothing to do with me.
12 So I let them go their own stubborn ways
 and follow their own advice.
13 If only my people would listen to me!
 If only Israel would follow me!
14 I would quickly defeat their enemies.
 I would turn my power against their foes.
15 Those who hate the LORD would cringe in front
 of him,
 and their time ˻for punishment˼ would
 last forever.
16 But I would feed Israel with the finest wheat
 and satisfy them with honey from a rock."

Psalm 82

A psalm by Asaph.

82:1–2 You can't make yourself any clearer. You don't tolerate unfair judgments. You're tired of people siding with the wicked.

1 God takes his place in his own assembly.
 He pronounces judgment among the gods:
2 "How long are you going to judge unfairly?
 How long are you going to side with
 wicked people?" *Selah*

82:3–5 You call me to defend the weak and orphaned. To protect the oppressed and poor. To rescue the weak and needy. Wicked people don't understand any of this.

3 Defend weak people and orphans.
 Protect the rights of the oppressed and the poor.
4 Rescue weak and needy people.
 Help them escape the power of wicked people.

5 Wicked people do not know or understand anything.
 As they walk around in the dark,
 all the foundations of the earth shake.
6 I said, "You are gods.
 You are all sons of the Most High.
7 You will certainly die like humans
 and fall like any prince."

82:6–8 The powerful will die like anyone else if they disregard your command. So rise up! Judge the world! We are yours!

8 Arise, O God!
 Judge the earth, because all the nations belong
 to you.

Psalm 83

A song; a psalm by Asaph.

[1] O God, do not remain silent.
Do not turn a deaf ear to me.
Do not keep quiet, O God.

[2] Look, your enemies are in an uproar.
Those who hate you hold their heads high.
[3] They make plans in secret against your people
and plot together against those you treasure.
[4] They say, "Let's wipe out their nation
so that the name of Israel will no longer
be remembered."
[5] They agree completely on their plan.
They form an alliance against you:
[6] the tents from Edom and Ishmael,
Moab and Hagar,
[7] Gebal, Ammon, and Amalek,
Philistia, along with those who live in Tyre.
[8] Even Assyria has joined them.
They helped the descendants of Lot.   *Selah*

[9] Do to them what you did to Midian,
to Sisera and Jabin at the Kishon River.
[10] They were destroyed at Endor.
They became manure to fertilize the ground.
[11] Treat their influential people as you treated Oreb
and Zeeb.
Treat all their leaders like Zebah and Zalmunna.
[12] They said, "Let's take God's pasturelands
for ourselves."
[13] O my God, blow them away like tumbleweeds,[a]
like husks in the wind.
[14] Pursue them with your storms,
and terrify them with your windstorms
[15] the way fire burns a forest
and flames set mountains on fire.[b]
[16] Let their faces blush with shame, O LORD,
so that they must look to you for help.
[17] Let them be put to shame and terrified forever.
Let them die in disgrace
[18] so that they must acknowledge you.
Your name is the LORD.
You alone are the Most High God of the
whole earth.

83:1–4 Don't stay silent. Don't pretend to be deaf. Your enemies plot to wipe out your people. They want to erase us so thoroughly that no one will know we ever existed.

83:5–8 This evil alliance already has a plan. The nations around us have all joined together.

83:9–14 Deal with your enemies as you have in the past. Make them manure and use them to fertilize the ground. Blow away evil leaders like tumbleweeds in the wind. Terrify them with your windstorms.

83:16–18 Make evil leaders blush with shame until they turn to you for help. Let them suffer disgrace until they acknowledge you as Lord, the Most High God of the whole world.

---

[a] 83:13 Or "whirling dust."
[b] 83:15 Verse 15 (in Hebrew) has been placed in front of verse 14 to express the complex Hebrew sentence structure more clearly in English.

Psalm 84

For the choir director; on the gittith; *a psalm by Korah's descendants.*

84:1–3 I ache for the beauty of your presence. My whole body shouts for joy to you. Near you even birds find a home, a safe place to hatch their young. You're my King and my God.

¹ Your dwelling place is lovely, O LORD of Armies!
² My soul longs and yearns
    for the LORD's courtyards.
  My whole body shouts for joy to the living God.
³   Even sparrows find a home,
        and swallows find a nest for themselves.
      There they hatch their young
        near your altars, O LORD of Armies,
          my king and my God.

84:4–5 You bless me when I stay close to you. I find abundant reasons to praise you. Drawing on your strength blesses me.

⁴ Blessed are those who live in your house.
  They are always praising you.   *Selah*
⁵ Blessed are those who find strength in you.
  Their hearts are on the road ⌞that leads to you⌟.ᵃ

84:5–7 My heart is on the road that leads to you. When I pass through dry valleys, you fill them with springs. With each step closer to you my strength grows.

⁶   As they pass through a valley where balsam
        trees grow,ᵇ
      they make it a place of springs.
      The early rains cover it with blessings.ᶜ
⁷   Their strength grows as they go along
            until each one of them appears
              in front of God in Zion.

⁸ O LORD God, commander of armies, hear my prayer.
  Open your ears, O God of Jacob.   *Selah*
⁹ Look at our shield, O God.
  Look with favor on the face of your anointed one.

84:10 A single day with you is better than a thousand anywhere else. I'd rather stand on your doorstep than live inside a wicked person's palace.

¹⁰ One day in your courtyards is better than a thousand
    ⌞anywhere else⌟.
  I would rather stand in the entrance to my God's house
    than live inside wicked people's homes.

84:11–12 You warm and protect me, giving me every blessing. All-powerful God, I'm happy because I trust in you.

¹¹ The LORD God is a sun and shield.
  The LORD grants favor and honor.
  He does not hold back any blessing
    from those who live innocently.

¹² O LORD of Armies, blessed is the person who trusts you.

Psalm 85

For the choir director; a psalm by Korah's descendants.

85:1–4 In the past you showed your people your favor. You restored our fortunes and forgave our sins. Restore us once again!

¹ You favored your land, O LORD.
  You restored the fortunes of Jacob.
² You removed your people's guilt.
  You pardoned all their sins.   *Selah*
³ You laid aside all your fury.

ᵃ 84:5 Hebrew meaning of this line uncertain.
ᵇ 84:6 Or "As they pass through the valley of Weeping."
ᶜ 84:6 Or "pools."

You turned away from your burning anger.

⁴ Restore us, O God, our savior.
Put an end to your anger against us.
⁵ Will you be angry with us forever?
Will you ever let go of your anger in the generations
to come?
⁶ Won't you restore our lives again
so that your people may find joy in you?
⁷ Show us your mercy, O LORD,
by giving us your salvation.

85:5–7 Quit your anger toward us. Don't burn against us forever. Rebuild us so we find joy in you once again. Let us experience your merciful gift of salvation.

⁸ I want to hear what God the LORD says,
because he promises peace to his people, to his
godly ones.
But they must not go back to their stupidity.
⁹ Indeed, his salvation is near those who fear him,
and ⌐his⌐ glory will remain in our land.

85:8–9 You promise us peace if we don't go back to our stupidity. Your salvation is near everyone who respects you fully.

¹⁰ Mercy and truth have met.
Righteousness and peace have kissed.
¹¹ Truth sprouts from the ground,
.and righteousness looks down from heaven.
¹² The LORD will certainly give us what is good,
and our land will produce crops.
¹³ Righteousness will go ahead of him
· and make a path for his steps.

85:10–12 Let us enjoy your mercy and truth, your righteousness and peace, your glory and everything good.

Psalm 86

A prayer by David.

¹ Turn your ear ⌐toward me⌐, O LORD.
Answer me, because I am oppressed and needy.
² Protect me, because I am faithful ⌐to you⌐.
Save your servant who trusts you. You are my God.
³ Have pity on me, O Lord,
because I call out to you all day long.
⁴ Give me joy, O Lord,
because I lift my soul to you.
⁵ You, O Lord, are good and forgiving,
full of mercy toward everyone who calls out to you.
⁶ Open your ears to my prayer, O LORD.
Pay attention when I plead for mercy.
⁷ When I am in trouble, I call out to you
because you answer me.
⁸ No god is like you, O Lord.
No one can do what you do.
⁹ All the nations that you have made
will bow in your presence, O Lord.
They will honor you.
¹⁰ Indeed, you are great, a worker of miracles.

86:1–2 Listen to me! Answer me! I live for you. I count on your protection.

86:3–4 Pity me, because I call to you all day long. Give me joy, because I've given my heart to you alone.

86:5–8 You're always good and forgiving, full of mercy to everyone who calls on you. I look to you because there's no one like you, none as able as you.

86:9–10 Your world will bow to you, great worker of miracles. You alone are God.

86:11–13 Teach me to live your truth with utter respect. I'll thank you with all my heart, giving you the honor you deserve for saving me from hell.

You alone are God.
[11] Teach me your way, O Lord,
  so that I may live in your truth.
Focus my heart on fearing you.
[12] I will give thanks to you with all my heart, O Lord
    my God.
  I will honor you forever
[13] because your mercy toward me is great.
    You have rescued me from the depths of hell.

86:14–17 Cruel people who think nothing of you want to kill me. But you're continually compassionate, merciful, patient, faithful, and forgiving. Strengthen me as I serve you. Prove your goodness to me and your world.

[14] O God, arrogant people attack me,
  and a mob of ruthless people seeks my life.
  They think nothing of you.
[15] But you, O Lord, are a compassionate and
    merciful God.
  You are patient, always faithful and ready to forgive.
[16] Turn toward me, and have pity on me.
  Give me your strength because I am your servant.
  Save me because I am the son of your female servant.
[17] Grant me some proof of your goodness
    so that those who hate me may see it and be put
      to shame.
  You, O Lord, have helped me and comforted me.

Psalm 87

By Korah's descendants; a psalm; a song.

87:1–3 You love your holy city and the people who live there. Others see it and say wonderful things.

[1] ˌThe cityˌ the Lord has founded ˌstandsˌ on
    holy mountains.
[2] The Lord loves the city of Zion
  more than any other place in Jacob.
[3] Glorious things are said about you, O city
    of God!   *Selah*

87:4–6 May every nation and race acknowledge you as God. Make the peoples of the world citizens of your kingdom. Let them enjoy the strength and security of your home.

[4] ˌThe Lord says,ˌ "I will add Egypt and Babylon
    as well as Philistia, Tyre, and Sudan
      to the list of those who acknowledge me.
        Each nation ˌwill claim that itˌ was born there."

[5] But it will be said of Zion,
    "Every race is born in it.
      The Most High will make it secure."
[6] The Lord will record this in the Book of Nations:
    "Every race ˌclaims that itˌ was
        born there."   *Selah*

[7] Singers and dancers will sing,
    "Zion is the source of all our blessings."

Psalm 88

A song; a psalm by Korah's descendants; for the choir director; according to mahalath leannoth;[a] *a maskil by Heman the Ezrahite.*

¹O LORD God, my savior,
   I cry out to you during the day and at night.
²   Let my prayer come into your presence.
     Turn your ear to hear my cries.
³My soul is filled with troubles,
   and my life comes closer to the grave.
⁴   I am numbered with those who go into the pit.
     I am like a man without any strength—
⁵   abandoned with the dead,
       like those who have been killed and lie in graves,
       like those whom you no longer remember,
         who are cut off from your power.
⁶You have put me in the bottom of the pit—in deep,
     dark places.
⁷Your rage lies heavily on me.
   You make all your waves pound on me.   *Selah*
⁸You have taken my friends far away from me.
   You made me disgusting to them.
     I'm shut in, and I can't get out.
⁹   My eyes grow weak because of my suffering.
     All day long I call out to you, O LORD.
     I stretch out my hands to you ⌐in prayer⌐.

¹⁰Will you perform miracles for those who are dead?
   Will the spirits of the dead rise and give thanks
     to you?   *Selah*
¹¹Will anyone tell about your mercy in Sheol
   or about your faithfulness in Abaddon?
¹²Will anyone know about your miracles in that dark place
   or about your righteousness in the place where
     forgotten people live?

¹³I cry out to you for help, O LORD,
   and in the morning my prayer will come into
     your presence.
¹⁴Why do you reject my soul, O LORD?
   Why do you hide your face from me?
¹⁵   Ever since I was young, I have been suffering and
     near death.
   I have endured your terrors, and now I am in despair.[b]
¹⁶   Your burning anger has swept over me.
     Your terrors have destroyed me.
¹⁷   They swirl around me all day long like water.

88:1–2 You are my God and Savior to whom I cry day and night. Welcome my prayers!

88:3–7 I'm filled with troubles and my death looms near. I feel already dead, abandoned with others long forgotten and beyond your help. In anger you've buried me in a grave's dark bottom.

88:8–9 You rob me of my friends. You make me repulsive to them. I'm trapped in this grave and can't get out. I can't see anything but my suffering.

88:10–12 What good are your miracles once I'm gone? How can I praise you from the grave? Dead people can't tell others about your mercy and faithfulness.

88:13–14 I cry for your help, approaching you every morning in prayer. Why do you reject me? Why do you hide from me?

88:15–18 I've been near death since I was born. The terrors I know too well cause me despair. Your anger swirls around me. I'm alone except for the darkness.

---

[a] 88:1 Unknown musical term.
[b] 88:15 Hebrew meaning uncertain.

They surround me on all sides.
18   You have taken my loved ones and friends far
away from me.
Darkness is my only friend![a]

Psalm 89

A maskil *by Ethan the Ezrahite.*

89:1 I'll sing now and forever of your mercy and faithfulness. I'll tell of the evidence I've seen with my own eyes.

[1] I will sing forever about the evidence of your mercy,
O Lord.
I will tell about your faithfulness to every generation.
[2] I said, "Your mercy will last forever.
Your faithfulness stands firm in the heavens."

89:3—4 You promised David a family line that lasts forever. You swore his throne will endure to every generation.

[3] ⌞You said,⌟ "I have made a promise[b] to my
chosen one.
I swore this oath to my servant David:
4   'I will make your dynasty continue forever.
I built your throne to last throughout
every generation.'"   *Selah*

89:5—7 Who in heaven compares with you? Who is greater or more awe-inspiring than you? You strike fear in the heart of every living thing.

[5] O Lord, the heavens praise your miracles
and your faithfulness in the assembly of the holy ones.
[6] Who in the skies can compare with the Lord?
Who among the heavenly beings is like the Lord?
[7] God is terrifying in the council of the holy ones.
He is greater and more awe-inspiring than those who
surround him.
[8] O Lord God of Armies, who is like you?
Mighty Lord, even your faithfulness surrounds you.

89:9—11 You rule the sea's raging waves. You crush chaos and scatter your enemies. Everything from heaven to earth belongs to you, because you made it all.

9   You rule the raging sea.
When its waves rise, you quiet them.
10   You crushed Rahab;[c] it was like a corpse.
With your strong arm you scattered your enemies.
[11] The heavens are yours.
The earth is also yours.
You made the world and everything in it.

89:12—14 You created every stretch of land. Majestic mountain heights sing your name with joy. Your strength rules with goodness and justice. Mercy and truth never leave you.

12   You created north and south.
Mount Tabor and Mount Hermon sing your
name joyfully.
13   Your arm is mighty.
Your hand is strong.
Your right hand is lifted high.
[14] Righteousness and justice are the foundations of
your throne.
Mercy and truth stand in front of you.

89:15—17 Happiness fills people who praise you, because your presence lights their paths.

[15] Blessed are the people who know how to praise you.
They walk in the light of your presence, O Lord.
16   They find joy in your name all day long.

---

[a] 88:18 Hebrew meaning uncertain.
[b] 89:3 Or "covenant."
[c] 89:10 Rahab is the name of a demonic creature who opposes God.

They are joyful in your righteousness

17 because you are the glory of their strength.

By your favor you give us victory.[a]

18 Our shield belongs to the LORD.

Our king belongs to the Holy One of Israel.

19 Once in a vision you said to your faithful ones:

"I set a boy above warriors.[b]

I have raised up one chosen from the people.

20 I found my servant David.

I anointed him with my holy oil.

21 My hand is ready to help him.

My arm will also give him strength.

22 No enemy will take him by surprise.

No wicked person will mistreat him.

23 I will crush his enemies in front of him

and defeat those who hate him.

24 My faithfulness and mercy will be with him,

and in my name he will be victorious.[c]

25 I will put his ⌊left⌋ hand on the sea

and his right hand on the rivers.

26 He will call out to me,

'You are my Father, my God, and the rock of

my salvation.'

27 Yes, I will make him the firstborn.

He will be the Most High to the kings of

the earth.

28 My mercy will stay with him forever.

My promise to him is unbreakable.

29 I will make his dynasty endure forever

and his throne like the days of heaven.

30 "If his descendants abandon my teachings

and do not live by my rules,

31 if they violate my laws

and do not obey my commandments,

32 then with a rod I will punish their rebellion

and their crimes with beatings.

33 But I will not take my mercy away from him

or allow my truth to become a lie.

34 I will not dishonor my promise

or alter my own agreement.

35 On my holiness I have taken an oath once and for all:

I will not lie to David.

36 His dynasty will last forever.

His throne will be in my presence like the sun.

37 Like the moon his throne will stand firm forever.

It will be like a faithful witness in heaven."

They never stop celebrating your good name. You strengthen them and give them victory.

89:19–20 You passed over warriors and picked a boy as your chosen one. You raised up David to rule your people.

89:21–24 You're always ready to help the king, strengthening him and protecting him from evil surprises. You crush everyone who hates him. He goes to battle accompanied by your faithfulness and mercy.

89:26–29 The king calls you Father and God. You exalt your firstborn as Most High over every earthly king. To him you make an unbreakable promise that his dynasty will last forever.

89:30–34 You promise to punish your people's disobedience, but you won't break your promise to the king. Your mercy will always endure.

89:35–39 You swore on your holiness that David's line will last forever. Like the sun and the moon it will endure. Yet you haven't kept your promise. You've rejected your people.

---

a 89:17 Hebrew meaning of "give us victory" uncertain.

b 89:19 Hebrew meaning of this line uncertain.

c 89:24 Hebrew meaning of "he will be victorious" uncertain.

89:40–45 You sent enemies through our walls, letting us be robbed and scorned. You grabbed the right hand of our enemies, lifting it high in victory. You left us defenseless, allowing our enemies to cut us down.

³⁸ But you have despised, rejected,
>   and become angry with your anointed one.
³⁹ You have refused to recognize the promise to
>   your servant
>   and have thrown his crown into the dirt.
⁴⁰ You have broken through all his walls
>   and have laid his fortified cities in ruins.
⁴¹   (Everyone who passed by robbed him.
>   He has become the object of his
>   neighbors' scorn.)
⁴² You held the right hand of his enemies high
>   and made all of his adversaries rejoice.
⁴³ You even took his sword out of his hand
>   and failed to support him in battle.
⁴⁴ You put an end to his splendor
>   and hurled his throne to the ground.
⁴⁵ You cut short the days of his youth
>   and covered him with shame.   *Selah*

89:46–47 Will you always hide from us? Will you always be angry? Life is too short for this!

⁴⁶ How long, O LORD? Will you hide yourself forever?
>   How long will your anger continue to burn like fire?
⁴⁷ Remember how short my life is!
>   Have you created Adam's descendants for no reason?
⁴⁸   Can a mortal go on living and never see death?
>   Who can set himself free from the power of
>   the grave?   *Selah*

89:49–51 Where's the proof of your mercy? Where's the evidence of your oath? My heart aches with the insults heaped on me and on your Messiah.

⁴⁹   Where is the evidence of your mercy, LORD?
>   You swore an oath to David
>   on ⌞the basis of⌟ your faithfulness.

⁵⁰ Remember, O LORD,^a how your servant^b has
>   been insulted.
>   Remember how I have carried in my heart ⌞the
>   insults⌟ from so many people.
⁵¹   Your enemies insulted ⌞me⌟.
>   They insulted your Messiah^c every step he took.

⁵²   Thank the LORD forever.
>   Amen and amen!

BOOK FOUR

(Psalms 90–106)

Psalm 90

A prayer by Moses, the man of God.

90:1–2 Forever and ever you've been our refuge. Before you

¹ O Lord, you have been our refuge throughout
>   every generation.

---

^a 89:50 Many Hebrew manuscripts; other Hebrew manuscripts "Lord."
^b 89:50 Many Hebrew manuscripts, Greek, Syriac; other Hebrew manuscripts "your servants."
^c 89:51 Or "anointed one."

2   Before the mountains were born,
        before you gave birth to the earth and the world, you
            were God.
        You are God from everlasting to everlasting.

3 You turn mortals back into dust
        and say, "Return, descendants of Adam."
4 Indeed, in your sight a thousand years are like a
        single day,
        like yesterday—already past—
        like an hour in the night.
5 You sweep mortals away.
        They are a dream.
        They sprout again in the morning like cut grass.
6   In the morning they blossom and sprout.
        In the evening they wither and dry up.

7 Indeed, your anger consumes us.
        Your rage terrifies us.
8   You have set our sins in front of you.
        You have put our secret sins in the light of
            your presence.
9 Indeed, all our days slip away because of your fury.
        We live out our years like one ⌞long⌟ sigh.
10   Each of us lives for 70 years—
        or even 80 if we are in good health.
            But the best of them[a] ⌞bring⌟ trouble
                and misery.
            Indeed, they are soon gone, and we fly away.
11 Who fully understands the power of your anger?
        A person fears you more when he better understands
            your fury.[b]
12 Teach us to number each of our days
        so that we may grow in wisdom.

13 Return, LORD! How long . . . ?
        Change your plans about ⌞us,⌟ your servants.
14 Satisfy us every morning with your mercy
        so that we may sing joyfully and rejoice all
            our days.
15 Make us rejoice for as many days as you have made
        us suffer,
        for as many years as we have experienced evil.
16 Let ⌞us,⌟ your servants, see what you can do.
        Let our children see your glorious power.
17 Let the kindness of the Lord our God be with us.
        Make us successful in everything we do.
            Yes, make us successful in everything we do.

formed the earth you reigned as the everlasting God.

90:3–5 You'll decide when my time on earth is up and then turn me back to dust. In your eyes a thousand years flicker like a single day. I'll come and go like a dream.

90:7–10 Your anger consumes me. Your brilliance exposes every one of my sins. Your fury makes my days slip away, so that my years add up to no more than one long sigh. The best years of my life bring trouble, and soon they'll all be gone.

90:11–12 Your fury teaches me to respect you. The shortness of my life tells me to live wisely.

90:14–15 Satisfy me morning by morning with your mercy. Give me reason to rejoice every day I have breath.

90:16–17 Show me your power. Lead me through life with your kindness. Make me successful in everything I do!

---

[a] 90:10 Hebrew meaning of "the best of them" uncertain.
[b] 90:11 Hebrew meaning of this line uncertain.

Psalm 91

91:1–2 You're my refuge, my God, the one I trust. I live in your safety and find rest in your presence.

[1] Whoever lives under the shelter of the Most High
 will remain in the shadow of the Almighty.
[2] I will say to the Lord,
 "⌐You are⌐ my refuge and my fortress, my God in
 whom I trust."

91:3–4 You rescue me from traps and deadly plagues. You pull me close and protect me. Your truth is my armor.

[3] He is the one who will rescue you from hunters' traps
 and from deadly plagues.
[4] He will cover you with his feathers,
 and under his wings you will find refuge.
 His truth is your shield and armor.

91:5–8 Because of your care I'm unafraid of terror, no matter where it might strike. Ten thousand might die next to me, but you'll spare me. I'll see with my own eyes how you punish evil.

[5] You do not need to fear
 terrors of the night,
 arrows that fly during the day,
[6] plagues that roam the dark,
 epidemics that strike at noon.
[7]   They will not come near you,
    even though a thousand may fall dead
     beside you
    or ten thousand at your right side.

[8] You only have to look with your eyes
 to see the punishment of wicked people.

91:9–13 God Most High, you're my home. Keep sickness and harm far from me. Command your angels to carry me through life. Let me trample on danger before it strikes.

[9] You, O Lord, are my refuge!

 You have made the Most High your home.
[10] No harm will come to you.
 No sickness will come near your house.
[11] He will put his angels in charge of you
 to protect you in all your ways.
[12]   They will carry you in their hands
    so that you never hit your foot against a rock.
[13]   You will step on lions and cobras.
 You will trample young lions and snakes.

91:14–16 Rescue me because you love me. Protect me because I'm yours. Answer me when I'm in trouble. Save me, honor me, and satisfy me with long life.

[14] Because you love me, I will rescue you.
 I will protect you because you know my name.
[15] When you call to me, I will answer you.
 I will be with you when you are in trouble.
 I will save you and honor you.
[16] I will satisfy you with a long life.
 I will show you how I will save you.

Psalm 92

A psalm; a song; for the day of worship.

92:1–3 I praise you at dawn and dusk and every hour in between. It's my chance

[1] It is good to give thanks to the Lord,
 to make music to praise your name, O Most High.
[2] It is good to announce your mercy in the morning
 and your faithfulness in the evening

3 on a ten-stringed instrument and a harp
and with a melody on a lyre.

4 You made me find joy in what you have done, O LORD.
I will sing joyfully about the works of your hands.
5 How spectacular are your works, O LORD!
How very deep are your thoughts!

6 A stupid person cannot know
and a fool cannot understand
7 that wicked people sprout like grass
and all troublemakers blossom ⌐like flowers⌐,
only to be destroyed forever.

8 But you, O LORD, are highly honored forever.
9 Now look at your enemies, O LORD.
Now look at your enemies.
They disappear, and all troublemakers
are scattered.

10 But you make me as strong as a wild bull,
and soothing lotion is poured on me.
11 My eyes gloat over those who spy on me.
My ears hear ⌐the cries⌐ of evildoers attacking me.

12 Righteous people flourish like palm trees
and grow tall like the cedars in Lebanon.
13 They are planted in the LORD's house.
They blossom in our God's courtyards.
14 Even when they are old, they still bear fruit.
They are always healthy and fresh.
15 They make it known that the LORD is decent.
He is my rock.
He is never unfair.

Psalm 93

1 The LORD rules as king! He is clothed with majesty.
The LORD has clothed himself; he has armed himself
with power.
The world was set in place; it cannot be moved.

2 Your throne was set in place a long time ago.
You are eternal.

3 The ocean rises, O LORD.
The ocean rises with a roar.
The ocean rises with its pounding waves.
4 The LORD above is mighty—
mightier than the sound of raging water,
mightier than the foaming waves of the sea.

5 Your written testimonies are completely reliable.

---

to declare your mercy and faithfulness. I sing and strum melodies to you.
92:4–5 Your spectacular handiwork gives me joy! Your thoughts are exceedingly deep!

92:6–8 Stupid people don't grasp that evildoers come and go like grass. But you deserve honor forever.

92:9–11 I've seen your enemies scatter even as you soothe me and make me strong. You keep me safe from lurking spies and evildoers on the attack.

92:12–15 I flourish like a palm planted in your courtyard, like a tree that will bear fruit even in old age. Keep me healthy and fresh. My well-being will declare your constant goodness and fairness.

93:1–2 You rule! You're clothed with majesty and armed with power. You've reigned forever and you'll never cease to exist.

93:3–4 I'm filled with awe as I watch the ocean roar and pound. Yet raging waters are feeble compared to you.

93:5 Your Word is completely

reliable. Your holiness makes heaven eternally beautiful.

O L0rd, holiness is what makes your house beautiful for days without end.

Psalm 94

94:1–7 Judge of the earth, arise and give proud people what they deserve. How long will you let them succeed?

[1] O Lord, God of vengeance,
O God of vengeance, appear!
[2] Arise, O Judge of the earth.
Give arrogant people what they deserve.
[3] How long, O Lord, will wicked people triumph?
How long?

94:4–7 Evildoers boast on and on. They crush your people. They kill widows and foreigners and orphans. Then they say you can't see them. They claim you aren't paying attention.

[4] They ramble.
They speak arrogantly.
All troublemakers brag about themselves.
[5] They crush your people, O Lord.
They make those who belong to you suffer.
[6] They kill widows and foreigners, and they murder orphans.
[7] They say, "The Lord doesn't see it.
The God of Jacob doesn't even pay attention to it."

94:8–9 Do stupid people really think you can't hear? You created our ears! Do they think you can't see? You formed our eyes!

[8] Pay attention, you stupid people!
When will you become wise, you fools?
[9] God created ears.
Do you think he can't hear?
He formed eyes.
Do you think he can't see?

94:10 Do fools actually think you won't punish? You discipline the nations! Do they think you know nothing? You're our teacher!

[10] He disciplines nations.
Do you think he can't punish?
He teaches people.
Do you think he doesn't know anything?

94:11–12 You know the pointlessness of human thoughts. I'm happy when you train and teach me.

[11] The Lord knows that people's thoughts are pointless.
[12] O Lord, blessed is the person whom you discipline and instruct from your teachings.

94:13–14 In troubled times you give me peace and quiet. Because I'm yours you'll never abandon me.

[13] You give him peace and quiet from times of trouble while a pit is dug to trap wicked people.
[14] The Lord will never desert his people or abandon those who belong to him.

94:15–16 Come lead our world. Make judges decide fairly and decent people work for justice. Take my side against evildoers.

[15] The decisions of judges will again become fair, and everyone whose motives are decent will pursue justice.[a]
[16] Who will stand up for me against evildoers?
Who will stand by my side against troublemakers?

94:17–23 I would have died if you hadn't helped me. I was

[17] If the Lord had not come to help me,
my soul would have quickly fallen silent ⌞in death⌟.

[a] 94:15 English equivalent of this verse difficult.

¹⁸ When I said, "My feet are slipping,"
  your mercy, O Lᴏʀᴅ, continued to hold me up.
¹⁹ When I worried about many things,
  your assuring words soothed my soul.

²⁰ Are wicked rulers who use the law to do unlawful things
    able to be your partners?
²¹   They join forces to take the lives of
        righteous people.
      They condemn innocent people to death.
²² The Lᴏʀᴅ has become my stronghold.
  My God has become my rock of refuge.
²³   He has turned their own wickedness against them.
      He will destroy them because of their sins.
        The Lᴏʀᴅ our God will destroy them.

slipping but you held me up. I was worried but you soothed my soul. You're my rock and my refuge. You turn the sins of the wicked against them.

Psalm 95

¹ Come, let's sing joyfully to the Lᴏʀᴅ.
  Let's shout happily to the rock of our salvation.
²   Let's come into his presence with a song
      of thanksgiving.
  Let's shout happily to him with psalms.
³ The Lᴏʀᴅ is a great God and a great king above all gods.
⁴   In his hand are the deep places of the earth,
      and the mountain peaks are his.
⁵   The sea is his.
      He made it, and his hands formed the dry land.

95:1–3 I shout my joy to you, rock of my salvation! I shout my happiness to you, great King above every so-called god!

95:4–5 You hold the depths and peaks of the earth in your hand. The land and sea belong to you. You made all of it.

⁶ Come, let's worship and bow down.
  Let's kneel in front of the Lᴏʀᴅ, our maker,
⁷   because he is our God
        and we are the people in his care,
          the flock that he leads.

95:6–7 I bow and worship you, Lord my maker. You're my God. You lead me as one of your flock.

If only you would listen to him today!
⁸   "Do not be stubborn like ⌊my people were⌋
      at Meribah,
      like the time at Massah in the desert.
⁹   Your ancestors challenged me and tested
        me there,
          although they had seen what I had done.
¹⁰ For 40 years I was disgusted with those people.
  So I said, 'They are a people whose hearts continue
    to stray.
      They have not learned my ways.'
¹¹ That is why I angrily took this solemn oath:
      'They will never enter my place of rest!'"

95:8–11 Your people witnessed your miracles yet they tested you. They constantly strayed from you and refused to learn your ways. Train me to obey you. Give me a heart that follows you. I want to enjoy your rest!

Psalm 96

¹ Sing to the Lᴏʀᴅ a new song!
  Sing to the Lᴏʀᴅ, all the earth!

96:1–3 My heart has fresh songs of praise for you. Day after day I announce how you save your people. I tell everyone about your glory and miracles.

96:4–5 You're worthy of higher praise than I know how to bring. You're nothing like false gods. You're fearsome and real.

96:6–8 Splendor and majesty fill your presence. Strength and beauty abound in your holy place. I promise to give you the glory you deserve.

96:9 Let me see your holy splendor. I tremble in your presence!

96:10–13 You reign over every human in every nation, judging without favoritism. So let heaven and earth rejoice. Let the sea roar. Let every field and forest sing your arrival. You'll judge the world with righteousness and truth.

² Sing to the Lord! Praise his name!
Day after day announce that the Lord saves his people.
³ Tell people about his glory.
Tell all the nations about his miracles.

⁴ The Lord is great!
He should be highly praised.
He should be feared more than all ⌐other⌐ gods
⁵ because all the gods of the nations are idols.
The Lord made the heavens.
⁶ Splendor and majesty are in his presence.
Strength and beauty are in his holy place.

⁷ Give to the Lord, you families of the nations.
Give to the Lord glory and power.
⁸ Give to the Lord the glory he deserves.
Bring an offering, and come into his courtyards.
⁹ Worship the Lord in ⌐his⌐ holy splendor.
Tremble in his presence, all the earth!

¹⁰ Say to the nations, "The Lord rules as king!"
The earth stands firm; it cannot be moved.
He will judge people fairly.
¹¹ Let the heavens rejoice and the earth be glad.
Let the sea and everything in it roar like thunder.
¹² Let the fields and everything in them rejoice.
Then all the trees in the forest will sing joyfully
¹³ in the Lord's presence because he is coming.
He is coming to judge the earth.
He will judge the world with righteousness
and its people with his truth.

Psalm 97

97:1–3 Because you rule as King I rejoice. You surround yourself with dark clouds. You build your throne on goodness and fairness. You scorch your enemies with purifying fire.

97:4–5 People see you light up the world with lightning and they tremble. Mountains melt in the heat of your presence.

97:6–9 The skies declare your goodness, showing off your glory for everyone to see. Maybe everyone will finally understand

¹ The Lord rules as king.
Let the earth rejoice.
Let all the islands be joyful.
² Clouds and darkness surround him.
Righteousness and justice are the foundations of his throne.
³ Fire spreads ahead of him.
It burns his enemies who surround him.
⁴ His flashes of lightning light up the world.
The earth sees them and trembles.
⁵ The mountains melt like wax in the presence of the Lord,
in the presence of the Lord of the whole earth.
⁶ The heavens tell about his righteousness,
and all the people of the world see his glory.

⁷ Everyone who worships idols
and brags about false gods will be put to shame.

All the gods will bow to him.

⁸ Zion hears about this and rejoices.
The people of Judah are delighted with your judgments,
O LORD.
⁹ You, O LORD, the Most High, are above the
whole earth.
You are highest. You are above all the gods.
¹⁰ Let those who love the LORD hate evil.
The one who guards the lives of his godly ones
will rescue them from the power of wicked people.
¹¹ Light dawns for righteous people^a
and joy for those whose motives are decent.
¹² Find joy in the LORD, you righteous people.
Give thanks to him as you remember how holy he is.

the worthlessness of false gods.
I rejoice when others discover
you're real. You're the Most High
God, Lord over all.

97:10–12 You'll make dawn
break through my darkness.
You'll give me joy in you. Your
holiness makes my heart well up
with thanks.

Psalm 98

A psalm.

¹ Sing a new song to the LORD
because he has done miraculous things.
His right hand and his holy arm have gained
victory for him.
² The LORD has made his salvation known.
He has uncovered his righteousness for the nations
to see.
³   He has not forgotten to be merciful and faithful
to Israel's descendants.
All the ends of the earth have seen how our God
saves ⌐them⌐.

98:1–3 I sing to celebrate your
miraculous acts, the power that
assured you of victory. Every
nation can see your salvation.
They witness your faithfulness to
your people.

⁴ Shout happily to the LORD, all the earth.
Break out into joyful singing, and make music.
⁵ Make music to the LORD with a lyre,
with a lyre and the melody of a psalm,
⁶   with trumpets and the playing of a ram's horn.
Shout happily in the presence of the king, the LORD.

98:4–6 Let the whole world
break out in music to you. Let
lyres and trumpets make
joyful tunes.

⁷ Let the sea, everything in it,
the world, and those who live in it roar like thunder.
⁸ Let the rivers clap their hands
and the mountains sing joyfully
⁹   in the LORD's presence
because he is coming to judge the earth.
He will judge the world with justice
and its people with fairness.

98:7–9 The sea roars with
worship and rivers clap their
hands to you. Mountains sing
because you're coming to judge
the earth with fairness.

Psalm 99

¹ The LORD rules as king.
Let the people tremble.

99:1–3 You rule as King. Let
everyone tremble! Let the earth

---

^a 97:11 One Hebrew manuscript, Greek, Syriac, Latin; other Hebrew
manuscripts "Light is planted for righteous people."

quake with respect! You reign over every angel and every human being. I offer thanks to your awesome name. You are holy!

He is enthroned over the angels.[a]
　　Let the earth quake.
[2] The LORD is mighty in Zion.
He is high above all people.
[3] 　Let them give thanks to your great and fearful name.

　　He is holy!

99:4–5 Your love of justice makes you strong. You're always fair and always right. You're worthy of the highest honor and I bow to you. You are holy!

[4] The king's strength is that he loves justice.
　　You have established fairness.
　　You have done what is fair and right for Jacob.

[5] Highly honor the LORD our God.
Bow down at his footstool.

　　He is holy!

99:6–9 You answered the prayers of Moses and Aaron and Samuel. You spoke to them from a column of smoke and put your laws in writing. You're a God who forgives yet you'll punish the unrepentant. You're worthy of the highest honor. I bow to you. You are holy!

[6] Moses and Aaron were among his priests.
Samuel was among those who prayed to him.
　　They called to the LORD, and he answered them.
[7] 　　He spoke to them from a column of smoke.
　　They obeyed his written instructions and the laws
　　　　that he gave them.
[8] O LORD, our God, you answered them.
　　You showed them that you are a forgiving God
　　　　and that you are a God who punishes their
　　　　⌐sinful⌐ deeds.

[9] Highly honor the LORD our God.
Bow at his holy mountain.

　　The LORD our God is holy!

Psalm 100

A psalm of thanksgiving.

100:1–3 I shout happily to you. I serve you gladly. I enter your presence with a joyful song. Why? Because you alone are God. You made me and I'm yours. I'm one of your flock.

[1] Shout happily to the LORD, all the earth.
[2] Serve the LORD cheerfully.
　　Come into his presence with a joyful song.
[3] Realize that the LORD alone is God.
　　He made us, and we are his.[b]
　　We are his people and the sheep in his care.
[4] Enter his gates with a song of thanksgiving.
　　Come into his courtyards with a song of praise.
　　Give thanks to him; praise his name.

100:4–5 I enter your presence with a song of praise and thanksgiving. Why? Because you're always good. Your faithfulness endures forever.

[5] The LORD is good.
　　His mercy endures forever.
　　His faithfulness endures throughout
　　　　every generation.

---

[a] 99:1 Or "cherubim."
[b] 100:3 Many Hebrew manuscripts, Greek, Targum, Latin; other Hebrew manuscripts "and not we ourselves."

Psalm 101

A psalm by David.

¹I will sing about mercy and justice.
O Lord, I will make music to praise you.
²I want to understand the path to integrity.
  When will you come to me?

I will live in my own home with integrity.
³ I will not put anything wicked in front of my eyes.
I hate what unfaithful people do.
  I want no part of it.
⁴I will keep far away from devious minds.
  I will have nothing to do with evil.
⁵I will destroy anyone who secretly slanders
    his neighbor.
  I will not tolerate anyone with a conceited look or
    arrogant heart.
⁶My eyes will be watching the faithful people in the land
  so that they may live with me.
    The person who lives with integrity will serve me.
⁷The one who does deceitful things will not stay in
    my home.
  The one who tells lies will not remain in my presence.

⁸Every morning I will destroy all the wicked people in
    the land
  to rid the Lord's city of all troublemakers.

101:2 Help me grasp what integrity is all about. Come and show me! I want to live with integrity toward my family.

101:3–5 I want nothing to do with unfaithfulness. I stay far from people who plot evil. I don't tolerate conceit.

101:6–8 I'm studying the people around me. I'm on the lookout for faithfulness and failure. I won't follow the lead of deceivers or liars. I'll stay far from troublemakers.

Psalm 102

A prayer by someone who is suffering, when he is weary and pours out his troubles in the Lord's presence.

¹O Lord, hear my prayer,
  and let my cry for help come to you.
²   Do not hide your face from me when I am
      in trouble.
    Turn your ear toward me.
    Answer me quickly when I call.
³My days disappear like smoke.
 My bones burn like hot coals.
⁴My heart is beaten down and withered like grass
  because I have forgotten about eating.
⁵I am nothing but skin and bones
  because of my loud groans.
⁶I am like a desert owl,
  like an owl living in the ruins.
⁷I lie awake.
 I am like a lonely bird on a rooftop.
⁸All day long my enemies insult me.
  Those who ridicule me use my name as a curse.
⁹I eat ashes like bread

102:1–2 Hear me when I cry to you for help. Don't turn away when I'm in trouble.

102:3–5 My life is going up in smoke. My bones burn and my heart is beaten down. I'm too sad to eat. I've shrunk to skin and bones.

102:8–10 My enemies use my name to curse. Ashes are all I eat and my tears fall into my cup—

all because of your anger. You've tossed me into the trash.

102:11–13 I'm dying like grass but you'll last forever. Soon you'll rise and show me compassion, because the time to show me favor has finally come.

102:16–22 One day you'll rebuild your people. You'll hear the prayers of the abandoned. You'll look down from heaven and see our suffering. You'll listen closely and hear our groans. You'll free us from death row. And one day all the world will gather to worship you.

102:23–24 You've taken strength from my body and days from my life. Don't cut me down now.

102:25–28 Long ago you formed the earth and the heavens. One day they'll be finished, but you'll live on. This world will wear out like old clothes. You'll toss it aside, but you'll live on. And your people will live forever in your presence.

and my tears are mixed with my drink

10   because of your hostility and anger,
      because you have picked me up and thrown
         me away.

11 My days are like a shadow that is getting longer,
      and I wither away like grass.

12 But you, O LORD, remain forever.
      You are remembered throughout every generation.

13   You will rise and have compassion on Zion,
         because it is time to grant a favor to it.
            Indeed, the appointed time has come.

14   Your servants value Zion's stones,
                  and they pity its rubble.

15 The nations will fear the LORD's name.
      All the kings of the earth will fear your glory.

16 When the LORD builds Zion,
      he will appear in his glory.

17   He will turn his attention to the prayers
         of those who have been abandoned.
      He will not despise their prayers.

18 This will be written down for a future generation
      so that a people yet to be created may praise the LORD:

19   "The LORD looked down from his holy place
         high above.
      From heaven he looked at the earth.

20   He heard the groans of the prisoners
            and set free those who were condemned
               to death.

21   The LORD's name is announced in Zion
               and his praise in Jerusalem

22   when nations and kingdoms gather
                  to worship the LORD."

23 He has weakened my strength along the way.
      He has reduced ⌐the number of⌐ my days.

24 I said, "My God, don't take me now in the middle of
         my life.
      Your years ⌐continue on⌐ throughout every generation.

25   Long ago you laid the foundation of the earth.
      Even the heavens are the works of your hands.

26   They will come to an end, but you will still go on.
      They will all wear out like clothing.
         You will change them like clothes,
            and they will be thrown away.

27   But you remain the same, and your life will
                  never end.

28   The children of your servants will go on living ⌐here⌐.
      Their descendants will be secure in your presence."

Psalm 103

By David.

¹Praise the LORD, my soul!
Praise his holy name, all that is within me.
²Praise the LORD, my soul,
  and never forget all the good he has done:
³   He is the one who forgives all your sins,
    the one who heals all your diseases,
⁴   the one who rescues your life from the pit,
    the one who crowns you with mercy
      and compassion,
⁵   the one who fills your life with blessings
      so that you become young again like an eagle.

⁶The LORD does what is right and fair
  for all who are oppressed.
⁷   He let Moses know his ways.
    He let the Israelites know the things he had done.
⁸The LORD is compassionate, merciful, patient,
  and always ready to forgive.

⁹He will not always accuse us of wrong
  or be angry ˪with us˩ forever.
¹⁰He has not treated us as we deserve for our sins
  or paid us back for our wrongs.

¹¹As high as the heavens are above the earth—
  that is how vast his mercy is toward those who
    fear him.
¹²As far as the east is from the west—
  that is how far he has removed our rebellious acts
    from himself.
¹³As a father has compassion for his children,
  so the LORD has compassion for those who fear him.

¹⁴He certainly knows what we are made of.
  He bears in mind that we are dust.
¹⁵Human life is as short-lived as grass.
  It blossoms like a flower in the field.
¹⁶   When the wind blows over the flower, it disappears,
    and there is no longer any sign of it.

¹⁷But from everlasting to everlasting,
  the LORD's mercy is on those who fear him.
    His righteousness belongs
      to their children and grandchildren,
¹⁸   to those who are faithful to his promise,ᵃ
    to those who remember to follow his
      guiding principles.
¹⁹The LORD has set his throne in heaven.

103:1–2 I praise you with all my might. I'll never forget the good you've done me.

103:3–6 You forgive my sins and heal my diseases. You rescue me from death and treat me with compassion. You fill my life with blessings and make me young again. You do right on behalf of all the oppressed.

103:8–10 Be compassionate to me. Be merciful, patient, and quick to forgive. Don't pay me back for my sins or give me what I deserve.

103:11–12 As far as the sky stretches above the earth—that's the vastness of your mercy to me. As far as the east runs from the west—that's how far you've cast away my rebellion.

103:14–16 You know I'm dust and my life is brief. Winds will blow over me and I will disappear.

103:17–18 Though my life is short your mercy lasts forever—mercy you give to those who live in awe of you. Your righteousness belongs to my children and grandchildren. Each of your promises and principles is a gift to us.

ᵃ 103:18 Or "covenant."

His kingdom rules everything.

103:19–22 You've established your throne in heaven and you rule everything that exists. Your angels will praise you. Your servants will praise you. Your creatures will praise you. And I too will praise you!

²⁰ Praise the LORD, all his angels,
  you mighty beings who carry out his orders
    and are ready to obey his spoken orders.
²¹ Praise the LORD, all his armies,
  his servants who carry out his will.
²² Praise the LORD, all his creatures
  in all the places of his empire.
Praise the LORD, my soul!

Psalm 104

104:1–5 Praise you! Praise your splendor and majesty! You wrap yourself in light. You stretch out the heavens. You lay the foundation of an unshakable earth.

¹ Praise the LORD, my soul!
O LORD my God, you are very great.
  You are clothed with splendor and majesty.
²   You cover yourself with light as though it were a robe.
  You stretch out the heavens as though they
    were curtains.
³   You lay the beams of your home in the water.
  You use the clouds for your chariot.
  You move on the wings of the wind.
⁴   You make your angels winds
    and your servants flames of fire.

⁵ You set the earth on its foundations
  so that it can never be shaken.

104:6–9 You covered the earth with water and raised the mountains to tower above the seas. You created peaks and valleys and hold back waters from flooding the earth.

⁶ You covered the earth with an ocean as though it were
    a robe.
  Water stood above the mountains
⁷   and fled because of your threat.
  Water ran away at the sound of your thunder.
⁸   The mountains rose and the valleys sank
    to the place you appointed for them.
⁹   Water cannot cross the boundary you set
    and cannot come back to cover the earth.

104:10–15 You make springs gush forth to give animals water to drink and birds a place to sing. You make grass grow for cattle and feed me with every good thing.

¹⁰ You make water gush from springs into valleys.
  It flows between the mountains.
¹¹   Every wild animal drinks ⌊from them⌋.
  Wild donkeys quench their thirst.
¹²   The birds live by the streams.
  They sing among the branches.
¹³ You water the mountains from your home above.
  You fill the earth with the fruits of your labors.

¹⁴ You make grass grow for cattle
  and make vegetables for humans to use
    in order to get food from the ground.
¹⁵ You make wine to cheer human hearts,
  olive oil to make faces shine,

and bread to strengthen human hearts.
¹⁶ The LORD's trees, the cedars in Lebanon which
    he planted,
    drink their fill.
¹⁷   Birds build their nests in them.
    Storks makes their homes in fir trees.
¹⁸ The high mountains are for wild goats.
    The rocks are a refuge for badgers.

¹⁹ He created the moon, which marks the seasons,
    and the sun, which knows when to set.
²⁰   He brings darkness, and it is nighttime,
        when all the wild animals in the forest come out.
²¹   The young lions roar for their prey
        and seek their food from God.
²²   When the sun rises,
        they gather and lie down in their dens.
²³   Then people go to do their work,
        to do their tasks until evening.

²⁴ What a large number of things you have made, O LORD!
    You made them all by wisdom.
        The earth is filled with your creatures.
²⁵   The sea is so big and wide with
            countless creatures,
            living things both large and small.
²⁶   Ships sail on it,
        and Leviathan,^a which you made, plays in it.
²⁷ All of them look to you to give them their food at the
    right time.
²⁸   You give it to them, and they gather it up.
    You open your hand, and they are filled
        with blessings.
²⁹   You hide your face, and they are terrified.
    You take away their breath, and they die and return
        to dust.
³⁰   You send out your Spirit, and they are created.
    You renew the face of the earth.

³¹ May the glory of the LORD endure forever.
    May the LORD find joy in what he has made.
³²   He looks at the earth, and it trembles.
    He touches the mountains, and they smoke.
³³   I will sing to the LORD throughout my life.
    I will make music to praise my God as long as
        I live.
³⁴ May my thoughts be pleasing to him.
    I will find joy in the LORD.
³⁵ May sinners vanish from the world.

---

^a 104:26 Hebrew meaning uncertain.

104:16–18 You plant the tallest trees and let them drink from the ground. You create a home on earth for every living thing.

104:19–23 You made the moon to mark the seasons and the sun to mark the day. By night young lions get their food from you. By day I arise and work.

104:24–25 You made countless things. You wisely created all of them, filling the earth and seas with living things both large and small.

104:27–30 All of your creatures look to you for food. At the right time you open your hand of blessing, and when you take away their breath they die. By your Spirit you continually renew the earth.

104:31–35 May your glory last forever. May you be happy with everything you made. I'll never stop singing to you. I want you to be happy with my joyful thoughts of you. Praise you!

May there no longer be any wicked people.
Praise the LORD, my soul!

Hallelujah!

Psalm 105

105:1–6 I thank you. I call on you. I tell the world what you have done. I make music to you and think hard about the miracles you've done for your people. Your amazing works give me reason upon reason to brag about you.

¹ Give thanks to the LORD.
Call on him.
Make known among the nations what he has done.
² Sing to him.
Make music to praise him.
Meditate on all the miracles he has performed.
³ Brag about his holy name.
Let the hearts of those who seek the LORD rejoice.
⁴ Search for the LORD and his strength.
Always seek his presence.
⁵ Remember the miracles he performed,
    the amazing things he did, and the judgments
        he pronounced,
⁶   you descendants of his servant Abraham,
        you descendants of Jacob, his chosen ones.

105:7–10 You are our God. And you always remember the promises you made long ago.

⁷ He is the LORD our God.
His judgments are pronounced throughout
    the earth.
⁸ He always remembers his promise,ᵃ
    the word that he commanded for a
        thousand generations,
⁹   the promise that he made to Abraham,
        and his sworn oath to Isaac.
¹⁰ He confirmed it as a law for Jacob,
    as an everlasting promise to Israel,
¹¹   by saying, "I will give you the land of Canaan.
        It is your share of the inheritance."

105:11–15 You promised Abraham, Isaac, and Jacob a homeland—just as you promise me rest. You didn't let anyone oppress your chosen ones.

¹² While the people of Israel were few in number,
    a small group of foreigners living in that land,
¹³   they wandered from nation to nation,
        from one kingdom to another.
¹⁴ He didn't permit anyone to oppress them.
He warned kings about them:
¹⁵   "Do not touch my anointed ones
        or harm my prophets."

105:16–22 You brought famine to the land, but you sent Joseph as a protector and provider. You allowed him to be sold into slavery, but you raised him up as a ruler of Egypt. You tested him

¹⁶ He brought famine to the land.
He took away their food supply.
¹⁷ He sent a man ahead of them.
He sent Joseph, who was sold as a slave.
¹⁸   They hurt his feet with shackles,
        and cut into his neck with an iron collar.

ᵃ 105:8 Or "covenant."

19 The Lord's promise tested him through
         fiery trials
         until his prediction came true.
20 The king sent someone to release him.
   The ruler of nations set him free.
21 He made Joseph the master of his palace
   and the ruler of all his possessions.
22 Joseph trained the king's officers the way
         he wanted
         and taught his respected leaders wisdom.

23 Then Israel came to Egypt.
   Jacob lived as a foreigner in the land of Ham.
24 The Lord made his people grow rapidly in number
   and stronger than their enemies.
25 He changed their minds so that they hated his people,
   and they dealt treacherously with his servants.
26 He sent his servant Moses, and he sent Aaron, whom
         he had chosen.
27 They displayed his miraculous signs among them
         and did amazing things in the land of Ham.
28 He sent darkness and made ⌞their land⌟ dark.
   They did not rebel against his orders.
29 He turned their water into blood
   and caused their fish to die.
30 He made their land swarm with frogs,
   even in the kings' bedrooms.
31 He spoke, and swarms of flies and gnats
   infested their whole territory.
32 He gave them hail and lightning
   instead of rain throughout their land.
33 He struck their grapevines and fig trees
   and smashed the trees in their territory.
34 He spoke, and countless locusts and
         grasshoppers came.
35 They devoured all the plants in the land.
   They devoured the crops in the fields.
36 He killed all the firstborn sons,
         the first ones born in the land when their fathers
         were young.
37 He brought Israel out with silver and gold,
   and no one among his tribes stumbled.
38 The Egyptians were terrified of Israel,
   so they were glad when Israel left.
39 He spread out a cloud as a protective covering
   and a fire to light up the night.
40 The Israelites asked, and he brought them quail
   and filled them with bread from heaven.
41 He opened a rock, and water gushed
   and flowed like a river through the dry places.

with fiery trials, but your promise
still held true.

105:24–36 You made your people many. You made them strong. When their enemies turned on them, you sent Moses and Aaron as deliverers. You sent darkness and plagues to defend your people—blood and frogs, flies and gnats, hail and lightning, locusts and death.

105:37–41 You freed Israel from slavery. You sent them into the desert loaded down with gifts of silver and gold from their slave masters. You led them through the wilderness with a cloud by day and a fire by night. You fed them with quail and manna. You quenched their thirst with water from a rock. You met their every need.

105:42–45 You'll always remember your promises to your people. You'll always save us with joy. You'll always bring us home and teach us to obey you. Hallelujah!

106:1–2 Hallelujah! Thanks for your goodness and unending mercy. Your mighty acts are too awesome for words.

106:3–5 I'll live in your blessing when I defend justice and do right. Save me so I can share in your people's happiness and brag about what you've done.

106:7–11 Back in Egypt your people forgot your mercy and miracles. They halted when you commanded them to move on. They couldn't see your path to freedom. But you made a way through the Red Sea. Help me always remember your miracles!

106:12–13 Your people saw what you did and believed. So they sang your praises. But

⁴²He remembered his holy promise to his servant Abraham.
⁴³He brought his people out with joy, his chosen ones with a song of joy.
⁴⁴He gave them the lands of ⌐other⌐ nations, and they inherited what others had worked for
⁴⁵ so that they would obey his laws and follow his teachings.

Hallelujah!

Psalm 106

¹Hallelujah!

Give thanks to the LORD because he is good, because his mercy endures forever.
²Who can speak about all the mighty things the LORD has done?
Who can announce all the things for which he is worthy of praise?
³Blessed are those who defend justice and do what is right at all times.

⁴Remember me, O LORD, when you show favor to your people.
Come to help me with your salvation
⁵ so that I may see the prosperity of your chosen ones, find joy in our people's happiness, and brag with the people who belong to you.

⁶We have sinned, and so did our ancestors.
We have done wrong.
We are guilty.
⁷ When our ancestors were in Egypt, they gave no thought to your miracles.
They did not remember your numerous acts of mercy, so they rebelled at the sea, the Red Sea.

⁸He saved them because of his reputation so that he could make his mighty power known.
⁹He angrily commanded the Red Sea, and it dried up.
He led them through deep water as though it were a desert.
¹⁰He rescued them from the power of the one who hated them.
He rescued them from the enemy.
¹¹ Water covered their adversaries.
Not one Egyptian survived.
¹² Then our ancestors believed what he said.
They sang his praise.

¹³They quickly forgot what he did.

They did not wait for his advice.

¹⁴ They had an unreasonable desire ∟for food⌐ in
the wilderness.

In the desert they tested God.

¹⁵   He gave them what they asked for.

He ∟also⌐ gave them a degenerative disease.

¹⁶ In the camp certain men became envious of Moses.

They also became envious of Aaron, the LORD's
holy one.

¹⁷   The ground split open and swallowed Dathan.

It buried Abiram's followers.

¹⁸   A fire broke out among their followers.

Flames burned up wicked people.

¹⁹ At Mount Horeb they made ∟a statue of⌐ a calf.

They worshiped an idol made of metal.

²⁰   They traded their glorious God[a]

for the statue of a bull that eats grass.

²¹ They forgot God, their savior,

the one who did spectacular things in Egypt,

²²   miracles in the land of Ham,

and terrifying things at the Red Sea.

²³ God said he was going to destroy them,

but Moses, his chosen one, stood in his way

to prevent him from exterminating them.

²⁴ They refused ∟to enter⌐ the pleasant land.

They did not believe what he said.

²⁵ They complained in their tents.

They did not obey the LORD.

²⁶   Raising his hand, he swore

that he would kill them in the wilderness,

²⁷   kill their descendants among the nations,

and scatter them throughout various lands.

²⁸ They joined in worshiping the god Baal while they
were at Peor,

and they ate what was sacrificed to the dead.

²⁹ They infuriated God by what they did,

and a plague broke out among them.

³⁰ Then Phinehas stood between God and the people,

and the plague was stopped.

³¹   Because of this, Phinehas was considered
righteous forever,

throughout every generation.

³² They made God angry by the water at Meribah.

Things turned out badly for Moses because of what
they did,

³³   since they made him bitter so that he
spoke recklessly.

they quickly forgot your mighty acts—and just as quickly they rebelled against you. Help me always remember your powerful kindness toward me!

106:19–21 Your people traded their glorious God for a metal statue of a grass-eating bull. They forgot you had spectacularly saved them. Help me always remember you've saved me!

106:24–28 Your people refused to enter the pleasant land you had sworn to them—all because they didn't believe your promises. Instead they grumbled and disobeyed. They infuriated you by bowing to the false god Baal. Help me always worship you as God!

---

[a] 106:20 Or "their glory."

³⁴ They did not destroy the people as the Lord had
told them.
³⁵   Instead, they intermarried with other nations.
They learned to do what other nations did,
³⁶   and they worshiped their idols,
which became a trap for them.
³⁷ They sacrificed their sons and daughters to demons.
³⁸   They shed innocent blood,
the blood of their own sons and daughters
whom they sacrificed to the idols of Canaan.
The land became polluted with blood.
³⁹ They became filthy because of what they did.
They behaved like prostitutes.
⁴⁰   The Lord burned with anger against his own people.
He was disgusted with those who belonged to him.
⁴¹   He handed them over to other nations,
and those who hated them ruled them.
⁴²   Their enemies oppressed them
and made them subject to their power.
⁴³   He rescued them many times,
but they continued to plot rebellion against him
and to sink deeper because of their sin.
⁴⁴   He saw that they were suffering
when he heard their cry for help.
⁴⁵   He remembered his promise^a to them.
In keeping with his rich mercy, he changed
his plans.
⁴⁶   He let them find compassion
from all those who held them captive.

⁴⁷ Rescue us, O Lord our God, and gather us from
the nations
so that we may give thanks to your holy name
and make your praise our glory.

⁴⁸   Thanks be to the Lord God of Israel
from everlasting to everlasting.
Let all the people say amen.

Hallelujah!

BOOK FIVE

(Psalms 107–150)

Psalm 107

¹ Give thanks to the Lord because he is good,
because his mercy endures forever.

² Let the people the Lord defended repeat these words.
They are the people he defended from the power of
their enemies

106:35–38 Your people married with people who didn't know you. They worshiped their neighbors' idols. They even sacrificed their children to false gods. Help me always obey your commands!

106:40–43 Your anger burned against your people and you handed them over to other nations. You rescued your people over and over, but they continued to rebel against you. Help me to make a clean break with sin!

106:43–48 You saw your people sinking and heard their cries. You remembered your promise and showed them compassion. Thanks to you now and forevermore! Amen! Hallelujah!

107:1–7 Thanks for your unending goodness and mercy. We were desert wanderers when you found us hungry, thirsty, and out of hope. You heard our

---
^a 106:45 Or "covenant."

³ and gathered from other countries,
from the east and from the west,
from the north and from the south.
⁴ They wandered around the desert on a deserted road
without finding an inhabited city.
⁵ They were hungry and thirsty.
They began to lose hope.
⁶ In their distress they cried out to the LORD.
He rescued them from their troubles.
⁷ He led them on a road that went straight to an
inhabited city.

⁸ Let them give thanks to the LORD because of his mercy.
He performed his miracles for Adam's descendants.
⁹ He gave plenty to drink to those who were thirsty.
He filled those who were hungry with good food.
¹⁰ Those who lived in the dark, in death's shadow
were prisoners in misery.
They were held in iron chains
¹¹ because they had rebelled against
God's words
and had despised the advice given by
the Most High.
¹² So he humbled them with hard work.
They fell down, but no one was there to
help them.
¹³ In their distress they cried out to the LORD.
He saved them from their troubles.
¹⁴ He brought them out of the dark, out of
death's shadow.
He broke apart their chains.

¹⁵ Let them give thanks to the LORD because of his mercy.
He performed his miracles for Adam's descendants.
¹⁶ He shattered bronze gates
and cut iron bars in two.
¹⁷ Fools suffered because of their disobedience
and because of their crimes.
¹⁸ All food was disgusting to them,
and they came near death's gates.
¹⁹ In their distress they cried out to the LORD.
He saved them from their troubles.
²⁰ He sent his message and healed them.
He rescued them from the grave.

²¹ Let them give thanks to the LORD because of his mercy.
He performed his miracles for Adam's descendants.
²² Let them bring songs of thanksgiving as their sacrifice.
Let them tell in joyful songs what he has done.
²³ Those who sail on the sea in ships,
who do business on the high seas,
²⁴ have seen what the LORD can do,

cries and saved us! You led us to everything we needed to live.

107:8–14 Thanks for your mercy and miracles. We were prisoners of misery, living in death's shadow. You kept us in chains for rebelling against your words. You humbled us with hard work. But you heard our cries and saved us! You brought us out of the darkness.

107:15–20 Thanks for your mercy and miracles. We were fools suffering for our disobedience and crimes. We couldn't stomach the sight of food and we came close to dying. But you heard our cries and saved us! You healed us and spared us from the grave.

107:21–30 Thanks for your mercy and miracles. We were sailing the sea when a storm began to blow. Our ship rose toward the sky and plunged to the depths. We staggered like drunks and our sailing skills became useless. But you heard our cries and saved us! You stilled the sea and guided us to safe harbor.

the miracles he performed in the depths of
the sea.
²⁵ He spoke, and a storm began to blow,
and it made the waves rise high.
²⁶ The sailors aboard ship rose toward the sky.
They plunged into the depths.
Their courage melted in ⌐the face of⌐ disaster.
²⁷ They reeled and staggered like drunks,
and all their skills as sailors became useless.
²⁸ In their distress they cried out to the LORD.
He led them from their troubles.
²⁹ He made the storm calm down,
and the waves became still.
³⁰ The sailors were glad that the storm was quiet.
He guided them to the harbor they had longed for.

107:31–32 Thanks for your mercy and miracles. We promise to praise you whenever we gather.

³¹ Let them give thanks to the LORD because of his mercy.
He performed his miracles for Adam's descendants.
³² Let them glorify him when the people are gathered
for worship.
Let them praise him in the company of
respected leaders.

107:33–38 You drive the wicked from the land and make us a place to live. You turn dry ground into springs and give us crops and cattle. You bless us and we multiply.

³³ He changes rivers into a desert,
springs into thirsty ground,
³⁴ and fertile ground into a layer of salt
because of the wickedness of the people
living there.
³⁵ He changes deserts into lakes
and dry ground into springs.
³⁶ There he settles those who are hungry,
and they build cities to live in.
³⁷ They plant in fields and vineyards
that produce crops.
³⁸ He blesses them, and their numbers multiply,
and he does not allow a shortage of cattle.

107:39–42 Our pride turned into humiliation. We suffered oppression, disaster, and sorrow. But you lift the needy high above suffering. You make us multiply again. Good people will see this and be glad.

³⁹ They became few in number and were humiliated
because of oppression, disaster, and sorrow.
⁴⁰ He poured contempt on their influential people
and made them stumble around in a
pathless desert.
⁴¹ But now he lifts needy people high
above suffering
and makes their families like flocks.
⁴² Decent people will see this and rejoice,
but all the wicked people will shut
their mouths.

107:43 Make me truly wise! I'll pay attention to the past so I can understand your blessings today.

⁴³ Let those who ⌐think⌐ they are wise
pay attention to these things
so that they may understand the LORD's blessings.

Psalm 108[a]

A song; a psalm by David.

[1] My heart is confident, O God.
I want to sing and make music even with my soul.[b]
[2] Wake up, harp and lyre!
I want to wake up at dawn.
[3] I want to give thanks to you among the people, O Lord.
I want to make music to praise you among the nations
[4] because your mercy is higher than the heavens.
Your truth reaches the skies.

[5] May you be honored above the heavens, O God.
Let your glory extend over the whole earth.

[6] Save ⌊us⌋ with your powerful hand, and answer us
so that those who are dear to you may be rescued.

[7] God has promised the following through his holiness:
"I will triumph!
I will divide Shechem.
I will measure the valley of Succoth.
[8] Gilead is mine.
Manasseh is mine.
Ephraim is the helmet on my head.
Judah is my scepter.
[9] Moab is my washtub.
I will throw my shoe over Edom.
I will shout in triumph over Philistia."

[10] Who will bring me into the fortified city?
Who will lead me to Edom?
[11] Isn't it you, O God, who rejected us?
Isn't it you, O God, who refused to accompany
our armies?

[12] Give us help against the enemy
because human assistance is worthless.
[13] With God we will display great strength.
He will trample our enemies.

Psalm 109

For the choir director; a psalm by David.

[1] O God, whom I praise, do not turn a deaf ear to me.
[2] Wicked and deceitful people have opened their
mouths against me.
They speak against me with lying tongues.
[3] They surround me with hateful words.
They fight against me for no reason.

108:1–3 In you my heart swells with confidence. I get up at dawn to worship. Let everyone everywhere hear!

108:4–5 Your mercy and truth reach past the heavens. Your glory shines to the whole earth. Receive the honor you deserve!

108:7 Your perfect holiness guarantees your promises. Thanks for every blessing you've sworn to your people!

108:10–13 You alone will lead me in triumph. No human can help me. Show me your strength!

109:1–5 Evildoers and liars speak hateful words against me. I show them love yet they accuse me. I pray for them but they pay me back with evil.

---

[a] 108:1 Verses 1–5 are virtually identical in wording to Psalm 57:7–11; verses 6–13 are virtually identical in wording to Psalm 60:5 12.
[b] 108:1 Or "my glory."

⁴ In return for my love, they accuse me,
but I pray for them.^a
⁵ They reward me with evil instead of good
and with hatred instead of love.

⁶ ⌞I said,⌟ "Appoint the evil one to oppose him.
Let Satan stand beside him.

109:7–8 I trust you to act with justice at my enemy's trial. Open my eyes to my sins large and small so I can see them and turn from them.

⁷   When he stands trial,
let him be found guilty.
Let his prayer be considered sinful.
⁸   Let his days be few ⌞in number⌟.
Let someone else take his position.

109:9–12 Teach me to show compassion to the fatherless and widowed and needy. Train me to imitate your kindness.

⁹   "Let his children become fatherless and his
wife a widow.
¹⁰   Let his children wander around and beg.
Let them seek help far from their
ruined homes.
¹¹   Let a creditor take everything he owns.
Let strangers steal what he has worked for.
¹²   Let no one be kind to him anymore.
Let no one show any pity to his
fatherless children.
¹³   Let his descendants be cut off
and their family name be wiped out by the
next generation.
¹⁴   Let the LORD remember the guilt of
his ancestors
and not wipe out his mother's sin.
¹⁵   Let their guilt and sin always remain
on record
in front of the LORD.
Let the LORD remove every memory of him^b from
the earth,

109:16–17 Prompt me to constant acts of kindness. Teach me to show mercy to the oppressed and needy and brokenhearted. Make me a blessing to everyone I encounter.

¹⁶   because he did not remember to be kind.

"He drove oppressed, needy,
and brokenhearted people to their graves.
¹⁷   He loved to put curses ⌞on others⌟,
so he, too, was cursed.
He did not like to bless ⌞others⌟,
so he never received a blessing.
¹⁸   He wore cursing as though it were clothing,
so cursing entered his body like water
and his bones like oil.
¹⁹   Let cursing be his clothing,
a belt he always wears."

109:20–24 Pain pierces my heart and my knees wobble. Grief

²⁰ This is how the LORD rewards those who accuse me,
those who say evil things against me.

---

^a 109:4 Or "but I am a man of prayer."
^b 109:15 Or "them."

²¹ O LORD Almighty, deal with me out of the goodness of
  your name.
    Rescue me because of your mercy.
²² I am oppressed and needy.
  I can feel the pain in my heart.
²³ I fade away like a lengthening shadow.
  I have been shaken off like a grasshopper.
²⁴   My knees give way because I have been fasting.
  My body has become lean, without any fat.
²⁵ I have become the victim of my enemies' insults.
  They look at me and shake their heads.
²⁶ Help me, O LORD my God.
  Save me because of your mercy.
²⁷   Then they will know that this is your doing,
    that you, O LORD, are the one who saved me.
²⁸ They may curse, but you will bless.
  Let those who attack me be ashamed,
    but let me rejoice.
²⁹ Let those who accuse me wear disgrace as though it
    were clothing.
  Let them be wrapped in their shame as though it were
    a robe.

³⁰ With my mouth I will give many thanks to the LORD.
  I will praise him among many people,
³¹   because he stands beside needy people
    to save them from those who would condemn
      them to death.

109:25–28 My enemies hurl insults at me. But when you save me they'll know you've come to my side. Bless me despite their curses. Let their attacks become their shame.

starves my body. So treat me with your goodness. Rescue me because of your mercy.

109:30–31 I'll shout my thanks so everyone can hear. You side with the needy and save them from death.

Psalm 110

A psalm by David.

¹ The LORD said to my Lord,
  "Sit in the highest position in heaven
    until I make your enemies your footstool."

² The LORD will extend your powerful scepter from Zion.
  Rule your enemies who surround you.

³   Your people will volunteer when you call up
    your army.
  Your young people will come to you in
    holy splendor
    like dew in the early morning.ᵃ

⁴ The LORD has taken an oath and will not change
    his mind:
  "You are a priest forever, in the way Melchizedek
    was a priest."

⁵ The Lord is at your right side.

110:1–2 You're seated at the highest position in heaven. You make your enemies a footstool and extend your reign in every direction. Let me gaze on your holy splendor.

110:4–7 The Lord's promise to his chosen one will not change: You'll be a priest forever. You'll crush kings and pass judgment on the nations. You'll hold your head high in victory.

ᵃ 110:3 Or "You have the dew of your youth."

He will crush kings on the day of his anger.
⁶ He will pass judgment on the nations
    and fill them with dead bodies.
        Throughout the earth he will crush ˻their˼ heads.
⁷ He will drink from the brook along the road.
    He will hold his head high.

Psalm 111[a]

¹Hallelujah!

I will give thanks to the LORD with all my heart
    in the company of decent people and in
        the congregation.
²The LORD's deeds are spectacular.
    They should be studied by all who enjoy them.
³His work is glorious and majestic.
His righteousness continues forever.
⁴He has made his miracles unforgettable.
    The LORD is merciful and compassionate.
⁵He provides food for those who fear him.
He always remembers his promise.[b]
⁶He has revealed the power of his works to his people
    by giving them the lands of other nations as
        an inheritance.
⁷His works are done with truth and justice.
    All his guiding principles are trustworthy.
⁸   They last forever and ever.
    They are carried out with truth and decency.
⁹He has sent salvation to his people.
He has ordered that his promise should
    continue forever.
    His name is holy and terrifying.
¹⁰The fear of the LORD is the beginning of wisdom.
Good sense is shown by everyone who follows
    ˻God's guiding principles˼.
His praise continues forever.

Psalm 112[c]

¹Hallelujah!

Blessed is the person who fears the LORD
    and is happy to obey his commands.
²   His descendants will grow strong on the earth.
    The family of a decent person will be blessed.
³   Wealth and riches will be in his home.
    His righteousness continues forever.

111:1–3 Your spectacular deeds command my attention. I enjoy studying your glorious and majestic work. Hallelujah!

111:3–7 Your goodness lasts forever and your miracles are unforgettable. You feed people who live with awe toward you. You do your work with truth and justice.

111:7–9 I can always count on your principles. They last forever like you. Your save your people and never stop keeping your promises.

111:10 I've begun to learn wisdom when I live in awe of you. Your principles give me good sense.

112:1–2 I live in your blessing as I happily follow your commands. My children grow strong and you show kindness to my family.

112:3–5 You're the source of my wealth. Train me to be

---

[a] 111:1 Psalm 111 is a poem in Hebrew alphabetical order.
[b] 111:5 Or "covenant."
[c] 112:1 Psalm 112 is a poem in Hebrew alphabetical order.

4 Light will shine in the dark for a
decent person.
He is merciful, compassionate, and fair.

merciful, compassionate, and
fair. Open doors for me to be
generous and do honest work.

5 All goes well for the person who is generous and
lends willingly.
He earns an honest living.
6 He will never fail.
A righteous person will always be remembered.
7 He is not afraid of bad news.
His heart remains secure, full of confidence in
the LORD.
8 His heart is steady, and he is not afraid.
In the end he will look triumphantly at
his enemies.

112:6–8 Because of you I'll
never really fail. I don't fear bad
news because my heart stays
confident in you. You sweep away
my worries.

9 He gives freely to poor people.
His righteousness continues forever.
His head is raised in honor.
10 The wicked person sees this and
becomes angry.
He angrily grits his teeth and disappears.
The hope that wicked people have
will vanish.

112:9 When I give freely to the
poor, you'll make my good acts
endure. You'll raise my head in
honor.

Psalm 113

1 Hallelujah!

You servants of the LORD, praise him.
Praise the name of the LORD.
2 Thank the name of the LORD now and forever.
3 From where the sun rises to where the sun sets,
the name of the LORD should be praised.
4 The LORD is high above all the nations.
His glory is above the heavens.
5 Who is like the LORD our God?
He is seated on his high throne.
6 He bends down to look at heaven and earth.
7 He lifts the poor from the dust.
He lifts the needy from a garbage heap.
8 He seats them with influential people,
with the influential leaders of his people.
9 He makes a woman who is in a childless home
a joyful mother.

Hallelujah!

113:1–3 Let all your servants
praise you now and forever. Let
people everywhere praise
your name.

113:4–5 You're more glorious
than anything in heaven or on
earth. No one compares to you.

113:5–8 You're seated on high,
yet you stoop to lift the poor out
of the dust. You honor the needy
and make them equals with
influential people. Teach me your
kind grace!

Psalm 114

1 When Israel left Egypt,
when Jacob's family left people who spoke a
foreign language,

114:1–4 You rescued your
people from slavery in Egypt.
You led them into your holy land.

You made the Red Sea and the Jordan River turn back. You made the mountains and the hills jump.

² Judah became his holy place and Israel became
     his kingdom.
³ The Red Sea looked at this and ran away.
    The Jordan River turned back.
⁴ The mountains jumped like rams.
    The hills jumped like lambs.
⁵ Red Sea, why did you run away?
    Jordan River, what made you turn back?
⁶ Mountains, what made you jump like rams?
    Hills, what made you jump like lambs?

114:7–8 The earth recognizes you as Lord and trembles before you. You turn rock into pools of water. You make flint into flowing springs.

⁷ Earth, tremble in the presence of the Lord,
    in the presence of the God of Jacob.
⁸ He turns a rock into a pool filled with water
    and turns flint into a spring flowing with water.

Psalm 115

115:1 Don't give me even a bit of glory. You deserve it all. Your mercy and faithfulness are boundless.

¹ Don't give glory to us, O Lord.
  Don't give glory to us.
    Instead, give glory to your name
    because of your mercy and faithfulness.

115:2–3 Others wonder where you are. But beyond any doubt I know you're in heaven. You do whatever you wish.

² Why should other nations say, "Where is their God?"
³ Our God is in heaven.
    He does whatever he wants.

115:4–8 Idols made by human hands can't speak or see. They can't smell or feel. They can't walk or make a noise. If I serve false gods I'll end up as senseless as the idols I worship.

⁴ Their idols are made of silver and gold.
    They were made by human hands.[a]
⁵ They have mouths, but they cannot speak.
    They have eyes, but they cannot see.
⁶ They have ears, but they cannot hear.
    They have noses, but they cannot smell.
⁷ They have hands, but they cannot feel.
    They have feet, but they cannot walk.
    They cannot ⌞even⌟ make a sound with
        their throats.
⁸ Those who make idols end up like them.
    So does everyone who trusts them.

115:9–13 I'll trust in you, my helper and shield. I fear and trust you. I count on you to remember me and bless me and my children. You bless everyone who respects you. You don't care whether the world thinks they're important or ordinary.

⁹ Israel, trust the Lord.
    He is your helper and your shield.
¹⁰ Descendants of Aaron, trust the Lord.
    He is your helper and your shield.
¹¹ If you fear the Lord, trust the Lord.
    He is your helper and your shield.

¹² The Lord, who is ⌞always⌟ thinking about us, will
        bless us.
    He will bless the descendants of Israel.
    He will bless the descendants of Aaron.
¹³ He will bless those who fear the Lord,
        from the least important to the most important.

---

[a] 115:4 Verses 4–8 are virtually identical in wording to Psalm 135:15–18.

¹⁴ May the Lord continue to bless you and your children.
¹⁵ You will be blessed by the Lord, the maker of heaven and earth.
¹⁶ The highest heaven belongs to the Lord,
    but he has given the earth to the descendants of Adam.
¹⁷ Those who are dead do not praise the Lord,
    nor do those who go into the silence ⌐of the grave⌐.
¹⁸ But we will thank the Lord now and forever.

Hallelujah!

Psalm 116

¹ I love the Lord because he hears my voice, my pleas
        for mercy.
² I will call on him as long as I live
    because he turns his ear toward me.
³ The ropes of death became tangled around me.
    The horrors of the grave took hold of me.
        I experienced pain and agony.
⁴ But I kept calling on the name of the Lord:
    "Please, Lord, rescue me!"

⁵ The Lord is merciful and righteous.
  Our God is compassionate.
⁶ The Lord protects defenseless people.
    When I was weak, he saved me.
⁷ Be at peace again, my soul,
    because the Lord has been good to you.

⁸ You saved me from death.
  You saved my eyes from tears ⌐and⌐ my feet
        from stumbling.
⁹ I will walk in the Lord's presence in this world of
        the living.
¹⁰ I kept my faith even when I said,
    "I am suffering terribly."
¹¹ I also said when I was panic-stricken,
    "Everyone is undependable."
¹² How can I repay the Lord
    for all the good that he has done for me?
¹³ I will take the cup of salvation
    and call on the name of the Lord.
¹⁴ I will keep my vows to the Lord
    in the presence of all his people.
¹⁵ Precious in the sight of the Lord
    is the death of his faithful ones.
¹⁶ O Lord, I am indeed your servant.
    I am your servant,
        the son of your female servant.
  You have freed me from my chains.
¹⁷ I will bring a song of thanksgiving to you as a sacrifice.

115:14–18 I boldly believe you will bless me and my family. Heaven belongs to you and you entrust the world to our care. We'll thank you now and forever! Hallelujah!

116:1–2 I love you because you hear my desperate pleas. I keep calling on you because you listen.

116:3–6 I was tangled in death and overcome with horror. But I begged you to rescue me and you showed me compassion. You saved me at my weakest.

116:7–9 I'm at peace because you did good to me. You dried my tears and steadied my feet. I'll walk in your presence as long as I live.

116:10–11 I kept trusting you even when I lamented my terrible suffering. I panicked when I couldn't count on anyone else.

116:12–15 How can I repay your amazing goodness? I'll gratefully accept your saving grace and keep calling on you. Everyone will see me keep my promises to you. My death will open the door to your presence.

116:16–19 Because you loosed my chains I'll always be your servant. I'll sing thanks to you and live close to you always. Hallelujah!

I will call on the name of the LORD.
¹⁸ I will keep my vows to the LORD
  in the presence of all his people,
¹⁹   in the courtyards of the LORD's house,
    in the middle of Jerusalem.

Hallelujah!

Psalm 117

117:1–2 I praise your powerful mercy! I praise your unending faithfulness! Hallelujah!

¹ Praise the LORD, all you nations!
  Praise him, all you people of the world!
²   His mercy toward us is powerful.
  The LORD's faithfulness endures forever.

Hallelujah!

Psalm 118

118:1–4 Thanks for your goodness and unending mercy. I'll say it once and I'll say it again: "Your mercy endures forever."

¹ Give thanks to the LORD because he is good,
  because his mercy endures forever.
²   Israel should say,
    "His mercy endures forever."
³   The descendants of Aaron should say,
    "His mercy endures forever."
⁴   Those who fear the LORD should say,
    "His mercy endures forever."

118:5–6 I called on you when I was in trouble. You showed that you're on my side. How can I ever again be afraid of mere people?

⁵ During times of trouble I called on the LORD.
  The LORD answered me ˻and˼ set me free ˻from all of them˼.
⁶ The LORD is on my side.
  I am not afraid.
    What can mortals do to me?
⁷ The LORD is on my side as my helper.
  I will see ˻the defeat of˼ those who hate me.

118:8–9 It's better to depend on you than trust people—even people with obvious power.

⁸ It is better to depend on the LORD
  than to trust mortals.
⁹ It is better to depend on the LORD
  than to trust influential people.

118:10–13 My enemies swarm around me like bees but you extinguish them. They push me hard but you hold me steady.

¹⁰ All the nations surrounded me,
  ˻but armed˼ with the name of the LORD, I
    defeated them.
¹¹ They surrounded me. Yes, they surrounded me,
  ˻but armed˼ with the name of the LORD, I
    defeated them.
¹² They swarmed around me like bees,
  but they were extinguished like burning thornbushes.
    ˻So armed˼ with the name of the LORD, I
      defeated them.
¹³ They pushed hard to make me fall,
  but the LORD helped me.

¹⁴ The L<small>ORD</small> is my strength and my song.
    He is my savior.

¹⁵ The sound of joyful singing and victory is heard
    in the tents of righteous people.
      The right hand of the L<small>ORD</small> displays strength.
¹⁶   The right hand of the L<small>ORD</small> is held high.
      The right hand of the L<small>ORD</small> displays strength.
¹⁷ I will not die,
    but I will live and tell what the L<small>ORD</small> has done.
¹⁸ The L<small>ORD</small> disciplined me severely,
    but he did not allow me to be killed.

118:15–17 I joyfully sing songs of victory because you showed your strength. You keep me alive to tell others what you've done.

118:18–21 You let me be struck down but you didn't allow me to die. Let me come close to you so I can thank you. You're my Savior!

¹⁹ Open the gates of righteousness for me.
    I will go through them ⌊and⌋ give thanks to the L<small>ORD</small>.
²⁰ This is the gate of the L<small>ORD</small>
    through which righteous people will enter.

²¹ I give thanks to you,
    because you have answered me.
      You are my savior.
²² The stone that the builders rejected
    has become the cornerstone.
²³ The L<small>ORD</small> is responsible for this,
    and it is amazing for us to see.
²⁴ This is the day the L<small>ORD</small> has made.
    Let's rejoice and be glad today!
²⁵ We beg you, O L<small>ORD</small>, save us!
    We beg you, O L<small>ORD</small>, give us success!
²⁶ Blessed is the one who comes in the name of
      the L<small>ORD</small>.
    We bless you from the L<small>ORD</small>'s house.
²⁷ The L<small>ORD</small> is God, and he has given us light.
    March in a festival procession
      with branches to the horns of the altar.
²⁸ You are my God, and I give thanks to you.
    My God, I honor you highly.

²⁹ Give thanks to the L<small>ORD</small> because he is good,
    because his mercy endures forever.

118:22–24 Builders rejected your hand-carved stone. But you made it the cornerstone of your work. You amaze me! I'll rejoice because you made this day.

118:25 I beg you to save me. I beg you to give me success!

118:27–29 You're my God and you've given me light. I'll march into your presence to say thanks and to honor you above everything else. Thanks for your goodness and unending mercy!

Psalm 119^a

¹ Blessed are those whose lives have integrity,
    those who follow the teachings of the L<small>ORD</small>.
² Blessed are those who obey his written instructions.
    They wholeheartedly search for him.
³   They do nothing wrong.
    They follow his directions.
⁴ You have commanded
    that your guiding principles be carefully followed.

119:1 When I follow your teachings I live in your blessing.

119:2–5 You wrote down your instructions so I could understand them. You command me to follow your principles carefully. Make me unwavering in obeying you.

---

^a 119:1 Psalm 119 is a poem in Hebrew alphabetical order.

⁵ I pray that my ways may become firmly established
so that I can obey your laws.
⁶   Then I will never feel ashamed
when I study all your commandments.
⁷ I will give thanks to you
as I learn your regulations, which are based on
your righteousness.
⁸ I will obey your laws.
Never abandon me.

⁹ How can a young person keep his life pure?
⌊He can do it⌋ by holding on to your word.
¹⁰ I wholeheartedly searched for you.
Do not let me wander away from
your commandments.
¹¹ I have treasured your promise in my heart
so that I may not sin against you.
¹² Thanks be to you, O LORD.
Teach me your laws.
¹³ With my lips I have repeated
every regulation that ⌊comes⌋ from your mouth.
¹⁴ I find joy in the way ⌊shown by⌋ your
written instructions
more than I find joy in all kinds of riches.
¹⁵ I want to reflect on your guiding principles
and study your ways.
¹⁶ Your laws make me happy.
I never forget your word.

¹⁷ Be kind to me so that I may live
and hold on to your word.
¹⁸ Uncover my eyes
so that I may see the miraculous things in
your teachings.
¹⁹ I am a foreigner in this world.
Do not hide your commandments from me.
²⁰ My soul is overwhelmed with endless longing for
your regulations.
²¹ You threaten arrogant people, who are condemned
and wander away from your commandments.
²² Remove the insults and contempt that have fallen on me
because I have obeyed your written instructions.
²³ Even though influential people plot against me,
I reflect on your laws.
²⁴ Indeed, your written instructions make me happy.
They are my best friends.

²⁵ I am close to death.
Give me a new life as you promised.
²⁶ I told you what I have done, and you answered me.
Teach me your laws.

119:7–8 Thank you for teaching me your rules, ways of living based on your own righteousness. Don't abandon me as I obey you.

119:9–10 How can I keep pure? By holding tight to your Word. I searched hard for you. Don't let me lose sight of you now.

119:11–13 I keep reminding myself of your promises to keep from sinning against you.

119:14–16 Your instructions give me more joy than anything else in life. The more I know of your laws the happier I become.

119:18–20 Open my eyes to your miraculous teachings. I can't understand them without your help. My heart aches for your instructions.

119:22–24 People mock me because I follow your teachings. But I won't let them scare me away from your laws. Your Word is my best friend.

119:25–28 When I'm close to death, I'll cling to your promise of new life. When I'm drowning in tears, I'll look for your strength.

²⁷ Help me understand your guiding principles
    so that I may reflect on your miracles.
²⁸ I am drowning in tears.
    Strengthen me as you promised.
²⁹ Turn me away from a life of lies.
    Graciously provide me with your teachings.
³⁰ I have chosen a life of faithfulness.
    I have set your regulations in front of me.
³¹ I have clung tightly to your written instructions.
    O LORD, do not let me be put to shame.
³² I will eagerly pursue your commandments
    because you continue to increase my understanding.

119:29–31 Don't let me get caught up in lies. Teach me to choose faithfulness instead. I cling tightly to your Word. Don't let others shame me.

³³ Teach me, O LORD, how to live by your laws,
    and I will obey them to the end.
³⁴ Help me understand so that I can follow your teachings.
    I will guard them with all my heart.
³⁵ Lead me on the path of your commandments,
    because I am happy with them.
³⁶ Direct my heart toward your written instructions
    rather than getting rich in underhanded ways.
³⁷ Turn my eyes away from worthless things.
    Give me a new life in your ways.
³⁸ Keep your promise to me
    so that I can fear you.
³⁹ Take away insults, which I dread,
    because your regulations are good.
⁴⁰ I long for your guiding principles.
    Give me a new life in your righteousness.

119:32–34 I hunt for your commandments because they always increase my understanding. Teach me to live what I know. Don't let me forget what I learn.

119:37–38 I refuse to lust for worthless things. New life with you is so much better. Keep your promises to me so I have abundant reasons to respect you.

⁴¹ Let your blessings reach me, O LORD.
    Save me as you promised.
⁴² Then I will have an answer for the one who insults me
    since I trust your word.
⁴³ Do not take so much as a single word of truth from
    my mouth.
    My hope is based on your regulations.
⁴⁴ I will follow your teachings forever and ever.
⁴⁵ I will walk around freely
    because I sought out your guiding principles.
⁴⁶ I will speak about your written instructions in the
    presence of kings
    and not feel ashamed.
⁴⁷ Your commandments, which I love, make me happy.
⁴⁸ I lift my hands ˻in prayer˼ because of
    your commandments,
    which I love.
    I will reflect on your laws.

119:41–42 Don't let me miss out on your blessings. Save me so I can silence people who insult me for trusting your Word.

119:43–45 Don't let me forget a single word of your truth. Your rules give me hope. Your principles make me free.

119:46–47 I'll talk about your Word to the most important people in my life. I won't feel ashamed because I love your commands.

⁴⁹ Remember the word ˻you gave˼ me.
    Through it you gave me hope.
⁵⁰ This is my comfort in my misery:

119:49–50 Don't forget what you've told me. Your words give me hope. They comfort me in misery and promise me new life.

119:51 The mocking of arrogant people won't keep me from obeying you.

119:54–55 Your laws are my songs in a lonely place. I remember you in the dark of night and resolve to obey you.

119:56–58 You're a gift to me in this world. I promise to keep my grip on your words. Please keep your kind promises to me.

119:59–61 I thought about running from you, but I came back to your instructions. I'll obey you without hesitation. I won't let wicked people drag me into disobedience.

119:63 I make friends with anyone who shows you the respect you deserve. Give me partners in following your principles.

119:66–71 Give me knowledge and good judgment as I trust your commands. I learned my lesson when I wandered from your Word. Learning your laws was worth the suffering I endured.

Your promise gave me a new life.
⁵¹ Arrogant people have mocked me with cruelty,
  yet I have not turned away from your teachings.
⁵² I remembered your regulations from long ago, O LORD,
  and I found comfort ⌊in them⌋.
⁵³ I am burning with anger because of wicked people,
  who abandon your teachings.
⁵⁴ Your laws have become like psalms to me
  in this place where I am only a foreigner.
⁵⁵ At night I remember your name, O LORD,
  and I follow your teachings.
⁵⁶ This has happened to me
  because I have obeyed your guiding principles.

⁵⁷ You are my inheritance, O LORD.
  I promised to hold on to your words.
⁵⁸ With all my heart I want to win your favor.
  Be kind to me as you promised.
⁵⁹ I have thought about my life,
  and I have directed my feet back to your
    written instructions.
⁶⁰ Without any hesitation I hurry to obey
  your commandments.
⁶¹ ⌊Though⌋ the ropes of wicked people are tied
    around me,
  I never forget your teachings.
⁶² At midnight I wake up to give thanks to you
  for the regulations, which are based on
    your righteousness.
⁶³ I am a friend to everyone who fears you
  and to everyone who follows your guiding principles.
⁶⁴ Your mercy, O LORD, fills the earth.
  Teach me your laws.

⁶⁵ You have treated me well, O LORD,
  as you promised.
⁶⁶ Teach me ⌊to use⌋ good judgment and knowledge,
  because I believe in your commandments.
⁶⁷ Before you made me suffer, I used to wander off,
  but now I hold on to your word.
⁶⁸ You are good, and you do good things.
  Teach me your laws.
⁶⁹ Arrogant people have smeared me with lies,
  ⌊yet⌋ I obey your guiding principles with all my heart.
⁷⁰ Their hearts are cold and insensitive,
  ⌊yet⌋ I am happy with your teachings.
⁷¹ It was good that I had to suffer
  in order to learn your laws.
⁷² The teachings ⌊that come⌋ from your mouth are worth
    more to me
  than thousands in gold or silver.

⁷³ Your hands created me and made me what I am.
　　Help me understand so that I may learn
　　　　your commandments.
⁷⁴ Those who fear you will see me and rejoice,
　　because my hope is based on your word.
⁷⁵ I know that your regulations are fair, O Lᴏʀᴅ,
　　and that you were right to make me suffer.
⁷⁶ Let your mercy comfort me
　　as you promised.
⁷⁷ Let your compassion reach me so that I may live,
　　because your teachings make me happy.
⁷⁸ Let arrogant people be put to shame
　　because they lied about me,
　　　└yet┘ I reflect on your guiding principles.
⁷⁹ Let those who fear you turn to me
　　so that they can come to know your
　　　　written instructions.
⁸⁰ Let my heart be filled with integrity in regard to
　　　your laws
　　so that I will not be put to shame.

⁸¹ My soul is weak from waiting for you to save me.
　　My hope is based on your word.
⁸² My eyes have become strained from looking for
　　　your promise.
　　I ask, "When will you comfort me?"
⁸³ Although I have become like a shriveled and dried
　　　out wineskin,
　　I have not forgotten your laws.
⁸⁴ What is left of my life?
　　When will you bring those who persecute me
　　　　to justice?
⁸⁵ 　Arrogant people have dug pits to trap me
　　　in defiance of your teachings.
⁸⁶ 　　　(All your commandments are reliable.)
　　Those people persecute me with lies. Help me!
⁸⁷ 　They almost wiped me off └the face of┘ the earth.
　　But I did not abandon your guiding principles.
⁸⁸ Give me a new life through your mercy
　　so that I may obey the written instructions,
　　　└which came┘ from your mouth.

⁸⁹ O Lᴏʀᴅ, your word is established in heaven forever.
⁹⁰ 　Your faithfulness endures throughout
　　　　every generation.
　　You set the earth in place, and it continues to stand.
⁹¹ 　　　All things continue to stand today because of
　　　　your regulations,
　　　　since they are all your servants.
⁹² If your teachings had not made me happy,
　　then I would have died in my misery.

119:73 Your hands made me all that I am. Help me know how to apply your commands to my life.

119:75–77 You're right when you use suffering to teach me. You show me mercy and compassion. You give me happiness through your teachings.

119:79 I long to teach people who respect you. Send them to me so I can pass on your instructions.

119:81–83 My soul can't wait much longer for you to save me. But your Word compels me to hope in you. My eyes hurt from watching for your promise. But I won't forget your laws.

119:85–87 Proud people entrap me. They persecute me with lies. They aim to wipe me off the face of the earth. But I won't stop following your principles.

119:88–91 Your Word lasts forever. Your faithfulness reaches every generation. Your rules hold everything together.

119:92–94 I would die in misery if I didn't have your

commands to make me happy. I can live a new life because of your principles. I belong to you.

119:96 Everything on earth has its limits. Only your commands know no bounds.

119:97–100 I love your teachings! I think of them all day long. I'm smarter than my teachers because your instructions fill my thoughts. I'm wiser than my elders because I obey your principles.

119:101–103 I won't venture down evil paths. I'll choose instead to obey your Word. I pay attention to everything you've taught me. Your promise is sweeter than honey.

119:105 Your Word lights my path so I don't stumble. Don't let me settle for walking in darkness.

119:106 I promised to keep your rules when I realized they flow from your goodness.

119:109 I face danger at every turn, but I rely on your teachings to keep me safe.

119:111–112 Your written instructions never wear out. They make me glad and give me an eternal reward.

119:113–117 I hate two-faced people, but your teachings never

---

[93] I will never forget your guiding principles,
   because you gave me a new life through them.
[94] I am yours.
   Save me, because I have searched for your
      guiding principles.
[95] The wicked people have waited for me in order to
      destroy me,
   ⌐yet⌐ I want to understand your written instructions.
[96] I have seen a limit to everything else,
   ⌐but⌐ your commandments have no limit.

[97] Oh, how I love your teachings!
   They are in my thoughts all day long.
[98] Your commandments make me wiser than my enemies,
   because your commandments are always with me.
[99] I have more insight than all my teachers,
   because your written instructions are in my thoughts.
[100] I have more wisdom than those with many years
      of experience,
   because I have obeyed your guiding principles.
[101] I have kept my feet ⌐from walking⌐ on any evil path
   in order to obey your word.
[102] I have not neglected your regulations,
   because you have taught me.
[103] How sweet the taste of your promise is!
   It tastes sweeter than honey.
[104] From your guiding principles I gain understanding.
   That is why I hate every path that leads to lying.

[105] Your word is a lamp for my feet
   and a light for my path.
[106] I took an oath, and I will keep it.
   I took an oath to follow your regulations,
      which are based on your righteousness.
[107] I have suffered so much.
   Give me a new life, O LORD, as you promised.
[108] Please accept the praise I gladly give you, O LORD,
   and teach me your regulations.
[109] I always take my life into my own hands,
   but I never forget your teachings.
[110] Wicked people have set a trap for me,
   but I have never wandered away from your
      guiding principles.
[111] Your written instructions are mine forever.
   They are the joy of my heart.
[112] I have decided to obey your laws.
   They offer a reward that never ends.

[113] I hate two-faced people,
   but I love your teachings.

[114] You are my hiding place and my shield.
My hope is based on your word.
[115] Get away from me, you evildoers,
so that I can obey the commandments of my God.
[116] Help me God, as you promised, so that I may live.
Do not turn my hope into disappointment.
[117] Hold me, and I will be safe,
and I will always respect your laws.
[118] You reject all who wander away from your laws,
because their lies mislead them.[a]
[119] You get rid of all wicked people on earth as if they
were rubbish.
That is why I love your written instructions.
[120] My body shudders in fear of you,
and I am afraid of your regulations.

[121] I have done what is fair and right.
Do not leave me at the mercy of those who
oppress me.
[122] Guarantee my well-being.
Do not let arrogant people oppress me.
[123] My eyes are strained from looking for you to save me
and from looking for the fulfillment of your
righteous promise.
[124] Treat me with kindness,
and teach me your laws.
[125] I am your servant.
Help me understand
so that I may come to know your
written instructions.
[126] It is time for you to act, O LORD.[b]
Even though people have abolished your teachings,
[127] I love your commandments more than gold, more
than pure gold.
[128] I follow the straight paths of your
guiding principles.
I hate every pathway that leads to lying.

[129] Your written instructions are miraculous.
That is why I obey them.
[130] Your word is a doorway that lets in light,
and it helps gullible people understand.
[131] I open my mouth and pant
because I long for your commandments.
[132] Turn toward me, and have pity on me
as you have pledged to do for those who love
your name.
[133] Make my steps secure through your promise,

deceive me. I count on you to protect me, and your words tell me why I should trust you. Hold me close, and I'll always be safe.

119:120 My body shudders when I think about your awesome greatness. I tremble when I hear your rules.

119:121–123 Don't leave me at the mercy of cruel oppressors. My eyes hurt from searching for you to fulfill your promise to save me.

119:125 I'm your servant. Help me understand your instructions so I can do your bidding.

119:126–127 Other people do away with your teachings, but I treasure your commands more than gold.

119:130 Your Word sheds light on life. Use it to help me understand your way.

119:131 My mouth opens wide panting for your Word. Fill me up!

---

[a] 119:118 Hebrew meaning of this line uncertain.
[b] 119:126 One Hebrew manuscript, Latin; other Hebrew manuscripts "It is time to act for the LORD."

119:133–134 Help me live obediently by relying on your promises. Don't let sin control me or people push me around.

119:135–136 You smile at me as you teach me your laws. But I weep when others don't listen.

119:137–140 Every one of your commands is fair and reliable. I've tested your promise and I love it.

119:141–143 On my own I'm insignificant. But your guiding principles make my life count. Even when I struggle your commands make me happy.

119:144–145 Your instructions lead to life. So help me understand them. With all my heart I want to obey you!

119:146–149 Rescue me from anything that keeps me from obeying you. Give me a fresh start in following your guidance.

119:150–151 People nearby plot to take my life. But you and your Word are even nearer.

119:152–153 Your instructions will last forever. Help me never to forget them.

119:155–156 Wicked people won't experience your salvation because they don't search your Word. I want your rules to guide me.

and do not let any sin control me.

[134] Save me from human oppression
so that I may obey your guiding principles.

[135] Smile on me,
and teach me your laws.

[136] Streams of tears flow from my eyes
because others do not follow your teachings.

[137] You are righteous, O Lord,
and your regulations are fair.

[138] You have issued your written instructions.
They are fair and completely dependable.

[139] My devotion ⌊for your words⌋ consumes me,
because my enemies have forgotten your words.

[140] Your promise has been thoroughly tested,
and I love it.

[141] I am unimportant and despised,
⌊yet⌋ I never forget your guiding principles.

[142] Your righteousness is an everlasting righteousness,
and your teachings are reliable.

[143] Trouble and hardship have found me,
but your commandments ⌊still⌋ make me happy.

[144] Your written instructions are always right.
Help me understand ⌊them⌋ so that I will live.

[145] I have called out with all my heart. Answer me,
O Lord.
I want to obey your laws.

[146] I have called out.
Save me, so that I can obey your written instructions.

[147] I got up before dawn, and I cried out for help.
My hope is based on your word.

[148] My eyes are wide-open throughout the nighttime hours
to reflect on your word.

[149] In keeping with your mercy, hear my voice.
O Lord, give me a new life guided by your regulations.

[150] Those who carry out plots against me are near,
⌊yet⌋ they are far away from your teachings.

[151] You are near, O Lord,
and all your commandments are reliable.

[152] Long ago I learned from your written instructions
that you made them to last forever.

[153] Look at my misery, and rescue me,
because I have never forgotten your teachings.

[154] Plead my case ⌊for me⌋, and save me.
Give me a new life as you promised.

[155] Wicked people are far from being saved,
because they have not searched for your laws.

[156] Your acts of compassion are many in number, O Lord.
Give me a new life guided by your regulations.

[157] I have many persecutors and opponents,
⌊yet⌋ I have not turned away from your
written instructions.
[158] I have seen traitors,
and I am filled with disgust.
They have not accepted your promise.
[159] See how I have loved your guiding principles!
O Lord, in keeping with your mercy, give me a new life.
[160] There is nothing but truth in your word,
and all of your righteous regulations endure forever.

[161] Influential people have persecuted me for no reason,
but it is only your words that fill my heart with terror.
[162] I find joy in your promise
like someone who finds a priceless treasure.
[163] I hate lying; I am disgusted with it.
I love your teachings.
[164] Seven times a day I praise you
for your righteous regulations.
[165] There is lasting peace for those who love your teachings.
Nothing can make those people stumble.
[166] I have waited with hope for you to save me, O Lord.
I have carried out your commandments.
[167] I have obeyed your written instructions.
I have loved them very much.
[168] I have followed your guiding principles and your
written instructions,
because my whole life is in front of you.

[169] Let my cry for help come into your presence, O Lord.
Help me understand as you promised.
[170] Let my plea for mercy come into your presence.
Rescue me as you promised.
[171] Let my lips pour out praise
because you teach me your laws.
[172] Let my tongue sing about your promise
because all your commandments are fair.
[173] Let your hand help me
because I have chosen ⌊to follow⌋ your
guiding principles.
[174] I have longed for you to save me, O Lord,
and your teachings make me happy.
[175] Let my soul have new life so that it can praise you.
Let your regulations help me.
[176] I have wandered away like a lost lamb.
Search for me,
because I have never forgotten
your commandments.

119:157–159 People rage against me, but they can't keep me from obeying your instructions. I love your principles because they lead me into life.

119:160–162 Your Word is wholly true and your rules last forever. Learning your promises is like unearthing priceless treasure.

119:163–165 I love your teachings. I praise you all day long for your goodness. Your teachings bring me peace.

119:167–168 You don't have to force me to keep your instructions. I love to obey them. I follow your principles and do life in your presence.

119:171–173 I praise you for teaching me your laws. I sing because your commands are fair. Help me live up to my choice to follow you.

119:174–176 My heart overflows with happiness because of your teachings. Give me new life so I have even more reason to praise you. When I wander away, search for me. I'll never forget your commands.

Psalm 120

A song for going up to worship.

120:1–2 You answer me when I cry about my troubles. I need you to save me from deceitful tongues.

[1] When I was in trouble, I cried out to the Lord,
  and he answered me.
[2] O Lord, rescue me from lying lips
  and from a deceitful tongue.

[3] You deceitful tongue, what can the Lord give you?
  What more can he do for you?
[4]   He will give you a warrior's sharpened arrows
  and red-hot coals.

120:5–7 I live in a world of peace haters. I dream of peace but they only want war. Bring us peace as only you can!

[5] How horrible it is to live as a foreigner in Meshech
  or to stay in the tents of Kedar.
[6]   I have lived too long with those who hate peace.
[7]   I am for peace, but when I talk about it,
  they only talk about war.

Psalm 121

A song for going up to worship.

121:1–2 I look toward your dwelling place. Where can I get help? Only from you, maker of heaven and earth.

[1] I look up toward the mountains.
  Where can I find help?
[2] My help comes from the Lord,
  the maker of heaven and earth.

121:3–4 You won't let me fall. You never doze off when you watch over me.

[3] He will not let you fall.
  Your guardian will not fall asleep.
[4] Indeed, the Guardian of Israel never rests or sleeps.

121:5–8 You shade me with your tender hand. You protect me from every bad thing. You guard me not only today but always.

[5] The Lord is your guardian.
  The Lord is the shade over your right hand.
[6]   The sun will not beat down on you during the day,
  nor will the moon at night.
[7] The Lord guards you from every evil.
  He guards your life.
[8] The Lord guards you as you come and go,
  now and forever.

Psalm 122

A song by David for going up to worship.

122:1–3 Thanks for giving me people who encourage me to worship you. Give us one heart and mind when we approach you.

[1] I was glad when they said to me,
  "Let's go to the house of the Lord."
[2] Our feet are standing inside your gates, Jerusalem.
[3] Jerusalem is built to be a city
  where the people are united.[a]
[4] All of the Lord's tribes go to that city
  because it is a law in Israel
    to give thanks to the name of the Lord.
[5] The court of justice sits there.
    It consists of ⌐princes who are⌐ David's descendants.

122:4–7 I worship you willingly. I'd bow before you even if worship weren't a command. I offer you thanks. I praise you for your justice. Give your peace and prosperity to everyone who loves you.

[a] 122:3 Hebrew meaning of this verse uncertain.

⁶ Pray for the peace of Jerusalem:
"May those who love you prosper.
⁷ May there be peace inside your walls
and prosperity in your palaces."
⁸ For the sake of my relatives and friends, let me say,
"May it go well for you!"
⁹ For the sake of the house of the LORD our God,
I will seek what is good for you.

122:8–9 Send your very best to my family and friends. They'll receive your good gifts and bow to you in worship.

Psalm 123

A song for going up to worship.

¹ I look up to you,
to the one who sits enthroned in heaven.
² As servants depend on their masters,
as a maid depends on her mistress,
so we depend on the LORD our God
until he has pity on us.
³ Have pity on us, O LORD.
Have pity on us
because we have suffered more than our share
of contempt.
⁴ We have suffered more than our share of ridicule
from those who are carefree.
We have suffered more than our share of contempt
from those who are arrogant.

123:1–2 You reign from your throne in heaven. Just as a servant depends on his master, I depend on your help here on earth.

123:3–4 Show me pity, because I've suffered more than my share of contempt. Raise me up, because arrogant people never stop ridiculing me.

Psalm 124

A song by David for going up to worship.

¹ "If the LORD had not been on our side . . ."
(Israel should repeat this.)
² "If the LORD had not been on our side when people
attacked us,
³ then they would have swallowed us alive
when their anger exploded against us.
⁴ Then the floodwaters would have swept us away.
An ⌞overflowing⌟ stream would have washed
us away.
⁵ Then raging water would have washed us away."

⁶ Thank the LORD, who did not let them sink their teeth
into us.
⁷ We escaped like a bird caught in a hunter's trap.
The trap was broken, and we escaped.
⁸ Our help is in the name of the LORD, the maker of
heaven and earth.

124:1–8 Without you on my side my enemies swallow me alive. Without you on my side raging floods sweep me away. Without you on my side my enemy's teeth sink deep in my flesh. Maker of heaven and earth, you're my one source of help.

Psalm 125

A song for going up to worship.

125:1–2 You hold me together and keep life from shaking me apart. You surround me with your strong protection like mountains ring your holy city.

125:3–5 Don't let evildoers rule over your followers. Do good to me because my motives are good, but discipline me when my heart becomes crooked.

¹Those who trust the Lord are like Mount Zion,
 which can never be shaken.
 It remains firm forever.
² ⌐As⌐ the mountains surround Jerusalem,
 so the Lord surrounds his people now and forever.

³A wicked ruler will not be allowed to govern
 the land set aside for righteous people.
 That is why righteous people do not use their power
 to do wrong.
⁴Do good, O Lord, to those who are good,
 to those whose motives are decent.
⁵But when people become crooked,
 the Lord will lead them away with troublemakers.

Let there be peace in Israel!

Psalm 126

A song for going up to worship.

126:1–2 When I finally experienced your goodness, it felt like a dream. My mouth spilled laughter and I sang joyful songs. Everyone sees the spectacular things you've done for me.

¹When the Lord restored the fortunes of Zion,
 it was as if we were dreaming.
²Then our mouths were filled with laughter
 and our tongues with joyful songs.
 Then the nations said,
 "The Lord has done spectacular things for them."

³The Lord has done spectacular things for us.
 We are overjoyed.

126:4–6 Make my life flow again like you make streams well up in the desert. Even if I weep during this season of planting, I'll sing for joy at the harvest.

⁴Restore our fortunes, O Lord,
 as you restore streams ⌐to dry riverbeds⌐ in
 the Negev.
⁵Those who cry while they plant
 will joyfully sing while they harvest.
⁶The person who goes out weeping, carrying his
 bag of seed,
 will come home singing, carrying his bundles
 of grain.

Psalm 127

A song by Solomon for going up to worship.

127:1 If I don't put you first in my planning and building, my work is useless. If I don't let you protect me and my loved ones, all my defenses are worthless.

127:2–3 You give me food and sleep as gifts, so call me back to your rhythm when I'm tempted

¹If the Lord does not build the house,
 it is useless for the builders to work on it.
 If the Lord does not protect a city,
 it is useless for the guard to stay alert.
² It is useless to work hard for the food you eat
 by getting up early and going to bed late.
 The Lord gives ⌐food⌐ to those he loves while
 they sleep.

³Children are an inheritance from the LORD.
They are a reward from him.
⁴ The children born to a man when he is young
    are like arrows in the hand of a warrior.
⁵   Blessed is the man who has filled his quiver
        with them.
        He will not be put to shame
            when he speaks with his enemies in the
                city gate.

to work myself to death. You give me children as a gift, so send me the help I need to raise them.

Psalm 128

A song for going up to worship.

¹Blessed are all who fear the LORD
    and live his way.

128:1–2 I'm blessed whenever I choose to live your way. You let me eat what I earn and make things go well for me.

²You will certainly eat what your own hands
    have provided.
    Blessings to you!
    May things go well for you!
³Your wife will be like a fruitful vine inside your home.
    Your children will be like young olive trees around
        your table.
⁴ This is how the LORD will bless the person who
    fears him.
⁵   May the LORD bless you from Zion
        so that you may see Jerusalem prospering
            all the days of your life.
⁶   May you live to see your children's children.

Let there be peace in Israel!

128:3–6 You sent my spouse as your blessing for every moment of life. My children come as gifts straight from your hand. Send us your blessing from heaven. Prosper us. Grant us long life. Give us peace!

Psalm 129

A song for going up to worship.

¹"From the time I was young, people have
    attacked me . . ."
    (Israel should repeat this.)
²"From the time I was young, people have attacked me,
    but they have never overpowered me.
³   They have plowed my back ˻like farmers
        plow fields˼.
    They made long slashes ˻like furrows˼."
⁴The LORD is righteous.
    He has cut me loose
        from the ropes that wicked people tied around me.
⁵Put to shame all those who hate Zion.
    Force them to retreat.
⁶   Make them be like grass on a roof,
        like grass that dries up before it produces a stalk.

129:1–4 People attack me again and again, but they never overpower me. They slice my back like a farmer plowing rows, but you always set me free.

129:5–8 Put to shame people who won't stop hating you. Let them dry up like sun-baked grass. Don't let me do evil and

die before the harvest. Don't let
me miss out on your blessings.

7   It will never fill the barns of those who harvest
         or the arms of those who gather bundles.
8   Those who pass by will never say ⌜to them⌟,
         "May you be blessed by the LORD"
         or "We bless you in the name of
            the LORD."

Psalm 130

A song for going up to worship.

130:1–2 I call to you from a
deep dark place. Can you hear
my prayers for mercy?

1 O LORD, out of the depths I call to you.
2 O Lord, hear my voice.
   Let your ears be open to my pleas for mercy.

130:3–4 I could never survive
your anger if you kept track of my
sins. But your forgiveness wins
my grateful respect.

3 O LORD, who would be able to stand
   if you kept a record of sins?
4 But with you there is forgiveness
   so that you can be feared.

130:5–8 I long for your help.
I hope for your mercy. I count
on your unlimited forgiveness.
I depend on you to rescue me
from sin.

5 I wait for the LORD, my soul waits,
   and with hope I wait for his word.
6 My soul waits for the LORD
   more than those who watch for the morning,
   more than those who watch for the morning.
7 O Israel, put your hope in the LORD,
   because with the LORD there is mercy
      and with him there is unlimited forgiveness.
8   He will rescue Israel from all its sins.

Psalm 131

A song by David for going up to worship.

131:1 Humble my heart and
keep me from looking down on
others. Don't let me think too
much of myself.

1 O LORD, my heart is not conceited.
   My eyes do not look down on others.
   I am not involved in things too big or too difficult
      for me.

131:2–3 I'll calm my soul as I
rest in your arms. I'll hope in you
now and always.

2 Instead, I have kept my soul calm and quiet.
   My soul is content as a weaned child is content in its
      mother's arms.
3 Israel, put your hope in the LORD now and forever.

Psalm 132

A song for going up to worship.

132:1–5 David longed to build
you a house of worship. He swore
he wouldn't sleep until it was
done. Give me that heart toward
you. I don't want to rest
until I give you the
worship you deserve.

1 O LORD, remember David and all the hardships
      he endured.
2   Remember how he swore an oath to the LORD
         and made this vow to the Mighty One of Jacob:
3   "I will not step inside my house,
4   get into my bed, shut my eyes, or close
               my eyelids
5   until I find a place for the LORD,
               a dwelling place for the Mighty One
                  of Jacob."

⁶Now, we have heard about the ark ⌞of the promise⌟
   being in Ephrathah.
We have found it in Jaar.
⁷Let's go to his dwelling place.
Let's worship at his footstool.
⁸O LORD, arise, and come to your resting place
   with the ark of your power.
⁹Clothe your priests with righteousness.
Let your godly ones sing with joy.
¹⁰For the sake of your servant David,
   do not reject your anointed one.
¹¹The LORD swore an oath to David.
   This is a truth he will not take back:
      "I will set one of your own descendants on
         your throne.
¹²   If your sons are faithful to my promise[a]
         and my written instructions that I will
            teach them,
         then their descendants will also sit on your
            throne forever."

¹³The LORD has chosen Zion.
He wants it for his home.
¹⁴   "This will be my resting place forever.
      Here I will sit enthroned because I want Zion.
¹⁵   I will certainly bless all that Zion needs.
      I will satisfy its needy people with food.
¹⁶   I will clothe its priests with salvation.
         Then its godly ones will sing joyfully.
¹⁷   There I will make a horn sprout up for David.
      I will prepare a lamp for my anointed one.
¹⁸   I will clothe his enemies with shame,
         but the crown on my anointed one will shine."

Psalm 133

A song by David for going up to worship.

¹See how good and pleasant it is
   when brothers and sisters live together in harmony!
²   It is like fine, scented oil on the head,
         running down the beard—down Aaron's beard—
         running over the collar of his robes.
³   It is like dew on ⌞Mount⌟ Hermon,
         dew which comes down on Zion's mountains.
         That is where the LORD promised
            the blessing of eternal life.

132:7–9 I want to come to your dwelling and worship at your feet. Clothe me with righteousness and teach me a joyful song.

132:11–12 Praise you for your unbreakable promise to David that his descendant will always reign from his throne. Praise you for the righteous King born to David's line.

132:14–18 You've made your chosen people your resting place. Bless me by meeting my every real need. Give me food and salvation and joyful songs. Crown me with your glory.

133:1–3 It's right and good when your people get along. It's like pouring fine perfume on your chosen ones. Train me to live in harmony with others!

---
a 132:12 Or "covenant."

Psalm 134

A song for going up to worship.

134:1–3 I stand to worship you. I lift my hands to praise you. I'll come to adore you night after night.

¹ Praise the Lord, all you servants of the Lord,
   all who stand in the house of the Lord night
      after night.
² Lift your hands toward the holy place, and praise
   the Lord.
³ May the Lord, the maker of heaven and earth, bless
   you from Zion.

Psalm 135

135:1–4 Hallelujah! I enter your presence to worship. I praise you because you're good. I make music because your name is beautiful. I thank you because you chose me to be your own special treasure.

¹ Hallelujah!

Praise the name of the Lord.
Praise him, you servants of the Lord
²   who are standing in the house of the Lord,
      in the courtyards of the house of our God.
³ Praise the Lord because he is good.
Make music to praise his name because his name
      is beautiful.
⁴   The Lord chose Jacob to be his own
      and chose Israel to be his own special treasure.

135:5–11 You're greater than every false god. You do whatever you want. You rule over nature and reign over your enemies. You defend your people and defeat anyone who dares rise up against you.

⁵ I know that the Lord is great,
   that our Lord is greater than all the false gods.
⁶ The Lord does whatever he wants in heaven or on earth,
   on the seas or in all the depths of the oceans.
⁷ He is the one who makes the clouds rise from the ends
      of the earth,
   who makes lightning for the thunderstorms,
      and who brings wind out of his storerooms.

⁸ He is the one who killed every firstborn male in Egypt.
   He killed humans and animals alike.
⁹ He sent miraculous signs and amazing things into the
      heart of Egypt
   against Pharaoh and all his officials.
¹⁰ He is the one who defeated many nations and killed
      mighty kings:
¹¹   King Sihon of the Amorites,
      King Og of Bashan,
         and all the kingdoms in Canaan.
¹²   He gave their land as an inheritance,
            an inheritance to his people Israel.

135:13–14 Your fame lasts forever. You always show me justice and compassion.

¹³ O Lord, your name endures forever.
   O Lord, you will be remembered throughout
         every generation.
¹⁴   The Lord will provide justice for his people
      and have compassion on his servants.

135:15–18 Idols are just

¹⁵ The idols of the nations are made of silver and gold.

They were made by human hands.[a]
16 They have mouths, but they cannot speak.
    They have eyes, but they cannot see.
17 They have ears, but they cannot hear.
    They cannot breathe.
18 Those who make idols end up like them.
    So does everyone who trusts them.

19 Descendants of Israel, praise the LORD.
   Descendants of Aaron, praise the LORD.
20 Descendants of Levi, praise the LORD.
   You people who fear the LORD, praise the LORD.
21 Thank the LORD in Zion.
    Thank the one who lives in Jerusalem.

Hallelujah!

135:19–21 I praise you because I'm one of your chosen people. I live for you with utter respect. Thank you for dwelling close to me!

Psalm 136

1 Give thanks to the LORD because he is good,
            because his mercy endures forever.
2 Give thanks to the God of gods
            because his mercy endures forever.
3 Give thanks to the Lord of lords
            because his mercy endures forever.

4 Give thanks to the only one who does
    miraculous things—
            because his mercy endures forever.
5 to the one who made the heavens by
    his understanding—
            because his mercy endures forever.
6 to the one who spread out the earth on the water
            because his mercy endures forever.
7 to the one who made the great lights—
            because his mercy endures forever.
8 the sun to rule the day—
            because his mercy endures forever.
9 the moon and stars to rule the night—
            because his mercy endures forever.

10 Give thanks to the one who killed the firstborn males
    in Egypt—
            because his mercy endures forever.
11 He brought Israel out from among them—
            because his mercy endures forever.
12 with a mighty hand and a powerful arm—
            because his mercy endures forever.

13 Give thanks to one who divided the Red Sea—
            because his mercy endures forever.
14 He led Israel through the middle of it—

136:1–3 I thank you because you're perfectly good—and your mercy lasts forever. I thank you because you're Lord of lords—and your mercy lasts forever.

136:4–9 I thank you because you do miracles—and your mercy lasts forever. I thank you because you made the skies by your wisdom. You strung out the sun, moon, and stars—and your mercy lasts forever.

136:11–15 I thank you because you rescued your people from slavery—and your mercy lasts forever. You saved us with your mighty power and swept away your enemies—and your mercy lasts forever.

[a] 135:15 Verses 15–18 are virtually identical in wording to Psalm 115:4–8.

metal objects shaped by human hands. They can't speak or see. They can't hear or breathe. If I serve false gods, I'll end up as senseless as the idols I worship.

because his mercy endures forever.
¹⁵ He swept Pharaoh and his army into the Red Sea—
because his mercy endures forever.

¹⁶ Give thanks to the one who led his people through
the desert—
because his mercy endures forever.

¹⁷ Give thanks to the one who defeated powerful kings—
because his mercy endures forever.
¹⁸ He killed mighty kings—
because his mercy endures forever.
¹⁹ King Sihon of the Amorites—
because his mercy endures forever.
²⁰ and King Og of Bashan—
because his mercy endures forever.
²¹ He gave their land as an inheritance—
because his mercy endures forever.
²² as an inheritance for his servant Israel—
because his mercy endures forever.

²³ He remembered us when we were humiliated—
because his mercy endures forever.
²⁴ He snatched us from the grasp of our enemies—
because his mercy endures forever.
²⁵ He gives food to every living creature—
because his mercy endures forever.

²⁶ Give thanks to the God of heaven
because his mercy endures forever.

Psalm 137

¹ By the rivers of Babylon, we sat down and cried
as we remembered Zion.
² We hung our lyres on willow trees.
³ It was there that those who had captured us demanded
that we sing.
Those who guarded us wanted us to entertain them.
⌞They said,⌟ "Sing a song from Zion for us!"

⁴ How could we sing the Lord's song in a foreign land?
⁵ If I forget you, Jerusalem,
let my right hand forget ⌞how to play the lyre⌟.
⁶ Let my tongue stick to the roof of my mouth
if I don't remember you,
if I don't consider Jerusalem my highest joy.

⁷ O Lord, remember the people of Edom.
Remember what they did the day Jerusalem
⌞was captured⌟.
They said, "Tear it down! Tear it down to
its foundation."

136:16–20 I thank you because you led your people through the wilderness—and your mercy lasts forever. I thank you because you defeated powerful enemies—and your mercy lasts forever.

136:23–25 I thank you because you didn't abandon us in our humiliation—and your mercy lasts forever. I thank you because you feed every living thing—and your mercy lasts forever.

137:1–3 I weep when I remember what it was like to live close to you. I ran away in sinful rebellion and you let me be captured. My captors make my praise a joke.

137:4–6 How can I sing when I'm so far from you? But how can I forget your holy city? I remember what it was like to live close to you. Oh how I long to return!

137:7–9 Don't overlook the evil others have done—the utter destruction they caused. I trust you to calm my rage.

8 You destructive people of Babylon,
   blessed is the one who pays you back
     with the same treatment you gave us.
9 Blessed is the one who grabs your little children
     and smashes them against a rock.

Psalm 138

By David.

1 I will give thanks to you with all my heart.
  I will make music to praise you in front of the
     false gods.
2 I will bow toward your holy temple.
  I will give thanks to your name because of your mercy
     and truth.
     You have made your name and your promise greater
       than everything.
3 When I called, you answered me.
   You made me bold by strengthening my soul.[a]
4 All the kings of the earth will give thanks to you,
     O Lord,
  because they have heard the promises you spoke.
5   They will sing this about the ways of the Lord:
     "The Lord's honor is great!"
6 Even though the Lord is high above, he sees humble
    people ⌞close up⌟,
   and he recognizes arrogant people from a distance.
7 Even though I walk into the middle of trouble,
   you guard my life against the anger of my enemies.
   You stretch out your hand,
     and your right hand saves me.
8 The Lord will do everything for me.
  O Lord, your mercy endures forever.
  Do not let go of what your hands have made.

138:1–2 I thank you with every part of my heart. I worship you even when so-called gods are watching. I bow to you and say thanks for your mercy and truth.

138:2–3 You and your promise are greater than anything I can imagine. You answer my cries and make me bold.

138:6 Even though you reign from on high, you know the humble up close. You spot the proud from miles away.

138:7–8 Even when I walk into trouble you guard my life. You reach out and save me. You mercifully do everything I need.

Psalm 139

For the choir director; a psalm by David.

1 O Lord, you have examined me, and you know me.
2   You alone know when I sit down and when I get up.
   You read my thoughts from far away.
3   You watch me when I travel and when I rest.
   You are familiar with all my ways.
4   Even before there is a ⌞single⌟ word on my tongue,
     you know all about it, Lord.
5   You are all around me—in front of me and in back
     of me.
   You lay your hand on me.

139:1–4 You've studied me up close and you see my every move. You know my thoughts before I think them and my words before I speak.

139:5–6 I can't escape your grip on me. There's nowhere I can go to get away from you.

---

[a] 138:3 Hebrew meaning of this line uncertain.

Up or down, right or left—you always hold me tight.

139:7–10 There's no corner of heaven where you can't find me. I can't escape to hell or the sun or a distant shore. You always hold me tight.

139:11–12 When I step into darkness, you see me as if it were broad daylight. You follow me wherever I go.

139:13–15 You made me inside and out, a pure miracle of complexity. My mother's womb couldn't hide me. It was you who was weaving me with great skill.

139:16–18 Your eyes saw me before I was born. You saw my whole life stretched out before me before a single day had passed. Your thoughts amaze me! You think of me all day long.

139:19–22 You know all things. You know I hate what the wicked do. Shouldn't I feel that way?

139:23–24 Examine me, my God. Keep checking my thoughts. Test me. Tell me when I'm headed into evil and put me back on the path toward you.

⁶Such knowledge is beyond my grasp.
It is so high I cannot reach it.

⁷Where can I go ˻to get away˼ from your Spirit?
Where can I run ˻to get away˼ from you?
⁸ If I go up to heaven, you are there.
If I make my bed in hell, you are there.
⁹ If I climb upward on the rays of the morning sun
˻or˼ land on the most distant shore of the sea
where the sun sets,
¹⁰ even there your hand would guide me
and your right hand would hold on to me.
¹¹ If I say, "Let the darkness hide me
and let the light around me turn into night,"
¹² even the darkness is not too dark for you.
Night is as bright as day.
Darkness and light are the same ˻to you˼.

¹³You alone created my inner being.
You knitted me together inside my mother.
¹⁴I will give thanks to you
because I have been so amazingly and
miraculously made.
Your works are miraculous, and my soul is fully
aware of this.
¹⁵My bones were not hidden from you
when I was being made in secret,
when I was being skillfully woven in an
underground workshop.
¹⁶Your eyes saw me when I was only a fetus.
Every day ˻of my life˼ was recorded in your book
before one of them had taken place.
¹⁷How precious are your thoughts concerning me, O God!
How vast in number they are!
¹⁸ If I try to count them,
there would be more of them than there are grains
of sand.
When I wake up, I am still with you.

¹⁹I wish that you would kill wicked people, O God,
and that bloodthirsty people would leave me alone.
²⁰ They say wicked things about you.
Your enemies misuse your name.
²¹Shouldn't I hate those who hate you, O LORD?
Shouldn't I be disgusted with those who attack you?
²² I hate them with all my heart.
They have become my enemies.

²³Examine me, O God, and know my mind.
Test me, and know my thoughts.
²⁴ See whether I am on an evil path.
Then lead me on the everlasting path.

Psalm 140

For the choir leader; a psalm by David.

¹Rescue me from evil people, O LORD.
Keep me safe from violent people.
² They plan evil things in their hearts.
They start fights every day.
³ They make their tongues as sharp as a snake's ⌐fang⌐.
Their lips hide the venom of poisonous snakes. *Selah*

⁴Protect me from the hands of wicked people, O LORD.
Keep me safe from violent people.
They try to trip me.
⁵Arrogant people have laid a trap for me.
They have spread out a net with ropes.
They have set traps for me along the road. *Selah*

⁶I said to the LORD, "You are my God."
O LORD, open your ears to hear my plea for pity.
⁷ O LORD Almighty, the strong one who saves me,
you have covered my head in the day of battle.
⁸ O LORD, do not give wicked people what they want.
Do not let their evil plans succeed,
⌐or⌐ they will become arrogant. *Selah*

⁹Let the heads of those who surround me
be covered with their own threats.
¹⁰Let burning coals fall on them.
Let them be thrown into a pit, never to rise again.
¹¹Do not let slanderers prosper on earth.
Let evil hunt down violent people with one blow
after another.

¹²I know that the LORD will defend the rights of those
who are oppressed
and the cause of those who are needy.
¹³ Indeed, righteous people will give thanks to
your name.
Decent people will live in your presence.

140:1–2 Rescue me from evildoers. Keep me safe from people who pick fights.

140:3–5 Protect me from violent people. Their words are like the fangs of venomous snakes. Their hands build traps to catch me unaware.

140:6–8 I declare to you that you're my God, so hear my plea for pity. You're the strong one, so save me. If you let evil people succeed, their plans will only get bigger.

140:9–11 Turn my enemies' threats back against them. Let them be caught in their own traps. Don't let them prosper until they turn to you.

140:12–13 You will defend the oppressed and needy. Good people will live close to you.

Psalm 141

A psalm by David.

¹O LORD, I cry out to you, "Come quickly."
Open your ears to me when I cry out to you.
² Let my prayer be accepted
as sweet-smelling incense in your presence.
Let the lifting up of my hands in prayer be accepted
as an evening sacrifice.

³O LORD, set a guard at my mouth.
Keep watch over the door of my lips.

141:1–2 I need you now! Accept my prayer like incense and my lifted hands as a sacrifice.

141:3–4 Silence me before I speak evil. Stop me when I'm about to step into wickedness. Don't let me taste the rewards of doing wrong and develop a liking for them.

141:5 I'll gladly accept the correction of good people. I need their help to avoid evil.

141:6–7 Put an end to evil judges at the time and place of your choosing.

141:8–9 I keep looking for you and your might. I count on your keeping me safe. Don't leave me to fight my battles on my own. And save me from traps meant to hurt me.

4 Do not let me be persuaded to do anything evil
  or to become involved with wickedness,
    with people who are troublemakers.
    Do not let me taste their delicacies.

5 A righteous person may strike me or correct me out
  of kindness.
  It is like lotion for my head.
    My head will not refuse it,
      because my prayer is directed against
      evil deeds.
6 When their judges are thrown off a cliff,
  they will listen to what I have to say.
    It will sound pleasant ⌞to them⌟.
7 As someone plows and breaks up the ground,
  so our bones will be planted at the mouth of
    the grave.[a]

8 My eyes look to you, LORD Almighty.
  I have taken refuge in you.
    Do not leave me defenseless.
9 Keep me away from the trap they set for me
    and from the traps set by troublemakers.
10 Let wicked people fall into their own nets,
    while I escape unharmed.

Psalm 142

A maskil[b] by David when he was in the cave; a prayer.

142:1–2 I cry out to you. I plead for mercy and pour out my complaints.

142:3–4 I'm losing hope—and you know why. My enemies want to trap me and there's no escape.

142:4–5 No one cares for me but you. So I cry out to you, my refuge. You're the only thing I have in this life.

142:6–7 Pay attention to me because I am far too weak to fight. Set me free from this prison and I will thank you again and again.

1 Loudly, I cry to the LORD.
  Loudly, I plead with the LORD for mercy.
2 I pour out my complaints in his presence
    and tell him my troubles.
3   When I begin to lose hope,
        you ⌞already⌟ know what I am experiencing.

  ⌞My enemies⌟ have hidden a trap for me on the path
    where I walk.
4 Look to my right and see that no one notices me.
  Escape is impossible for me.
    No one cares about me.

5 I call out to you, O LORD.
  I say, "You are my refuge,
    my own inheritance in this world of the living."
6 Pay attention to my cry for help
    because I am very weak.
  Rescue me from those who pursue me
    because they are too strong for me.

---

[a] 141:7 Hebrew meaning of verses 5–7 uncertain.
[b] 142:1 Unknown musical term.

7 Release my soul from prison
  so that I may give thanks to your name.
  Righteous people will surround me
  because you are good to me.

Psalm 143

A psalm by David.

1 O LORD, listen to my prayer.
  Open your ears to hear my urgent requests.
  Answer me because you are faithful and righteous.
2 Do not take me to court for judgment,
  because there is no one alive
  who is righteous in your presence.

3 The enemy has pursued me.
  He has ground my life into the dirt.
  He has made me live in dark places
  like those who have died long ago.
4   That is why I begin to lose hope
  and my heart is in a state of shock.

5 I remember the days long ago.
  I reflect on all that you have done.
  I carefully consider what your hands have made.
6 I stretch out my hands to you in prayer.
  Like parched land, my soul thirsts for you.   *Selah*

7 Answer me quickly, O LORD.
  My spirit is worn out.
  Do not hide your face from me,
  or I will be like those who go into the pit.
8 Let me hear about your mercy in the morning,
  because I trust you.
  Let me know the way that I should go,
  because I long for you.
9 Rescue me from my enemies, O LORD.
  I come to you for protection.

10 Teach me to do your will, because you are my God.
  May your good Spirit lead me on level ground.
11 O LORD, keep me alive for the sake of your name.
  Because you are righteous, lead me out of trouble.
12 In keeping with your mercy, wipe out my enemies
  and destroy all who torment me,
  because I am your servant.

Psalm 144

By David.

1 Thank the LORD, my rock,
  who trained my hands to fight
  and my fingers to do battle,

143:1–2 Hear my urgent request! Answer me because you are good! Don't judge me, because no human can measure up to your standards.

143:3–6 The enemy has ground me into the dirt and made me lose hope. My heart is in shock. I feel parched as I pray. Yet I recall one by one all the awesome things you have done.

143:7–8 Answer me soon because my spirit is worn out. I'm as good as dead if you keep hiding from me. Send your mercy and show me what to do. I long for you!

143:9–12 Rescue me when I come to you for protection. You're my Lord, so train me to do your will. I'm your servant, so keep me alive for the sake of your good reputation.

144:1–2 Thank you, my rock, for making me tough. Train me to stay in the fight. You're my merciful one, my stronghold and Savior.

2   my merciful one, my fortress,
   my stronghold, and my savior,
   my shield, the one in whom I take refuge,
      and the one who brings people under my authority.

144:3–4 Why do you care about me? I'm nothing more than a breath of air. My life comes and goes like a shadow.

3 O Lord, what are humans that you should care
      about them?
   What are mere mortals that you should think
      about them?
4   Humans are like a breath of air.
      Their life span is like a fleeting shadow.

144:5–8 Bring heaven to me here on earth. Come down to me now. Battle against my enemies. Scatter and confuse them. They tell lies and make phony promises.

5 O Lord, bend your heaven low, and come down.
   Touch the mountains, and they will smoke.
6   Hurl bolts of lightning, and scatter them.
   Shoot your arrows, and throw them into confusion.
7   Stretch out your hands from above.
   Snatch me, and rescue me from raging waters
      and from foreigners' hands.
8   Their mouths speak lies.
      Their right hands take false pledges.

144:9–11 I'll sing a fresh song to you because you give me victory. You snatch me from my enemies, the ones who tell lies and make promises they don't intend to keep.

9 O God, I will sing a new song to you.
   I will sing a psalm to you on a ten-stringed harp.
10 You are the one who gives victory to kings.
   You are the one who snatches your servant David
      away from a deadly sword.
11   Snatch me, and rescue me from foreigners' hands.
      Their mouths speak lies.
      Their right hands take false pledges.

144:12–15 Make my children strong and mature. Fill our house with food. Protect us from enemies who want to break into our lives and snatch us away. Keep our world free from distress. We're blessed to call you our Lord!

12 May our sons be like full-grown, young plants.
   May our daughters be like stately columns
      that adorn the corners of a palace.
13 May our barns be filled with all kinds of crops.
   May our sheep give birth to thousands of lambs,
      tens of thousands in our fields.
14 May our cattle have many calves.[a]

   May no one break in, and may no one be dragged out.
   May there be no cries of distress in our streets.

15   Blessed are the people who have these blessings!
   Blessed are the people whose God is the Lord!

Psalm 145[b]

A song of praise by David.

145:1–3 I have endless reasons to praise you, so I'll praise you

1 I will highly praise you, my God, the king.
   I will bless your name forever and ever.

---

[a] 144:14 Hebrew meaning of this verse uncertain.
[b] 145:1 Psalm 145 is a poem in Hebrew alphabetical order.

²I will bless you every day.
I will praise your name forever and ever.

³The Lord is great, and he should be highly praised.
His greatness is unsearchable.
⁴One generation will praise your deeds to the next.
Each generation will talk about your mighty acts.
⁵I will think about the glorious honor of your majesty
and the miraculous things you have done.
⁶People will talk about the power of your
terrifying deeds,
and I will tell about your greatness.
⁷They will announce what they remember of your
great goodness,
and they will joyfully sing about your righteousness.
⁸The Lord is merciful, compassionate, patient,
and always ready to forgive.
⁹The Lord is good to everyone
and has compassion for everything that he has made.
¹⁰Everything that you have made will give thanks to you,
O Lord,
and your faithful ones will praise you.
¹¹Everyone will talk about the glory of your kingdom
and will tell the descendants of Adam about
your might
¹²   in order to make known your mighty deeds
and the glorious honor of your kingdom.
¹³Your kingdom is an everlasting kingdom.
Your empire endures throughout every generation.

¹⁴The Lord supports everyone who falls.
He straightens ⌊the backs⌋ of those who are bent over.
¹⁵   The eyes of all creatures look to you,
and you give them their food at the proper time.
¹⁶   You open your hand,
and you satisfy the desire of every living thing.
¹⁷The Lord is fair in all his ways
and faithful in everything he does.
¹⁸The Lord is near to everyone who prays to him,
to every faithful person who prays to him.
¹⁹He fills the needs of those who fear him.
He hears their cries for help and saves them.
²⁰The Lord protects everyone who loves him,
but he will destroy all wicked people.

²¹My mouth will speak the praise of the Lord,
and all living creatures will praise his holy name
forever and ever.

today and forever. Your greatness is more than I can comprehend.

145:4–7 Let each generation of your people tell the next what you've done. We'll all sing of your goodness when I tell of your glorious honor and miraculous deeds.

145:8–10 You're merciful and ready to forgive. You're compassionate toward everything you've made. Everything you've made thanks you.

145:11–13 All of your followers praise you as they talk about your glorious might. Your kingdom lasts forever.

145:14–17 You support the fallen. You straighten the bent over. You feed us and satisfy our every desire. You're always fair and faithful.

145:18–21 You're near to everyone who prays to you, and you meet the needs of people who live for you with utter respect. When we ask you for help, you save us. Praise you now and forever!

Psalm 146

146:1–2 Hallelujah! Praise you! I'll live my whole life as an act of worship. I'll sing to you each day of my life.

146:3–6 I'm done with depending on influential people. They die and their plans die with them. Real help comes from you, the maker of heaven and earth. Your faithfulness never ends.

146:7–10 You grant justice to the oppressed and feed the hungry. You free prisoners and open blind eyes. You raise up the hurting, defend the outcast, and care for the needy. Rule as our King forever and ever!

¹Hallelujah!

Praise the Lord, my soul!
²I want to praise the Lord throughout my life.
I want to make music to praise my God as long as I live.

³Do not trust influential people,
    mortals who cannot help you.
⁴   When they breathe their last breath, they return to
        the ground.
    On that day their plans come to an end.
⁵Blessed are those who receive help from the God
    of Jacob.
    Their hope rests on the Lord their God,
⁶   who made heaven, earth,
        the sea, and everything in them.
    The Lord remains faithful forever.
⁷   He brings about justice for those who are oppressed.
    He gives food to those who are hungry.
    The Lord sets prisoners free.
⁸The Lord gives sight to blind people.
    The Lord straightens ⌊the backs⌋ of those who are
        bent over.
    The Lord loves righteous people.
⁹The Lord protects foreigners.
    The Lord gives relief to orphans and widows.
        But he keeps wicked people from reaching their goal.
¹⁰The Lord rules as king forever.
    Zion, your God rules throughout every generation.

Hallelujah!

Psalm 147

147:1 Hallelujah! It's good to sing beautiful songs to you.

147:2–6 You make outcasts into a people and bandage the brokenhearted. You set stars in the sky and name each one. There's no limit to your power and knowledge. You relieve the oppressed and bring down evildoers.

147:7–9 I'll sing thanks to you for sending rain and growing grass and feeding every living thing.

¹Hallelujah!

It is good to sing psalms to our God.
It is pleasant to sing ⌊his⌋ praise beautifully.

²The Lord is the builder of Jerusalem.
    He is the one who gathers the outcasts of
        Israel together.
³   He is the healer of the brokenhearted.
    He is the one who bandages their wounds.
⁴   He determines the number of stars.
    He gives each one a name.
⁵Our Lord is great, and his power is great.
    There is no limit to his understanding.
⁶The Lord gives relief to those who are oppressed.
    He brings wicked people down to the ground.

⁷Sing to the Lord a song of thanksgiving.
Make music to our God with a lyre.

8 He covers the sky with clouds.
   He provides rain for the ground.
   He makes grass grow on the mountains.
9 He is the one who gives food to animals
      and to young ravens when they call out.
10 He finds no joy in strong horses,
      nor is he pleased by brave soldiers.
11 The LORD is pleased with those who fear him,
      with those who wait with hope for his mercy.

12 Praise the LORD, Jerusalem!
   Praise your God, Zion!
13   He makes the bars across your gates strong.
      He blesses the children within you.
14   He is the one who brings peace to your borders
      and satisfies your ⌐hunger⌐ with the finest wheat.
15   He is the one who sends his promise throughout
         the earth.
      His word travels with great speed.
16   He is the one who sends snow like wool
      and scatters frost like ashes.
17   He is the one who throws his hailstones
         like breadcrumbs.
      Who can withstand his chilling blast?
18   He sends out his word and melts his hailstones.
      He makes wind blow ⌐and⌐ water flow.
19   He speaks his word to Jacob,
         his laws and judicial decisions to Israel.
20   He has done nothing like this for any other nation.
         The other nations do not know the decisions he has
            handed down.

Hallelujah!

147:10–11 You aren't impressed by human strength. You love hearts that hold you in awe and look to you for mercy.

147:13–14 Strengthen our cities and build up our children. Bring peace to our land and satisfy our hunger.

147:15–20 Your promises speed around the world. They carry out your will and convey wisdom to your people. Hallelujah!

Psalm 148

1 Hallelujah!

Praise the LORD from the heavens.
Praise him in the heights above.
2 Praise him, all his angels.
Praise him, his entire heavenly army.
3 Praise him, sun and moon.
Praise him, all shining stars.
4 Praise him, you highest heaven
   and the water above the sky.
5 Let them praise the name of the LORD
   because they were created by his command.
6 He set them in their places forever and ever.
He made it a law that no one can break.

7 Praise the LORD from the earth.
Praise him, large sea creatures and all the ocean depths,

148:3 Hallelujah! Let your praises sound from the heavens. Let them ring from sun, moon, and stars.

148:5–6 The heavens exist because of your command. They stay in place because of your law.

148:7–9 Let your praises sound from the earth. Let them

ring from sea and sky, from
mountains and hills, from snow
and fog, from strong winds that
obey you.

148:10–12 Let your praises
sound from your creatures. Let
them ring from animals and
birds, kings and commoners,
women and men, old and young.

148:13–14 Let your praises
keep sounding forever. Your
name is above any other name.
Hallelujah!

⁸ lightning and hail,
snow and fog,
strong winds that obey his commands,
⁹ mountains and all hills,
fruit trees and all cedar trees,
¹⁰ wild animals and all domestic animals,
crawling animals and birds,
¹¹ kings of the earth and all its people,
officials and all judges on the earth,
¹² young men and women,
old and young together.
¹³ Let them praise the name of the LORD
because his name is high above all others.
His glory is above heaven and earth.
¹⁴ He has given his people a strong leader,[a]
someone praiseworthy for his faithful ones,
for the people of Israel, the people who are close
to him.

Hallelujah!

Psalm 149

¹ Hallelujah!

149:1–2 Hallelujah! I'll sing a
new song to you. My Creator, I
find joy in you. My King,
I rejoice in you.

Sing a new song to the LORD.
Sing his praise in the assembly of godly people.
² Let Israel find joy in their creator.
Let the people of Zion rejoice over their king.
³ Let them praise his name with dancing.
Let them make music to him with tambourines
and lyres,

149:3–4 I'll praise you with
dancing and music. You smile at
me and crown me with victory.

⁴ because the LORD takes pleasure in his people.
He crowns those who are oppressed with victory.
⁵ Let godly people triumph in glory.
Let them sing for joy on their beds.
⁶ Let the high praises of God be in their throats
and two-edged swords in their hands
⁷ to take vengeance on the nations,
to punish the people of the world,
⁸ to put their kings in chains
and their leaders in iron shackles,
⁹ to carry out the judgment that is written
against them.
This is an honor that belongs to all his
godly ones.

149:5–9 You declare judgment
and avenge your honor. You
shackle kings and punish people.
Spare me from your day of wrath.

Hallelujah!

---
[a] 148:14 Or "given his people strength."

Psalm 150

¹Hallelujah!

Praise God in his holy place.
Praise him in his mighty heavens.
²Praise him for his mighty acts.
Praise him for his immense greatness.
³Praise him with sounds from horns.
Praise him with harps and lyres.
⁴Praise him with tambourines and dancing.
Praise him with stringed instruments and flutes.
⁵Praise him with loud cymbals.
Praise him with crashing cymbals.

⁶Let everything that breathes praise the LORD!

Hallelujah!

150:1–2 Hallelujah! I'll praise your holiness here on earth. I'll praise you when I come home to heaven. I'll praise you for your immense greatness.

150:3–6 I'll praise you with instruments and dancing. I'll praise you with loud crashing cymbals. Let every living thing join me in worship. Hallelujah!

Introduction to Proverbs

Like no other book of the Bible, Proverbs instructs you to sit down and listen closely. Again and again it plainly tells the good it seeks to accomplish. It offers "wisdom and discipline," "deep thoughts." It provides everything you need to "acquire the discipline of wise behavior" along with "righteousness and justice and fairness." It gives "insight to gullible people" and "knowledge and foresight to the young." It lets even the wise "listen and continue to learn" and the discerning "gain direction" (Proverbs 1:1–5).

The first part of this book (Proverbs 1–9) introduces wisdom, explaining what it is and why you need it. The remainder of the book contains pithy sayings. A mostly random collection of 375 of these proverbs (Proverbs 10:1–22:16) comes from Solomon, a man uniquely gifted with God's wisdom (1 Kings 3:12). Other sayings of the wise fill out the book, with material arranged more thematically (Proverbs 22:17–31:31).

Though the topics covered range from relationships and money to work, sex, parenting, and more, a single truth connects them all: Wisdom begins and ends with respect for God (Proverbs 1:7). The sayings in the book frequently use parallelism to make a point, repeating similar and contrasting thoughts.

Praying this book invites you to open yourself to God's wisdom, to ask God to let these words permeate your heart and mind and change your life. Explore Proverbs not just as a collection of human sayings but as a gift of insight to you from the all-wise God.

PROVERBS

The Reasons for Proverbs

1 ¹The proverbs of Solomon, David's son who was king
of Israel, ⌐given⌐

² to grasp wisdom and discipline,
to understand deep thoughts,
³ to acquire the discipline of wise behavior—
righteousness and justice and fairness—
⁴ to give insight to gullible people,
to give knowledge and foresight to the young—
⁵ a wise person will listen and continue to learn,
and an understanding person will
gain direction—
⁶ to understand a proverb and a clever saying,
the words of wise people and their riddles.

⁷The fear of the LORD is the beginning of knowledge.
Stubborn fools despise wisdom and discipline.

Listen to Wisdom

⁸My son,
listen to your father's discipline,
and do not neglect your mother's teachings,
⁹ because discipline and teachings
are a graceful garland on your head
and a ⌐golden⌐ chain around your neck.

¹⁰My son,
if sinners lure you, do not go along.
¹¹ If they say,
"Come with us.
Let's set an ambush to kill someone.
Let's hide to ambush innocent people for fun.
¹² We'll swallow them alive like the grave,
like those in good health who go into the pit.
¹³ We'll find all kinds of valuable possessions.
We'll fill our homes with stolen goods.
¹⁴ Join us.
We'll split the loot equally."

¹⁵My son,
do not follow them in their way.
Do not even set foot on their path,
¹⁶ because they rush to do evil
and hurry to shed blood.

1:1–4 I crave wisdom! I need discipline! Teach me deep thoughts that train me to be good and fair. Expose my blind spots and give me insight beyond my years.

1:5–7 I'm willing to learn and keep learning from smart people you put in my path. I'm finally starting to wise up when I give you the respect you deserve.

1:8–9 I won't shut out my parents' words or resent the ways they discipline me. I'll let their wisdom grace my life.

1:10–14 Help me be on guard against anyone aiming to lure me into sin. I won't let them sell me on the so-called fun of hurting innocent people or taking what isn't mine.

1:15–19 I choose not to take a single step down the path to sin, because people who rush to do evil will get what they deserve. They'll be killed in the ambush they set for others. Sooner or later their greed will catch up with them.

¹⁷ It does no good to spread a net
within the sight of any bird.
¹⁸ But these people set an ambush for their
own murder.
They go into hiding only to lose their lives.
¹⁹ This is what happens to everyone
who is greedy for unjust gain.
Greed takes away his life.

1:20–22 Your wisdom sings to me. You call me by name. You want to know how much longer I'll be so gullible. You can't figure out why I hate knowledge.

²⁰ Wisdom sings her song in the streets.
In the public squares she raises her voice.
²¹ At the corners of noisy streets she calls out.
At the entrances to the city she speaks her words,
²² "How long will you gullible people love being
so gullible?
How long will you mockers find joy in
your mocking?
How long will you fools hate knowledge?

1:23–25 Warn me. Pour out your Spirit for me. Teach me wise words. I won't let your efforts go to waste. I'll act on your advice.

²³ "Turn to me when I warn you.
I will generously pour out my spirit for you.
I will make my words known to you.

²⁴ "I called, and you refused to listen.
I stretched out my hands to you, and no one
paid attention.
²⁵ You ignored all my advice.
You did not want me to warn you.

1:26–29 I refuse to bring calamity on myself or give people reason to laugh at my panic. I don't want anyone to say I ignored your advice. Don't ever stop trying to get through to me!

²⁶ I will laugh at your calamity.
I will make fun of you
when panic strikes you,
²⁷ when panic strikes you like a violent storm,
when calamity strikes you like a wind storm,
when trouble and anguish come to you.

²⁸ "They will call to me at that time, but I will
not answer.
They will look for me, but they will not find me,
²⁹ because they hated knowledge
and did not choose the fear of the Lord.
³⁰ They refused my advice.
They despised my every warning.
³¹ They will eat the fruit of their lifestyle.
They will be stuffed with their own schemes.

1:32–33 I have enough problems in life without bringing trouble on myself. I'd rather listen to you and live without worry.

³² "Gullible people kill themselves because of their
turning away.
Fools destroy themselves because of
their indifference.
³³ But whoever listens to me will live
without worry
and will be free from the dread of disaster."

The Benefit of Wisdom

2 ¹My son,
if you take my words ⌐to heart⌐
and treasure my commands within you,
² if you pay close attention to wisdom,
and let your mind reach for understanding,
³ if indeed you call out for insight,
if you ask aloud for understanding,
⁴ if you search for wisdom as if it were money
and hunt for it as if it were hidden treasure,
⁵ then you will understand the fear of the LORD
and you will find the knowledge of God.
⁶ The LORD gives wisdom.
From his mouth come knowledge
and understanding.
⁷ He has reserved priceless wisdom for
decent people.
He is a shield for those who walk in integrity
⁸ in order to guard those on paths of justice
and to watch over the way of his godly ones.
⁹ Then you will understand what is right and just
and fair—
every good course ⌐in life⌐.

¹⁰ Wisdom will come into your heart.
Knowledge will be pleasant to your soul.
¹¹ Foresight will protect you.
Understanding will guard you.

¹² ⌐Wisdom will⌐ save you
from the way of evil,
from the person who speaks devious things,
¹³ from those who abandon the paths of righteousness
to walk the ways of darkness,
¹⁴ from those who enjoy doing evil,
from those who find joy in the deviousness of evil.
¹⁵ Their paths are crooked.
Their ways are devious.

¹⁶ ⌐Wisdom will⌐ also save you
from an adulterous woman,
from a loose woman with her smooth talk,
¹⁷ who leaves ⌐her husband,⌐ the closest friend of
her youth,
and forgets her marriage vows to her God.
¹⁸ Her house sinks down to death.
Her ways lead to the souls of the dead.
¹⁹ None who have sex with her come back.
Nor do they ever reach the paths of life.

²⁰ So walk in the way of good people
and stay on the paths of righteous people.

2:1–5 Your wisdom never comes cheap or easy. So I'll take your words to heart. I'll pay close attention to everything you say. I'll cry for understanding and hunt for wisdom like buried treasure. Then I'll know and fear you.

2:6–9 Wisdom comes straight from you—and you save your best wisdom for people who won't squander it. Guard me as I act on your wisdom. Show me how and where to do good.

2:10–15 Your wisdom pleases me. It guards me and saves me from evil. It protects me from people who want to pull me down dark crooked paths.

2:16–19 Wisdom saves me from sinning against my spouse. It shows me the stupidity of abandoning my best friend and the vows we made in your presence. Wisdom shouts that sexual sin will ravage my world and kill my soul.

2:21–22 I'll live in your blessings when I follow your ways. Don't let anything tear me away from you!

21   Decent people will live in the land.
        People of integrity will remain in it.
22   But wicked people will be cut off from the land
            and treacherous people will be torn[a] from it.

Using Wisdom

3 ¹My son,
    do not forget my teachings,
        and keep my commands in mind,
2   because they will bring you
            long life, good years, and peace.

3:1–4 Your teachings bring me long life, good years, and peace. So I'll never forget your commands. I'll keep mercy and truth close to my heart. They bring me success.

3   Do not let mercy and truth leave you.
        Fasten them around your neck.
        Write them on the tablet of your heart.
4   Then you will find favor and much success
            in the sight of God and humanity.

5   Trust the Lord with all your heart,
        and do not rely on your own understanding.
6   In all your ways acknowledge him,
        and he will make your paths smooth.[b]
7   Do not consider yourself wise.
        Fear the Lord, and turn away from evil.
8   ⌐Then⌐ your body will be healed,
            and your bones will have nourishment.

3:5–6 I trust you with all my heart. Your wisdom is so much bigger than mine. I count on you to lead my every step. Smooth my path!

3:7–10 When I turn from evil, you heal and nourish me. When I honor you with my wealth, you surprise me with abundance.

9   Honor the Lord with your wealth
        and with the first and best part of all your income.[c]
10   Then your barns will be full,
            and your vats will overflow with fresh wine.

11   Do not reject the discipline of the Lord, my son,
        and do not resent his warning,
12   because the Lord warns the one he loves,
            even as a father warns a son with whom he is pleased.

3:11–12 I welcome your discipline as a sign you love me. I accept your warnings as proof I'm your child.

13 Blessed is the one who finds wisdom
    and the one who obtains understanding.
14   The profit ⌐gained⌐ from ⌐wisdom⌐ is greater than the profit ⌐gained⌐ from silver.
        Its yield is better than fine gold.
15 ⌐Wisdom⌐ is more precious than jewels,
    and all your desires cannot equal it.
16   Long life is in ⌐wisdom's⌐ right hand.
        In ⌐wisdom's⌐ left hand are riches and honor.
17 ⌐Wisdom's⌐ ways are pleasant ways,

3:14–15 Your wisdom brings riches greater than pure gold, true wealth more precious than my largest desires.

---

[a] 2:22 Or "will be swept away."
[b] 3:6 Or "straight."
[c] 3:9 Or "harvest."

and all its paths lead to peace.
¹⁸ ⌐Wisdom⌐ is a tree of life
for those who take firm hold of it.
Those who cling to it are blessed.

¹⁹ By Wisdom the LORD laid the foundation of the earth.
By understanding he established the heavens.
²⁰ By his knowledge the deep waters were divided,
and the skies dropped dew.

²¹ My son,
do not lose sight of these things.
Use priceless wisdom and foresight.
²²   Then they will mean life for you,
and they will grace your neck.
²³   Then you will go safely on your way,
and you will not hurt your foot.
²⁴   When you lie down, you will not be afraid.
As you lie there, your sleep will be sweet.

²⁵   Do not be afraid of sudden terror
or of the destruction of wicked people when
it comes.
²⁶   The LORD will be your confidence.
He will keep your foot from getting caught.

²⁷   Do not hold back anything good
from those who are entitled to it
when you have the power to do so.
²⁸   When you have the good thing with you, do not tell
your neighbor,
"Go away!
Come back tomorrow.
I'll give you something then."

²⁹   Do not plan to do something wrong to your neighbor
while he is sitting there with you and
suspecting nothing.
³⁰   Do not quarrel with a person for no reason
if he has not harmed you.
³¹   Do not envy a violent person.
Do not choose any of his ways.
³²   The devious person is disgusting to the LORD.
The LORD's intimate advice is with decent people.

³³ The LORD curses the house of wicked people,
but he blesses the home of righteous people.
³⁴ When he mocks the mockers,
he is gracious to humble people.
³⁵ Wise people will inherit honor,
but fools will bear disgrace.

3:17–18 Your wisdom points me down pleasant paths, leading me to life and peace. I'll forever cling to your insights.

3:21–26 I'll never let your wisdom out of my sight. It brings me life and leads me to safety. It lets me lie down unafraid and sleep sweetly. It spares me from fear. You are my confidence!

3:27–28 You have the power to give me everything I truly need. Don't hold back! I'll share everything you give me.

3:29–32 I won't plot evil against my neighbor or quarrel without cause. I won't envy or imitate the violent. You guide and empower people intent on doing good.

3:33–35 If I chase wickedness, I miss your blessing. I suffer disgrace when I act like a fool.

Cherish Wisdom

4 ¹Sons,
  listen to ⌐your¬ father's discipline,
   and pay attention in order to gain understanding.
²   After all, I have taught you well.
  Do not abandon my teachings.
³ When I was a boy ⌐learning¬ from my father,
  when I was a tender and only child of my mother,
⁴   they used to teach me and say to me,
   "Cling to my words wholeheartedly.
   Obey my commands so that you may live.
⁵   Acquire wisdom.
   Acquire understanding.
   Do not forget.
   Do not turn away from the words that I
    have spoken.
⁶   Do not abandon wisdom, and it will watch
    over you.
   Love wisdom, and it will protect you.
⁷   The beginning of wisdom is to
    acquire wisdom.
   Acquire understanding with all that
    you have.
⁸   Cherish wisdom.
    It will raise you up.
    It will bring you honor when you
     embrace it.
⁹   It will give you a graceful garland for
     your head.
    It will hand you a beautiful crown."

Stay on the Path of Wisdom

¹⁰ My son,
  listen and accept my words,
   and they will multiply the years of your life.
¹¹   I have taught you the way of wisdom.
   I have guided you along decent paths.
¹²   When you walk, your stride will not
    be hampered.
    Even if you run, you will not stumble.
¹³ Cling to discipline.
   Do not relax your grip on it.
   Keep it because it is your life.
¹⁴ Do not stray onto the path of wicked people.
  Do not walk in the way of evil people.
¹⁵   Avoid it.
   Do not walk near it.
    Turn away from it,
     and keep on walking.

4:1–4 You use my parents to discipline me and give me understanding. They teach me your life-giving commands.

4:5–6 I'm determined to acquire your wisdom. I won't forget what you teach, and I'll stay true to the words you speak. They guard and protect me.

4:8–9 I love your wisdom. It raises me up and honors me. It graces my head like a beautiful crown.

4:10–12 Your wisdom lengthens my life and leads me down good paths. With your wisdom I run strong and don't stumble.

4:13 I'll grab hold of your wisdom and never let go. Your wisdom is my life.

4:14–16 Lead me out of evil habits. Help me run fast and hard from evil ways. I want the peaceful slumber that comes from doing right.

¹⁶ Wicked people cannot sleep
  unless they do wrong,
    and they are robbed of their sleep
      unless they make someone stumble.
¹⁷   They eat food obtained
          through wrongdoing
        and drink wine obtained
          through violence.

¹⁸ But the path of righteous people is like the light
  of dawn
    that becomes brighter and brighter until it
      reaches midday.
¹⁹ The way of wicked people is like deep darkness.
  They do not know what makes them stumble.

4:18–19 You light up my path like the dawn, shining brighter and brighter as the hours pass. You keep me from stumbling in darkness.

Stay Focused on Wisdom

²⁰ My son,
  pay attention to my words.
  Open your ears to what I say.
²¹ Do not lose sight of these things.
  Keep them deep within your heart
²²   because they are life to those who find them
      and they heal the whole body.
²³ Guard your heart more than anything else,
    because the source of your life flows from it.
²⁴ Remove dishonesty from your mouth.
  Put deceptive speech far away from your lips.
²⁵ Let your eyes look straight ahead
    and your sight be focused in front of you.
²⁶ Carefully walk a straight path,
    and all your ways will be secure.
²⁷ Do not lean to the right or to the left.
  Walk away from evil.

4:20–22 I'll listen closely to your words. Your wisdom gives me life and heals my whole body.

4:23 Whatever I let flourish in my heart flows out to my whole life. So I'll guard my heart above all else.

4:25–27 Keep me focused straight ahead as I walk toward you. Don't let me veer off the path into evil.

Avoid Adultery

5 ¹ My son,
  pay attention to my wisdom.
  Open your ears to my understanding
²   so that you may act with foresight
      and speak with insight.

³ The lips of an adulterous woman drip with honey.
  Her kiss is smoother than oil,
⁴   but in the end she is as bitter as wormwood,
      as sharp as a two-edged sword.
⁵ Her feet descend to death.
  Her steps lead straight to hell.
⁶   She doesn't even think about the path of life.
    Her steps wander, and she doesn't realize it.

5:1–2 I won't plug my ears to your wisdom. I'll listen and act with understanding.

5:3–6 Sexual sin sounds sweet and smooth, but it cuts like a double-bladed sword. It leads straight to death.

5:7–8 I won't run from your wise advice. I won't go anywhere near the door of sexual sin. I'll stay far from every person, place, or situation that tempts me to unfaithfulness. Help me!

5:11–14 The cost of adultery is total destruction, consuming bodies and hearts that hate correction. Convince me my teachers are right so I don't end in ruin.

5:15–19 I'll share myself only with my spouse, because my body and heart belong to my love and no one else. I'll delight in my spouse today even more than the day we wed. Fill us with intoxicating love!

5:21–23 You see everything I do. Keep me from stumbling into deeper and deeper sin. Don't let me die as a result of my own stupidity.

6:1–5 Don't let me be so dumb I make disastrous promises. Show

⁷ But now, sons,
    listen to me,
        and do not turn away from what I say to you.
⁸ Stay far away from her.
    Do not even go near her door.
⁹   Either you will surrender your reputation
            to others
        and ⌐the rest of⌐ your years to some
            cruel person,
¹⁰   or strangers will benefit from your strength
        and you will have to work hard in a
            pagan's house.
¹¹   Then you will groan when your end comes,
        when your body and flesh are consumed.
    You will say,
¹²   "Oh, how I hated discipline!
        How my heart despised correction!
¹³   I didn't listen to what my teachers said to me,
            nor did I keep my ear open to
                my instructors.
¹⁴   I almost reached total ruin
                in the assembly and in the congregation."

¹⁵ Drink water out of your own cistern
        and running water from your own well.
¹⁶   Why should water flow out of your spring?
        Why should your streams flow into the streets?
¹⁷   They should be yours alone,
            so do not share them with strangers.
¹⁸ Let your own fountain be blessed,
        and enjoy the girl you married when you
            were young,
¹⁹   a loving doe and a graceful deer.[a]
    Always let her breasts satisfy you.
    Always be intoxicated with her love.
²⁰   Why should you, my son,
            be intoxicated with an adulterous woman
            and fondle a loose woman's breast?

²¹ Each person's ways are clearly seen by the LORD,
        and he surveys all his actions.
²² A wicked person will be trapped by his own wrongs,
        and he will be caught in the ropes of his own sin.
²³ He will die for his lack of discipline
        and stumble around because of his great stupidity.

Avoid Disaster

6 ¹My son,
    if you guarantee a loan for your neighbor
        or pledge yourself for a stranger with a handshake,

---

[a] 5:19 Or "graceful goat."

2   you are trapped by the words of your own mouth,
         caught by your own promise.
3 Do the following things, my son, so that you may
         free yourself,
      because you have fallen into your
         neighbor's hands:
      Humble yourself,
         and pester your neighbor.
4   Don't let your eyes rest
         or your eyelids close.
5   Free yourself like a gazelle from the hand of
         a hunter
      and like a bird from the hand of a hunter.

6 Consider the ant, you lazy bum.
   Watch its ways, and become wise.
7   Although it has no overseer, officer, or ruler,
8   in summertime it stores its food supply.
      At harvest time it gathers its food.

9 How long will you lie there, you lazy bum?
   When will you get up from your sleep?
10   "Just a little sleep,
      just a little slumber,
      just a little nap."
11   Then your poverty will come ⌞to you⌟ like a drifter,
         and your need will come ⌞to you⌟ like a bandit.

12 A good-for-nothing scoundrel is a person who has a
         dishonest mouth.
13   He winks his eye,
      makes a signal with his foot,
         ⌞and⌟ points with his fingers.
14   He devises evil all the time with a twisted mind.
   He spreads conflict.
15   That is why disaster will come on him suddenly.
         In a moment he will be crushed beyond recovery.

16 There are six things that the LORD hates,
   even seven that are disgusting to him:
17   arrogant eyes,
      a lying tongue,
      hands that kill innocent people,
18   a mind devising wicked plans,
      feet that are quick to do wrong,
19   a dishonest witness spitting out lies,
         and a person who spreads conflict
            among relatives.

More Advice about Avoiding Adultery
20 My son,
      obey the command of your father,
      and do not disregard the teachings of your mother.

6:6–8 Teach me to take charge of myself and work hard even when no one stands over me telling me what to do. Train me not to squander seasons of ease and plenty.

6:9–11 Wake me when I want to doze off instead of working hard at everything you plan for me. Don't let me sleep my life away or make rest my highest goal.

6:16–19 Free me from everything that displeases you—from arrogance and deceit, from rage and evil schemes, from chasing after sin, from speaking lies instead of truth, from provoking conflict in my family.

me how to break free of pledges I've come to regret.

6:20–23 My parents taught me right from wrong, so I'll

continually remind myself of what they said. Their wisdom watches over me and fills my ears. It warns me and puts me on your path to life.

6:24–29 Keep my mind clear when sexual sin beckons me. Remind me that beauty is a trap and charming eyes deceive. Sexual sin always burns.

6:30–31 It's too easy to explain away and justify my sins. Remind me that I can't escape the consequences of doing wrong.

6:32–35 Sexual sin makes no sense. Don't let me ever forget how it leads to destruction, disease, and dishonor. It arouses a spouse's fury

7:1–2 I pay close attention to your words. I treasure your commands deep in my heart. I keep your teachings as carefully as I protect my own eyes.

21 Fasten them on your heart forever.
Hang them around your neck.
22 When you walk around, they will lead you.
When you lie down, they will watch over you.
When you wake up, they will talk to you
23 because the command is a lamp,
the teachings are a light,
and the warnings from discipline are the path of life
24 to keep you from an evil woman
and from the smooth talk of a loose woman.

25 Do not desire her beauty in your heart.
Do not let her catch you with her eyes.
26 A prostitute's price is ⌐only¬ a loaf of bread,
but a married woman hunts for ⌐your¬ life itself.
27 Can a man carry fire in his lap
without burning his clothes?
28 Can anyone walk on red-hot coals
without burning his feet?
29 So it is with a man who has sex with his neighbor's wife.
None who touch her will escape punishment.
30 People do not despise a thief who is hungry
when he steals to satisfy his appetite,
31 but when he is caught,
he has to repay it seven times.
He must give up all the possessions in his house.

32 Whoever commits adultery with a woman has no sense.
Whoever does this destroys himself.
33 An adulterous man will find disease[a] and dishonor,
and his disgrace will not be blotted out,
34 because jealousy arouses a husband's fury.
The husband will show no mercy when he takes revenge.
35 No amount of money will change his mind.
The largest bribe will not satisfy him.

7 ¹My son,
pay attention to my words.
Treasure my commands that are within you.
2 Obey my commands so that you may live.
Follow my teachings just as you protect the pupil of your eye.
3 Tie them on your fingers.
Write them on the tablet of your heart.

---

[a] 6:33 Or "wounds."

4 Say to wisdom, "You are my sister."
Give the name "my relative" to understanding
5   in order to guard yourself from an
            adulterous woman,
        from a loose woman with her smooth talk.

6 From a window in my house I looked through
    my screen.
7 I was looking at gullible people
    when I saw a young man without much sense
        among youths.
8 He was crossing a street near her corner
    and walking toward her house
9   in the twilight,
        in the evening,
        in the dark hours of the night.

10 A woman with an ulterior motive meets him.
    She is dressed as a prostitute.
11 She is loud and rebellious.
    Her feet will not stay at home.
12   One moment she is out on the street,
        the next she is at the curb,
            on the prowl at every corner.
13 She grabs him and kisses him and brazenly says to him,
14   "I have some sacrificial meat.
        Today I kept my vows.
15   That's why I came to meet you.
        Eagerly, I looked for you,
            and I've found you.
16   I've made my bed,
        with colored sheets of Egyptian linen.
17   I've sprinkled my bed with myrrh, aloes,
        and cinnamon.
18   Come, let's drink our fill of love until morning.
        Let's enjoy making love,
19   because my husband's not home.
            He has gone on a long trip.
20   He took lots of money with him.
            He won't be home for a couple of weeks."

21 With all her seductive charms, she persuades him.
    With her smooth lips, she makes him give in.
22   He immediately follows her
        like a steer on its way to be slaughtered,
        like a ram hobbling into captivity[a]
23   until an arrow pierces his heart,
        like a bird darting into a trap.
    He does not realize that it will cost him his life.

---

[a] 7:22 Hebrew meaning of this line uncertain.

7:4–12 Your wisdom guards me from sexual sin. But I'm surrounded by gullible people. I see them everywhere I look. Young men hook up with women on the prowl. They're blind to each others' evil motives. Give me more sense than that!

7:13–21 Temptation never stays on the edge of my life. It hunts me down and grabs hold of me. It recites all the reasons I should give in to sin, promising me evil pleasures at no cost. Make your truth louder than these lies.

7:22–23 Sexual sin will lead me to slaughter. It will hobble me and pierce my heart. It will cost me my life. Remind me of these realities!

7:24–27 I want a heart stubbornly committed to staying on your path. Help me see sexual sin for what it is—a stop on the way to the darkest place in hell.

24 Now, sons,
　　listen to me.
　　Pay attention to the words from my mouth.
25　　Do not let your heart be turned to her ways.
　　Do not wander onto her paths,
26　　　　because she has brought down many victims,
　　　　　and she has killed all too many.
27　　　　Her home is the way to hell
　　　　　and leads to the darkest vaults of death.

Wisdom's Announcement

8:1–5 Your wisdom calls out to every human being. It shouts from high ground so the crowds can hear. Let your wisdom teach me good sense. Let it give me the understanding I need for real life.

8 ¹Does not wisdom call out?
　　Does not understanding raise its voice?
　²⌊Wisdom⌋ takes its stand on high ground,
　　by the wayside where the roads meet,
³　near the gates to the city.
　　At the entrance ⌊wisdom⌋ sings its song,
4　　"I am calling to all of you,
　　　and my appeal is to all people.
5　　　　You gullible people, learn how to be sensible.
　　　　You fools, get a heart that has understanding.ᵃ

8:6–9 In a world full of lies you speak pure truth. Your every word is fair. Not a single one twists the facts. Your wisdom is clear to anyone who wants it.

6　Listen! I am speaking about noble things,
　　and my lips will say what is right.
7　My mouth expresses the truth,
　　and wickedness is disgusting to my lips.
8　Everything I say is fair,
　　and there is nothing twisted or crooked in it.
9　　All of it is clear to a person who
　　　has understanding
　　　and right to those who have
　　　　acquired knowledge.

8:10–11 I want your discipline more than silver, your knowledge more than gold, your wisdom more than jewels. Nothing in the world equals your wisdom.

10　Take my discipline, not silver,
　　and my knowledge rather than fine gold,
11　　because wisdom is better than jewels.
　　　Nothing you desire can equal it.

Wisdom's Authority

8:12–16 Your wisdom gives insight and knowledge. It teaches me to hate evil—whether pride or arrogance, evil acts or twisted words. It gives kings power and compels judges to be fair.

12　"I, Wisdom, live with insight,
　　and I acquire knowledge and foresight.
13　　To fear the LORD is to hate evil.
　　I hate pride, arrogance, evil behavior, and
　　　twisted speech.
14　　Advice and priceless wisdom are mine.
　　I, Understanding, have strength.
15　　Through me kings reign,
　　　and rulers decree fair laws.
16　　Through me princes rule,
　　　so do nobles and all fair judges.

8:17–21 You love those who love your insights, and you

17　I love those who love me.
　　Those eagerly looking for me will find me.

ᵃ 8:5 English equivalent difficult.

18   I have riches and honor,
           lasting wealth and righteousness.
19   What I produce is better than gold, pure gold.
       What I yield is better than fine silver.
20   I walk in the way of righteousness, on the paths
           of justice,
21   to give an inheritance to those who love me
           and to fill their treasuries.

Wisdom as Creator
22   "The LORD already possessed me long ago,
           when his way began,
               before any of his works.
23   I was appointed from everlasting
           from the first,
               before the earth began.
24   I was born
           before there were oceans,
           before there were springs filled with water.
25   I was born
           before the mountains were settled in their places
               and before the hills,
26   when he had not yet made land or fields
               or the first dust of the world.

27   "When he set up the heavens, I was there.
       When he traced the horizon on the surface of
               the ocean,
28   when he established the skies above,
       when he determined the currents in the ocean,
29   when he set a limit for the sea
           so the waters would not overstep his command,
       when he traced the foundations of the earth,
30   I was beside him as a master craftsman.[a]
       I made him happy day after day,
           I rejoiced in front of him all the time,
31   found joy in his inhabited world,
               and delighted in the human race.

Wisdom as Lifegiver
32   "Now, sons, listen to me.
           Blessed are those who follow my ways.
33   Listen to discipline, and become wise.
           Do not leave my ways.
34   Blessed is the person who listens to me,
           watches at my door day after day,
           and waits by my doorposts.
35   Whoever finds me finds life
           and obtains favor from the LORD.
36   Whoever sins against me harms himself.
       All those who hate me love death."

grant your wisdom to anyone who eagerly looks for it. Your wisdom bestows riches greater than pure gold. It points me to righteousness and justice.

8:22–23 Your wisdom is an indispensable part of your heart and mind. It comes from the core of who you are. Your wisdom is as ancient as you.

8:24–29 Your wisdom existed before earth began, before oceans and mountains, before fields and skies. It's been around since before anything began.

8:30–31 Your wisdom makes you a master craftsman. It gives you joy in everything you made. It makes you happy with the people you created.

8:32–36 When I live according to your wisdom, I experience your blessing. So I listen to your every word. I watch and wait for your advice. Finding your wisdom brings me life, but forsaking your insights puts me in harm's way.

---

[a] 8:30 Hebrew meaning of "master craftsman" uncertain.

Wisdom's Hosts a Banquet

9 ¹Wisdom has built her house.
  She has carved out her seven pillars.
² She has prepared her meat.
  She has mixed her wine.
  She has set her table.
³ She has sent out her servant girls.
  She calls from the highest places in the city,
⁴   "Whoever is gullible turn in here!"

She says to a person without sense,
⁵   "Come, eat my bread,
      and drink the wine I have mixed.
⁶   Stop being gullible and live.
    Start traveling the road to understanding."

9:1–6 Your wisdom stands like a well-built house, beautiful and complete. Your wisdom prepares a feast, calling out to me and other gullible people. It invites us to eat and enjoy.

Wisdom Prolongs Life

⁷ Whoever corrects a mocker receives abuse.
  Whoever warns a wicked person gets hurt.
⁸   Do not warn a mocker, or he will hate you.
    Warn a wise person, and he will love you.
⁹   Give ⌐advice⌐ to a wise person,
        and he will become even wiser.
    Teach a righteous person,
        and he will learn more.

9:7–9 I fear correcting belligerent people, but often I have no choice. Make me brave and bold. Help me notice opportunities to share wisdom with people who want it. We can help each other grow.

¹⁰ The fear of the Lᴏʀᴅ is the beginning of wisdom.
  The knowledge of the Holy One is understanding.

¹¹ You will live longer because of me,
      and years will be added to your life.
¹² If you are wise, your wisdom will help you.
  If you mock, you alone will be held responsible.

9:10–12 I'm finally starting to wise up when I give you the respect you deserve. Your wisdom will add years to my life. But if I mock your ways, I'll never get the insight I need.

Stupidity Imitates Wisdom's Banquet

¹³ The woman Stupidity is loud, gullible, and ignorant.[a]
¹⁴ She sits at the doorway of her house.
  She is enthroned on the high ground of the city
¹⁵   and calls to those who pass by,
        those minding their own business,
¹⁶   "Whoever is gullible turn in here!"

She says to a person without sense,
¹⁷   "Stolen waters are sweet,
      and food eaten in secret is tasty."
¹⁸ But he does not know
      that the souls of the dead are there,
      that her guests are in the depths of hell.

9:13–18 Wisdom calls out to me. But so does stupidity—in a loud and gullible and ignorant voice. I'm trying hard to do right, but stupidity still makes its case for doing wrong. Remind me that stupidity puts my soul on a path to death.

[a] 9:13 Hebrew meaning of this verse uncertain.

10 ¹The proverbs of Solomon:

A Wise Son Is Righteous

A wise son makes his father happy,
  but a foolish son brings grief to his mother.

²Treasures gained dishonestly profit no one,
  but righteousness rescues from death.
³The LORD will not allow a righteous person to starve,
  but he intentionally ignores the desires of a
    wicked person.

⁴Lazy hands bring poverty,
  but hard-working hands bring riches.
⁵Whoever gathers in the summer is a wise son.
  Whoever sleeps at harvest time brings shame.

⁶Blessings cover the head of a righteous person,
  but violence covers the mouths of wicked people.

⁷The name of a righteous person remains blessed,
  but the names of wicked people will rot away.

Proverbs Concerning the Mouth

⁸The one who is truly wise accepts commands,
  but the one who talks foolishly will be thrown
    down headfirst.
⁹Whoever lives honestly will live securely,
  but whoever lives dishonestly will be found out.
¹⁰Whoever winks with his eye causes heartache.
  The one who talks foolishly will be thrown
    down headfirst.
¹¹ The mouth of a righteous person is a fountain of life,
    but the mouths of wicked people
      conceal violence.
¹²Hate starts quarrels,
  but love covers every wrong.

¹³Wisdom is found on the lips of a person who
    has understanding,
  but a rod is for the back of one without sense.
¹⁴Those who are wise store up knowledge,
  but the mouth of a stubborn fool invites ruin.
¹⁵The rich person's wealth is ⌐his⌐ strong city.
  Poverty ruins the poor.
¹⁶ A righteous person's reward is life.
    A wicked person's harvest is sin.
¹⁷Whoever practices discipline is on the way to life,
  but whoever ignores a warning strays.

¹⁸Whoever conceals hatred has lying lips.
  Whoever spreads slander is a fool.

10:2–4 Train me to do right in every part of life, because living your way will rescue me from death. You won't let me go hungry, and my hard work will bear fruit.

10:5–7 Teach me to seize moments when I need to put wisdom into action. I'll miss out on your blessings if I don't act.

10:8–11 Foolish words hurl me down headfirst. Save me from tripping myself up with my words. Let my words be a fountain of life to everyone who listens.

10:12 I'm quick to talk on and on about how I've been wronged. Teach me to make up and move ahead.

10:14 I don't want your wisdom to come in one ear and go out the other. I promise to remember everything you teach me.

10:18–20 I'm a fake when my words don't match my thoughts.

I'm a fool when I spread insults. Whenever I open my mouth too much I'm bound to sin. So help me make my every word count for good.

10:22 I can't take credit for anything I've accomplished in life. Even my ability to work hard is a gift from you. Thank you!

10:25–28 You're my everlasting foundation, my place to stand in a storm. Give me long days as I live completely for you. Give me joy as I hope in you.

10:29 Your ways protect me like a fortress. They're my place to run when evil comes my way. Troublemakers can't make sense of you.

10:31–32 Good people's words make me wise. Wicked people say nothing that helps me.

11:1–3 You won't settle for subtle changes in me. You aim to make me righteous in everything I do. You want honesty rather than lies, humility instead of arrogance, integrity in place of hypocrisy. Build those qualities in me!

[19] Sin is unavoidable when there is much talk,
  but whoever seals his lips is wise.
[20] The tongue of a righteous person is pure silver.
  The hearts of wicked people are worthless.
[21] The lips of a righteous person feed many,
  but stubborn fools die because they have no sense.

[22] It is the LORD's blessing that makes a person rich,
  and hard work adds nothing to it.
[23] Like the laughter of a fool when he carries out an
    evil plan,
  so is wisdom to a person who has understanding.

Righteous People Contrasted to Wicked People

[24] That which wicked people dread happens to them,
  but ⌊the LORD⌋ grants the desire of righteous people.
[25] When the storm has passed, the wicked person
    has vanished,
  but the righteous person has an
      everlasting foundation.
[26] Like vinegar to the teeth,
  like smoke to the eyes,
    so is the lazy person to those who send him ⌊on
      a mission⌋.
[27] The fear of the LORD lengthens ⌊the number of⌋ days,
  but the years of wicked people are shortened.
[28] The hope of righteous people ⌊leads to⌋ joy,
  but the eager waiting of wicked people comes
      to nothing.
[29] The way of the LORD is a fortress for an innocent person
  but a ruin to those who are troublemakers.
[30] A righteous person will never be moved,
  but wicked people will not continue to live in the land.
[31] The mouth of a righteous person increases wisdom,
  but a devious tongue will be cut off.
[32] The lips of a righteous person announce good will,
  but the mouths of wicked people are devious.

The Value of Righteousness

11 [1] Dishonest scales are disgusting to the LORD,
  but accurate weights are pleasing to him.
[2] Arrogance comes,
    then comes shame,
      but wisdom remains with humble people.
[3] Integrity guides decent people,
  but hypocrisy leads treacherous people to ruin.

[4] Riches are of no help on the day of fury,
  but righteousness saves from death.

⁵ The righteousness of innocent people makes their
　　road smooth,
　　but wicked people fall by their own wickedness.
⁶ Decent people are saved by their righteousness,
　　but treacherous people are trapped by their own greed.
⁷　　At the death of a wicked person, hope vanishes.
　　Moreover, his confidence in strength vanishes.

⁸ A righteous person is rescued from trouble,
　　and a wicked person takes his place.
⁹ With his talk a godless person can ruin his neighbor,
　　but righteous people are rescued by knowledge.

¹⁰ When righteous people prosper, a city is glad.
　　When wicked people die, there are songs of joy.
¹¹　　With the blessing of decent people a city is raised up,
　　　　but by the words of wicked people, it is torn down.

¹² A person who despises a neighbor has no sense,
　　but a person who has understanding keeps quiet.
¹³ Whoever gossips gives away secrets,
　　but whoever is trustworthy in spirit can keep a secret.
¹⁴ A nation will fall when there is no direction,
　　but with many advisers there is victory.
¹⁵ Whoever guarantees a stranger's loan will get
　　　　into trouble,
　　but whoever hates the closing of a deal
　　　　remains secure.
¹⁶ A gracious woman wins respect,
　　but ruthless men gain riches.
¹⁷ A merciful person helps himself,
　　but a cruel person hurts himself.
¹⁸ A wicked person earns dishonest wages,
　　but whoever spreads righteousness earns honest pay.
¹⁹ As righteousness leads to life,
　　so whoever pursues evil finds his own death.

²⁰ Devious people are disgusting to the LORD,
　　but he is delighted with those whose ways
　　　　are innocent.
²¹ Certainly, an evil person will not go unpunished,
　　but the descendants of righteous people will escape.
²² ⌞Like⌟ a gold ring in a pig's snout,
　　⌞so⌟ is a beautiful woman who lacks good taste.
²³ The desire of righteous people ends only in good,
　　but the hope of wicked people ends only in fury.

²⁴ One person spends freely and yet grows richer,
　　while another holds back what he owes and yet
　　　　grows poorer.
²⁵　　A generous person will be made rich,

11:5–10 Let your warnings about wickedness sink deep in my soul. Sin trips me up and entraps me. It steals my hope and strength. It puts me in line for trouble. And the more I sin, the louder people will rejoice when I die.

11:11–13 Evil words can destroy a whole city. They spill secrets and senselessly expose a neighbor. Show me when my words go bad.

11:14 Without vision a nation falls. Point our country in your direction.

11:18–21 Righteousness opens the door to honest work and leads me into life. You delight in my innocence and won't let evil go unpunished.

11:22 Grant me good taste or I'll be a pig with a gold ring in its snout.

11:25 Convince me I can trust you with my money. As I meet others' needs I count on you to meet mine.

11:27 I don't have to look hard to find evil. Keep me searching for real good.

11:28 Riches aren't enough to keep me going. But following your ways will make me flourish.

11:30 Make me wise. Show me how to win people to you.

12:1 I hate when I act like a mindless beast. I'll choose to learn from your discipline.

12:3 I can't build a life on wickedness. I'll make righteousness my unshakable foundation.

12:5–6 I want my thoughts to be fair and my advice truly helpful. Warn me when I'm about to ambush others with my words.

12:8 Give me insights worth hearing. Shield others from my twisted moments.

12:11 Teach me to work hard at the jobs you provide me. Give me sense to know when my dreams won't work out.

and whoever satisfies others will himself
be satisfied.[a]

[26] People will curse the one who hoards grain,
but a blessing will be upon the head of the one who
sells it.

[27] Whoever eagerly seeks good searches for good will,
but whoever looks for evil finds it.

[28] Whoever trusts his riches will fall,
but righteous people will flourish like a green leaf.

[29] Whoever brings trouble upon his family inherits
⌐only⌐ wind,
and that stubborn fool becomes a slave to the wise
in heart.

[30] The fruit of a righteous person is a tree of life,
and a winner of souls is wise.

[31] If the righteous person is rewarded on earth,
how much more the wicked person and the sinner!

12 [1] Whoever loves discipline loves to learn,
but whoever hates correction is a dumb animal.

[2] A good person obtains favor from the LORD,
but the LORD condemns everyone who schemes.

[3] A person cannot stand firm on a foundation
of wickedness,
and the roots of righteous people cannot be moved.

[4] A wife with strength of character is the crown of
her husband,
but the wife who disgraces him is like bone cancer.

[5] The thoughts of righteous people are fair.
The advice of wicked people is treacherous.

[6] The words of wicked people are a deadly ambush,
but the words[b] of decent people rescue.

[7] Overthrow wicked people, and they are no more,
but the families of righteous people continue to stand.

[8] A person will be praised based on his insight,
but whoever has a twisted mind will be despised.

[9] Better to be unimportant and have a slave
than to act important and have nothing to eat.

[10] A righteous person cares ⌐even⌐ about the life of
his animals,
but the compassion of wicked people is ⌐nothing
but⌐ cruelty.

[11] Whoever works his land will have plenty to eat,
but the one who chases unrealistic dreams has
no sense.

---

[a] 11:25 Or "and whoever gives someone a drink will also get a drink."
[b] 12:6 Or "mouths."

[12] A wicked person delights in setting a trap for ⌐other⌐
   evil people,
   but the roots of righteous people produce ⌐fruit⌐.[a]
[13] An evil person is trapped by his own sinful talk,
   but a righteous person escapes from trouble.
[14] One person enjoys good things as a result of his
   speaking ability.
   Another is paid according to what his hands
   have accomplished.

12:13 When I do evil, my own words will convict me. Keep my speech straightforward and true.

[15] A stubborn fool considers his own way the right one,
   but a person who listens to advice is wise.
[16] When a stubborn fool is irritated, he shows
   it immediately,
   but a sensible person hides the insult.

12:15–16 Don't let me think I'm too smart to listen to others' advice. Don't let me be so sensitive that I react to every insult.

[17] A truthful witness speaks honestly,
   but a lying witness speaks deceitfully.
[18] Careless words stab like a sword,
   but the words of wise people bring healing.
[19] The word of truth lasts forever,
   but lies last only a moment.
[20] Deceit is in the heart of those who plan evil,
   but joy belongs to those who advise peace.

12:18 Give me a taste of the pain I inflict on others when I stab them with my words. Make my words wise and soothing.

[21] No ⌐lasting⌐ harm comes to a righteous person,
   but wicked people have lots of trouble.
[22] Lips that lie are disgusting to the LORD,
   but honest people are his delight.
[23] A sensible person ⌐discreetly⌐ hides knowledge,
   but foolish minds preach stupidity.
[24] Hard-working hands gain control,
   but lazy hands do slave labor.
[25] A person's anxiety will weigh him down,
   but an encouraging word makes him joyful.
[26] A righteous person looks out for his neighbor,
   but the path of wicked people leads others astray.
[27] A lazy hunter does not catch[b] his prey,
   but a hard-working person becomes wealthy.[c]
[28] Everlasting life is on the way of righteousness.
   Eternal death is not along its path.

12:21 I won't stop following your ways. Help me bounce back from every hurt I endure.

12:23 Stop me when I show off my knowledge—and when I put my stupidity on display.

12:25 Free me from the weight of my anxieties. Lift me up with an encouraging word.

12:26 Show me when I'm only looking out for myself. I want to lead people to real life.

A Wise Son Lives Righteously

13 [1] A wise son listens to his father's discipline,
   but a mocker does not listen to reprimands.
[2] A person eats well as a result of his speaking ability,
   but the appetite of treacherous people
   ⌐craves⌐ violence.

13:1 I choose to embrace my father's discipline. I won't plug my ears to reprimands.

---

[a] 12:12 Hebrew meaning of this verse uncertain.

[b] 12:27 Hebrew meaning uncertain.

[c] 12:27 Hebrew meaning of this line uncertain.

13:3 At times my mouth puts my life at risk. Teach me to filter.

13:5–6 Good people hate lying. They always stand up for honesty. Teach me to speak truth without compromise.

13:7 Don't let me pretend to be rich when I'm not. Don't let me brag about the things I have.

13:10 Make me wise through the advice of others. Help me escape stupid arguments.

13:12 When hope dies I feel sick. I count on you to keep my dreams alive.

13:13 You won't let me escape the terrible consequences of despising your words. But you never let me miss the rewards of following your commands.

13:15–16 Give me good sense and wide-ranging knowledge. I'm beyond stupid without your help.

13:18 Lack of discipline will send me into poverty. Thanks for helpful criticism that keeps me alive.

13:20 Give me wise people to walk through life with. I won't let fools drag me in the wrong direction.

13:23 Show me when my own bad habits keep the poor from

³ Whoever controls his mouth protects his own life.
  Whoever has a big mouth comes to ruin.
⁴ A lazy person craves food and there is none,
  but the appetite of hard-working people is satisfied.
⁵ A righteous person hates lying,
  but a wicked person behaves with shame and disgrace.
⁶ Righteousness protects the honest way of life,
  but wickedness ruins a sacrifice for sin.
⁷ One person pretends to be rich but has nothing.
  Another pretends to be poor but has great wealth.
⁸ A person's riches are the ransom for his life,
  but the poor person does not pay attention to threats.
⁹ The light of righteous people beams brightly,
  but the lamp of wicked people will be snuffed out.
¹⁰ Arrogance produces only quarreling,
  but those who take advice gain wisdom.
¹¹ Wealth ⌐gained⌐ through injustice dwindles away,
  but whoever gathers little by little has plenty.
¹² Delayed hope makes one sick at heart,
  but a fulfilled longing is a tree of life.
¹³ Whoever despises ⌐God's⌐ words will pay the penalty,
  but the one who fears ⌐God's⌐ commands will
    be rewarded.
¹⁴ The teachings of a wise person are a fountain of life
  to turn ⌐one⌐ away from the grasp of death.
¹⁵ Good sense brings favor,
  but the way of treacherous people is always
    the same.ᵃ
¹⁶ Any sensible person acts with knowledge,
  but a fool displays stupidity.
¹⁷ An undependable messenger gets into trouble,
  but a dependable envoy brings healing.
¹⁸ Poverty and shame come to a person who
    ignores discipline,
  but whoever pays attention to constructive criticism
    will be honored.
¹⁹ A fulfilled desire is sweet to the soul,
  but turning from evil is disgusting to fools.
²⁰ Whoever walks with wise people will be wise,
  but whoever associates with fools will suffer.
²¹ Disaster hunts down sinners,
  but righteous people are rewarded with good.
²² Good people leave an inheritance to their grandchildren,
  but the wealth of sinners is stored away for a
    righteous person.
²³ When poor people are able to plow, there is much food,
  but a person is swept away where there is no justice.

ᵃ 13:15 Masoretic Text; Greek "is their disaster."

²⁴Whoever refuses to spank his son hates him,
 but whoever loves his son disciplines him from
 early on.
²⁵A righteous person eats to satisfy his appetite,
 but the bellies of wicked people are always empty.

Wise People Live Righteously

14 ¹The wisest of women builds up her home,
 but a stupid one tears it down with her own hands.
²Whoever lives right fears the LORD,
 but a person who is devious in his ways despises him.
³Because of a stubborn fool's words a whip is lifted
 against him,
 but wise people are protected by their speech.

⁴Where there are no cattle, the feeding trough is empty,
 but the strength of an ox produces plentiful harvests.
⁵A trustworthy witness does not lie,
 but a dishonest witness breathes lies.
⁶A mocker searches for wisdom without finding it,
 but knowledge comes easily to a person who
 has understanding.

⁷Stay away from a fool,
 because you will not receive knowledge from his lips.
⁸The wisdom of a sensible person guides his way of life,
 but the stupidity of fools misleads them.
⁹Stubborn fools make fun of guilt,
 but there is forgiveness among decent people.

¹⁰The heart knows its own bitterness,
 and no stranger can share its joy.
¹¹The houses of wicked people will be destroyed,
 but the tents of decent people will continue to expand.
¹²There is a way that seems right to a person,
 but eventually it ends in death.
¹³Even while laughing a heart can ache,
 and joy can end in grief.

¹⁴A heart that turns ⌞from God⌟ becomes bored with its
 own ways,
 but a good person is satisfied with God's ways.
¹⁵A gullible person believes anything,
 but a sensible person watches his step.
¹⁶A wise person is cautious and turns away from evil,
 but a fool is careless^a and overconfident.
¹⁷A short-tempered person acts stupidly,
 and a person who plots evil is hated.
¹⁸Gullible people are gifted with stupidity,
 but sensible people are crowned with knowledge.

---

^a 14:16 Hebrew meaning uncertain.

earning a living. Alert me to my unjust ways.

14:2 I want my whole life to show I respect you. Teach me to live right in every way.

14:4 I can't even feed myself without your help. I count on you for the resources I need to live and thrive.

14:7–8 Fools can't give me the knowledge I need for life. They stumble over their own advice. Show me when I'm allowing fools to lead me.

14:9 Fools make fun of guilt and refuse to admit their wrongs. Show me when I'm not owning up to my sins.

14:12 I can be completely convinced I'm right and still be dead wrong. I welcome your correction!

14:14 My life fades to nothing when my heart turns from you. You and your ways satisfy me fully!

14:15–18 Free me from my foolish faults—gullibility, carelessness, overconfidence, a short temper, and outright stupidity.

14:19–20 I don't want cheap admiration. Help me earn respect through genuine acts of goodness and generosity.

[19] Evil people will bow to good people.
Wicked people will bow at the gates of a
righteous person.

[20] A poor person is hated even by his neighbor,
but a rich person is loved by many.
[21] Whoever despises his neighbor sins,
but blessed is the one who is kind to humble people.

14:22 Good acts don't happen by accident. Help me plan good deeds that flow from the mercy and faithfulness you show me.

[22] Don't those who stray plan what is evil,
while those who are merciful and faithful plan what
is good?
[23] In hard work there is always something gained,
but idle talk leads only to poverty.
[24] The crown of wise people is their wealth.
The stupidity of fools is just that—stupidity!
[25] An honest witness saves lives,
but one who tells lies is dangerous.

14:26–27 Respect for you gives me strong confidence. It creates a hiding place for my children. Respect for you is a life-giving fountain flowing inside me.

[26] In the fear of the LORD there is strong confidence,
and his children will have a place of refuge.
[27] The fear of the LORD is a fountain of life
to turn ⌞one⌟ away from the grasp of death.
[28] A large population is an honor for a king,
but without people a ruler is ruined.

14:29 I won't ever be patient if I don't first take time to understand. Stop me when I make assumptions and rush to conclusions.

[29] A person of great understanding is patient,
but a short temper is the height of stupidity.
[30] A tranquil heart makes for a healthy body,
but jealousy is ⌞like⌟ bone cancer.

14:31 When I oppress the poor I insult not just people but you. I want to honor you through acts of kindness.

[31] Whoever oppresses the poor insults his maker,
but whoever is kind to the needy honors him.
[32] A wicked person is thrown down by his
own wrongdoing,
but even in his death a righteous person has a refuge.

14:33 Fill my heart with so much wisdom that everyone can see that it comes from you.

[33] Wisdom finds rest in the heart of an
understanding person.
Even fools recognize this.[a]

Wise Ways to Live

[34] Righteousness lifts up a nation,
but sin is a disgrace in any society.
[35] A king is delighted with a servant who acts wisely,
but he is furious with one who acts shamefully.

15:1–2 My harsh words only make a situation worse. Train me to answer gently and turn away rage. Don't let my words pour out a flood of stupidity.

15 [1] A gentle answer turns away rage,
but a harsh word stirs up anger.
[2] The tongues of wise people give good expression
to knowledge,
but the mouths of fools pour out a flood of stupidity.

15:3 You see everything I do. Comfort and warn me with that fact!

[3] The eyes of the LORD are everywhere.
They watch evil people and good people.

---

[a] 14:33 Hebrew meaning of this line uncertain.

⁴A soothing tongue is a tree of life,
   but a deceitful tongue breaks the spirit.
⁵A stubborn fool despises his father's discipline,
   but whoever appreciates a warning shows good sense.
⁶Great treasure is in the house of a righteous person,
   but trouble comes along with the income of a
      wicked person.
⁷The lips of wise people spread knowledge,
   but a foolish attitude does not.

⁸A sacrifice brought by wicked people is disgusting to
      the LORD,
   but the prayers of decent people please him.
⁹The way of wicked people is disgusting to the LORD,
   but he loves those who pursue righteousness.

¹⁰Discipline is a terrible ˌburdenˌ to anyone who leaves
      the ˌrightˌ path.
   Anyone who hates a warning will die.
¹¹If Sheol and Abaddon lie open in front of the LORD
   how much more the human heart!
¹²A mocker does not appreciate a warning.
   He will not go to wise people.

¹³A joyful heart makes a cheerful face,
   but with a heartache comes depression.
¹⁴The mind of a person who has understanding searches
      for knowledge,
   but the mouths of fools feed on stupidity.
¹⁵Every day is a terrible day for a miserable person,
   but a cheerful heart has a continual feast.

¹⁶Better to have a little with the fear of the LORD
   than great treasure and turmoil.
¹⁷Better to have a dish of vegetables where there is love
   than juicy steaks where there is hate.

¹⁸A hothead stirs up a fight,
   but one who holds his temper calms disputes.
¹⁹The path of lazy people is like a thorny hedge,
   but the road of decent people is an ˌopenˌ highway.

A Wise Son Brings Blessings to Others
²⁰A wise son makes his father happy,
   but a foolish child despises its mother.

²¹Stupidity is fun to the one without much sense,
   but a person who has understanding forges
      straight ahead.
²²Without advice plans go wrong,
   but with many advisers they succeed.

15:5 I welcome the discipline of my parents and other wise people. Send them my way when I need their advice.

15:8–9 My prayers and religious rituals disgust you when I keep making a habit of sin. Call me to account.

15:11 If you can see into the darkest corners of death, I know you can see straight through my heart!

15:13–15 Let the joy of my heart show on my face. Quiet the pains that linger inside me. I'll make every day a celebration of you.

15:16–17 I'm content with having little as long as I can hang on to you. I'm happy with simple things as long as I have love in my home.

15:21 Stupidity feels fun until I obtain good sense. Teach me wisdom that takes me in a good direction.

15:22 I'm not smart enough to

do life on my own. Lead me to advisers who can help my plans succeed.

15:24–26 Lead me upward. Turn me away from hell. Watch over my property. Don't tear down my house. Let my words please you. Push evil from my mind.

15:27 Take away my greed for unjust gain. Show me when I'm wrongly working the system to my advantage.

15:29–30 Be close to me and hear my prayers. Refresh my body with good news.

15:31–33 I want to hear your life-giving warnings. I long to hear them and gain understanding. I'll humble myself and accept your discipline.

16:1–3 I can make plans and even put them into action, but you still check my motives. You want me to put all my efforts in your hands.

16:5–6 It doesn't please you when I put myself first or make myself most important. I won't live at peace with you as long as I stray from mercy and faithfulness. So I'll humble myself and follow your ways.

---

²³ A person is delighted to hear an answer from his own mouth,
  and a timely word—oh, how good!

²⁴ The path of life for a wise person leads upward
  in order to turn him away from hell below.

²⁵ The LORD tears down the house of an arrogant person,
  but he protects the property of widows.

²⁶ The thoughts of evil people are disgusting to the LORD,
  but pleasant words are pure to him.

²⁷ Whoever is greedy for unjust gain brings trouble to his family,
  but whoever hates bribes will live.

²⁸ The heart of a righteous person carefully considers how to answer,
  but the mouths of wicked people pour out a flood of evil things.

²⁹ The LORD is far from wicked people,
  but he hears the prayers of righteous people.

³⁰ A twinkle in the eye delights the heart.
  Good news refreshes the body.

³¹ The ear that listens to a life-giving warning
  will be at home among wise people.

³² Whoever ignores discipline despises himself,
  but the person who listens to warning gains understanding.

³³ The fear of the LORD is discipline ⌐leading to⌐ wisdom,
  and humility comes before honor.

Wisdom's Blessings Come from the LORD

16 ¹ The plans of the heart belong to humans,
  but an answer on the tongue comes from the LORD.

² A person thinks all his ways are pure,
  but the LORD weighs motives.

³ Entrust your efforts to the LORD,
  and your plans will succeed.

⁴ The LORD has made everything for his own purpose,
  even wicked people for the day of trouble.

⁵ Everyone with a conceited heart is disgusting to the LORD.
  Certainly, ⌐such a person⌐ will not go unpunished.

⁶ By mercy and faithfulness, peace is made with the LORD.
  By the fear of the LORD, evil is avoided.

⁷ When a person's ways are pleasing to the LORD,
  he makes even his enemies to be at peace with him.

⁸ Better a few ⌐possessions⌐ gained honestly

than many gained through injustice.
⁹ A person may plan his own journey,
  but the LORD directs his steps.

16:9 No matter how many plans I make, you still control where I go. I count on you to lead me.

¹⁰ When a divine revelation is on a king's lips,
   he cannot voice a wrong judgment.
¹¹ Honest balances and scales belong to the LORD.
   He made the entire set of weights.

16:11 You alone decide what's honest. I submit to your truth.

¹² Wrongdoing is disgusting to kings
   because a throne is established
     through righteousness.
¹³ Kings are happy with honest words,
   and whoever speaks what is right is loved.
¹⁴ A king's anger announces death,
   but a wise man makes peace with him.
¹⁵ When the king is cheerful, there is life,
   and his favor is like a cloud bringing spring rain.

16:12–15 Give the authorities in my life a love for righteousness and honesty. Make their judgments fair and full of life.

¹⁶ How much better it is to gain wisdom than gold,
   and the gaining of understanding should be chosen
     over silver.
¹⁷ The highway of decent people turns away from evil.
   Whoever watches his way preserves his own life.

16:16 Your wisdom is more important than money. I'll choose it over any kind of wealth.

¹⁸ Pride precedes a disaster,
   and an arrogant attitude precedes a fall.
¹⁹ Better to be humble with lowly people
   than to share stolen goods with arrogant people.

16:18 When I'm proud I'm headed for disaster. When I'm arrogant I'm about to fall.

²⁰ Whoever gives attention to the LORD's word prospers,
   and blessed is the person who trusts the LORD.
²¹ The person who is truly wise is called understanding,
   and speaking sweetly helps others learn.
²² Understanding is a fountain of life to the one who has it,
   but stubborn fools punish themselves with
     their stupidity.
²³ A wise person's heart controls his speech,
   and what he says helps others learn.
²⁴ Pleasant words are ⌐like⌐ honey from a honeycomb—
   sweet to the spirit and healthy for the body.

16:20 I'll pay attention to your Word and trust everything I learn from you.

16:21–24 Make my words sweet to people who long to learn. Give us all greater understanding as you help me choose my words.

Words of Advice to a Wise Son
²⁵ There is a way that seems right to a person,
   but eventually it ends in death.
²⁶ A laborer's appetite works to his advantage,
   because his hunger drives him on.
²⁷ A worthless person plots trouble,
   and his speech is like a burning fire.
²⁸ A devious person spreads quarrels.
   A gossip separates the closest of friends.
²⁹ A violent person misleads his neighbor
   and leads him on a path that is not good.

16:25 Stop me when I think I'm going in the right direction but I'm actually headed toward death.

16:27–29 There's no end to the troubles I cause when I let my mouth run. I ignite fires and spread quarrels. I separate friends and send people down evil paths. Teach me a better way!

³⁰Whoever winks his eye is plotting something devious.
Whoever bites his lips has finished his evil work.

³¹Silver hair is a beautiful crown found in a righteous life.
³² Better to get angry slowly than to be a hero.
Better to be even-tempered than to capture a city.
³³The dice are thrown,
but the LORD determines every outcome.

17

¹Better a bite of dry bread ⌐eaten⌐ in peace
than a family feast filled with strife.
²A wise slave will become master over a son who
acts shamefully,
and he will share the inheritance with the brothers.
³The crucible is for refining silver and the smelter
for gold,
but the one who purifies hearts ⌐by fire⌐ is the LORD.
⁴An evildoer pays attention to wicked lips.
A liar opens his ears to a slanderous tongue.
⁵ Whoever makes fun of a poor person insults
his maker.
Whoever is happy ⌐to see someone's⌐ distress will not
escape punishment.
⁶Grandchildren are the crown of grandparents,
and parents are the glory of their children.

The Consequences of Being a Fool

⁷Refined speech is not fitting for a godless fool.
How much less does lying fit a noble person!
⁸A bribe seems ⌐like⌐ a jewel to the one who gives it.[a]
Wherever he turns, he prospers.
⁹Whoever forgives an offense seeks love,
but whoever keeps bringing up the issue separates
the closest of friends.
¹⁰A reprimand impresses a person who
has understanding
more than a hundred lashes impress a fool.
¹¹A rebel looks for nothing but evil.
Therefore, a cruel messenger will be sent ⌐to
punish⌐ him.
¹²Better to meet a bear robbed of its cubs
than a fool ⌐carried away⌐ with his stupidity.
¹³Whoever pays back evil for good—
evil will never leave his home.
¹⁴Starting a quarrel is ⌐like⌐ opening a floodgate,
so stop before the argument gets out of control.
¹⁵Whoever approves of wicked people
and whoever condemns righteous people
is disgusting to the LORD.

---

[a] 17:8 Or "who receives it."

16:33 Everything changes when you get involved in a situation. You decide every outcome.

17:1 Peace at home matters more than fancy feasts. Put your peace at the heart of my family.

17:3 You purify my heart like a crucible refines silver. I need your refining fire.

17:5 When I make fun of the poor, I insult you. I won't escape punishment if I smile when others suffer.

17:6 My grandparents are my crown and my parents my glory. I'll look for ways to honor them.

17:9 I have love as my goal. I commit myself to forgiving wrongs instead of bringing them up again and again.

17:10 I want to be quick to respond to your discipline. Don't let me miss your words of correction.

17:13 When others wrong me, give me your strength to pay them back with good.

¹⁶ Why should a fool have money in his hand to
buy wisdom
when he doesn't have a mind to grasp anything?
¹⁷ A friend always loves,
and a brother is born to share trouble.
¹⁸ A person without good sense closes a deal with
a handshake.
He guarantees a loan in the presence of his friend.
¹⁹ Whoever loves sin loves a quarrel.
Whoever builds his city gate high invites destruction.
²⁰ A twisted mind never finds happiness,
and one with a devious tongue ⌐repeatedly⌐ gets
into trouble.
²¹ The parent of a fool has grief,
and the father of a godless fool has no joy.
²² A joyful heart is good medicine,
but depression drains one's strength.
²³ A wicked person secretly accepts a bribe to corrupt the
ways of justice.
²⁴ Wisdom is directly in front of an understanding person,
but the eyes of a fool ⌐are looking around⌐ all over
the world.

How Fools Live

²⁵ A foolish son is a heartache to his father
and bitter grief to his mother.

²⁶ To punish an innocent person is not good.
To strike down noble people is not right.
²⁷ Whoever has knowledge controls his words,
and a person who has understanding is
even-tempered.

²⁸ Even a stubborn fool is thought to be wise if he
keeps silent.
He is considered intelligent if he keeps his lips sealed.

18 ¹ A loner is out to get what he wants for himself.
He opposes all sound reasoning.
² A fool does not find joy in understanding
but only in expressing his own opinion.

³ When wickedness comes, contempt also comes,
and insult comes along with disgrace.
⁴ The words of a person's mouth are like deep waters.
The fountain of wisdom is an overflowing stream.
⁵ It is not good to be partial toward a wicked person,
thereby depriving an innocent person of justice.

⁶ By talking, a fool gets into an argument,
and his mouth invites a beating.
⁷ A fool's mouth is his ruin.
His lips are a trap to his soul.

17:17 I need friends who love me nonstop and share my troubles. Guide me to people who will share the worst and best of our lives.

17:20 Straighten out my mind so I find happiness in life. Make me see the world like you do.

17:22 Joy fills my heart and fixes my whole body. Give me strength when my heart grows weary.

17:24 You don't make wisdom hard to find. You want me to act on what I already know is right.

17:27–28 Train me to filter what comes from my lips. People will think I'm wise if I keep my foolish thoughts to myself.

18:1–2 Don't let me go through life only looking out for myself. I need to stop talking and understand what other people think.

18:4 My words reveal who I am inside. Make wisdom spill from me like an overflowing stream.

18:6–7 At times I use words to pick fights or to make sure I end them. Change me before my mouth ruins me.

⁸The words of a gossip are swallowed greedily,
   and they go down into a person's innermost being.

How to Avoid Fools and Foolishness

⁹Whoever is lazy in his work is related to a vandal.
¹⁰The name of the LORD is a strong tower.
   A righteous person runs to it and is safe.
¹¹A rich person's wealth is his strong city
   and is like a high wall in his imagination.

18:10 Your name is a strong tower. When I run to it I find safety.

¹²Before destruction a person's heart is arrogant,
   but humility comes before honor.
¹³Whoever gives an answer before he listens is stupid
   and shameful.
¹⁴A person's spirit can endure sickness,
   but who can bear a broken spirit?
¹⁵The mind of a person who has understanding
   acquires knowledge.
   The ears of wise people seek knowledge.
¹⁶A gift opens doors for the one who gives it
   and brings him into the presence of great people.

18:12 Arrogance leads to my destruction. Humility brings me honor. Why do I allow my pride to live?

18:14 Heal the places I'm broken. Mend me in both body and spirit.

¹⁷The first to state his case seems right
   ⌐until⌐ his neighbor comes to cross-examine him.
¹⁸Flipping a coin ends quarrels
   and settles ⌐issues⌐ between powerful people.
¹⁹An offended brother is more ⌐resistant⌐ than a
      strong city,
   and disputes are like the locked gate of a castle tower.

18:17 Don't let me fall for the first argument I hear. Teach me to think critically and not swallow everything whole.

²⁰A person's speaking ability provides for his stomach.
   His talking provides him a living.
²¹The tongue has the power of life and death,
   and those who love to talk will have to eat their
      own words.

18:21 My tongue can kill or give life. But talking too much always gets me in trouble.

²²Whoever finds a wife finds something good
   and has obtained favor from the LORD.
²³A poor person is timid when begging,
   but a rich person is blunt when replying.
²⁴Friends can destroy one another,[a]
   but a loving friend can stick closer than family.

18:22 My spouse is my life's greatest blessing, a gift straight from your hand.

19 ¹Better to be a poor person who lives innocently
   than to be one who talks dishonestly and is a fool.
²A person without knowledge is no good.
   A person in a hurry makes mistakes.
³The stupidity of a person turns his life upside down,
   and his heart rages against the LORD.
⁴Wealth adds many friends,
   but a poor person is separated from his friend.

19:1 I'd rather be innocent and poor than dishonest and rich.

19:2–3 Grant me the knowledge I need to get through life. Teach me to pace myself and do things right the first time. Don't let me turn my life upside down by stupidly raging against you.

ᵃ 18:24 Or "A person has friends as companions."

5 A lying witness will not go unpunished.
One who tells lies will not escape.
6 Many try to win the kindness of a generous person,
         and everyone is a friend to a person who gives gifts.
7 The entire family of a poor person hates him.
         How much more do his friends keep their
               distance from him!
               When he chases them with words, they
                     are gone.
8 A person who gains sense loves himself.
      One who guards understanding finds
         something good.
9 A lying witness will not go unpunished.
   One who tells lies will die.

10 Luxury does not fit a fool,
      much less a slave ruling princes.
11 A person with good sense is patient,
      and it is to his credit that he overlooks an offense.
12 The rage of a king is like the roar of a lion,
      but his favor is like dew on the grass.

A Foolish Son Brings Ruin to Others
13 A foolish son ruins his father,
      and a quarreling woman is like constantly
         dripping water.
14 Home and wealth are inherited from fathers,
      but a sensible wife comes from the Lord.

15 Laziness throws one into a deep sleep,
      and an idle person will go hungry.
16 Whoever obeys the law preserves his life,
      ⌐but⌐ whoever despises the Lord's ways will be put
         to death.

17 Whoever has pity on the poor lends to the Lord,
      and he will repay him for his good deed.
18 Discipline your son while there is still hope.
      Do not be the one responsible for his death.
19 A person who has a hot temper will pay for it.
      If you rescue him, you will have to do it over and over.
20 Listen to advice and accept discipline
      so that you may be wise the rest of your life.
21 Many plans are in the human heart,
      but the advice of the Lord will endure.
22 Loyalty is desirable in a person,
      and it is better to be poor than a liar.

23 The fear of the Lord leads to life,
      and such a person will rest easy without suffering
         harm.[a]

---
[a] 19:23 Hebrew meaning of this line uncertain.

19:5 Sooner or later even little lies will catch up with me. With your help I'll aim for total honesty.

19:8 Getting your wisdom is good for me. Gaining understanding benefits my entire life.

19:11 I want to have the same patience with others that you show to me. Help me see when it's smart just to overlook an offense.

19:14 My family can give me wealth, but a good spouse comes only from you.

19:16 Obeying you gives me life. Despising your ways leads to certain death.

19:18 Show me how and when to discipline my children. When I set boundaries, I protect them from self-destruction.

19:21 I can dream enormous dreams, but your advice allows me to build a life that lasts.

19:23 Living with proper fear of you brings me peace and rest.

19:25 I hate to learn lessons the hard way. I'm open to whatever you want to teach me.

19:27 I won't quit listening to your wisdom. I won't stray from anything you teach me.

20:1 Warn me whenever alcohol makes me anything less than you want me to be.

20:3 Help me think clearly and step back from fights.

20:4 I can't expect a harvest if I never put seed in the ground. Work in me so I learn to work hard.

20:6 Teach me true loyalty— not just words but constant trustworthiness.

20:9 I can't escape when you charge me with sin. I can't claim to be pure, inside or out. I can't cleanse myself, but you can. Wash me clean.

20:11 You've seen the real me since my first day of life. Even though I've failed in the past, make me pure and right.

24 A lazy person puts his fork in his food.
He doesn't even bring it back to his mouth.
25 Strike a mocker, and a gullible person may learn a lesson.
Warn an understanding person, and he will gain more knowledge.

Foolproof Instructions

26 A son who assaults his father ˻and˼ who drives away his mother
brings shame and disgrace.
27 If you stop listening to instruction, my son,
you will stray from the words of knowledge.

28 A worthless witness mocks justice,
and the mouths of wicked people swallow up trouble.
29 Punishments are set for mockers
and beatings for the backs of fools.

20 ¹Wine ˻makes people˼ mock,
liquor ˻makes them˼ noisy,
and everyone under their influence is unwise.
2 The rage of a king is like the roar of a lion.
Whoever makes him angry forfeits his life.
3 Avoiding a quarrel is honorable.
After all, any stubborn fool can start a fight.

4 A lazy person does not plow in the fall.[a]
He looks for something in the harvest but
finds nothing.
5 A motive in the human heart is like deep water,
and a person who has understanding draws it out.
6 Many people declare themselves loyal,
but who can find someone who is
˻really˼ trustworthy?
7 A righteous person lives on the basis of his integrity.
Blessed are his children after he is gone.
8 A king who sits on his throne to judge sifts out every
evil with his eyes.

9 Who can say,
"I've made my heart pure.
I'm cleansed from my sin"?
10 A double standard of weights and measures—
both are disgusting to the LORD.
11 Even a child makes himself known by his actions,
whether his deeds are pure or right.
12 The ear that hears,
the eye that sees—
the LORD made them both.
13 Do not love sleep or you will end up poor.

---

a 20:4 Fall was the start of the planting season in Palestine.

Keep your eyes open, and you will have plenty to eat.

[14] "Bad! Bad!" says the buyer.
Then, as he goes away, he brags ⌐about his bargain⌐.
[15] There are gold and plenty of jewels,
but the lips of knowledge are precious gems.
[16] Hold on to the garment of one who guarantees a
stranger's loan,
and hold responsible the person who makes a loan
on behalf of a foreigner.
[17] Food gained dishonestly tastes sweet to a person,
but afterwards his mouth will be filled with gravel.
[18] Plans are confirmed by getting advice,
and with guidance one wages war.
[19] Whoever goes around as a gossip tells secrets.
Do not associate with a person whose mouth is
always open.

[20] The lamp of the person who curses his father
and mother
will be snuffed out in total darkness.[a]
[21] An inheritance quickly obtained in the beginning
will never be blessed in the end.
[22] Do not say, "I'll get even with you!"
Wait for the LORD, and he will save you.
[23] A double standard of weights is disgusting to the LORD,
and dishonest scales are no good.
[24] The LORD is the one who directs a person's steps.
How then can anyone understand his own way?
[25] It is a trap for a person to say impulsively, "This is a
holy offering!"
and later to have second thoughts about those vows.

[26] A wise king scatters the wicked
and then runs them over.
[27] A person's soul is the LORD's lamp.
It searches his entire innermost being.
[28] Mercy and truth protect a king,
and with mercy he maintains his throne.
[29] While the glory of young men is their strength,
the splendor of older people is their silver hair.
[30] Brutal beatings cleanse away wickedness.
Such beatings cleanse the innermost being.

The LORD Controls Wise and Foolish People

21 [1] The king's heart is like streams of water.
Both are under the LORD's control.
He turns them in any direction he chooses.
[2] A person thinks everything he does is right,
but the LORD weighs hearts.
[3] Doing what is right and fair

20:15 Your wise words are more precious than gemstones. Keep speaking to me.

20:17 Catch me when I cheat or steal or deceive to get what I want. Don't let me get by with anything less than honesty and integrity.
20:19 You hate gossip. Nudge me when my mouth hangs open.

20:22 My bones ache to take revenge on my enemies. But I'll wait for you to save me.

20:24 I need you to direct my steps. As hard as I try, I can't find my way through life.

20:27 You light up my soul and see everything going on inside me. Thanks that there are no secrets between us.

20:29 Let me enjoy being young and strong. But let me celebrate being silver and wise.

21:2–3 I'm forever convinced I'm right, but you see the sin in my heart. Make me intent on doing right instead of looking good.

---

[a] 20:20 Or "snuffed out as darkness approaches."

21:4 You leave no room for debate—conceit and arrogance are sin.

21:6–7 Getting rich by lying courts death. Refusing to do what is just will get me dragged away.

21:9 Bring peace to my household before one of us needs to move to the roof.

21:11 Help me watch and learn from the punishments others endure. Don't let me repeat their mistakes.

21:13 You always hear the cry of the poor. Don't let me refuse their pleas.

21:15 I'm glad to see justice in this world. Troublemakers are the only ones who are terrified when good triumphs.

21:17 Loving pleasure will make me poor. Expensive tastes will keep me from building wealth.

21:19 Bring peace to my marriage before one of us runs away and pitches a tent in the desert.

21:21 The only way I'll find life and honor is by pursuing righteousness and mercy.

is more acceptable to the LORD than offering a sacrifice.

4 A conceited look and an arrogant attitude, which are the lamps of wicked people, are sins.

5 The plans of a hard-working person lead to prosperity, but everyone who is ˻always˼ in a hurry ends up in poverty.

6 Those who gather wealth by lying are wasting time. They are looking for death.

7 The violence of wicked people will drag them away since they refuse to do what is just.

8 The way of a guilty person is crooked, but the behavior of those who are pure is moral.[a]

9 Better to live on a corner of a roof than to share a home with a quarreling woman.

10 The mind of a wicked person desires evil and has no consideration for his neighbor.

11 When a mocker is punished, a gullible person becomes wise, and when a wise person is instructed, he gains knowledge.

12 A righteous person wisely considers the house of a wicked person. He throws wicked people into disasters.

13 Whoever shuts his ear to the cry of the poor will call and not be answered.

14 A gift ˻given˼ in secret calms anger, and a secret bribe calms great fury.

15 When justice is done, a righteous person is delighted, but troublemakers are terrified.

16 A person who wanders from the way of wise behavior will rest in the assembly of the dead.

17 Whoever loves pleasure will become poor. Whoever loves wine and expensive food will not become rich.

18 Wicked people become a ransom for righteous people, and treacherous people will take the place of decent people.

19 Better to live in a desert than with a quarreling and angry woman.

20 Costly treasure and wealth are in the home of a wise person, but a fool devours them.

21 Whoever pursues righteousness and mercy will find life, righteousness, and honor.

22 A wise man attacks a city of warriors

[a] 21:8 Hebrew meaning of this verse uncertain.

and pulls down the strong defenses in which
　　they trust.
23 Whoever guards his mouth and his tongue keeps himself
　　out of trouble.
24 An arrogant, conceited person is called a mocker.
　　His arrogance knows no limits.

21:24 Don't allow me to become a mocker, a person with unlimited arrogance.

25 The desire of a lazy person will kill him
　　because his hands refuse to work.
26 　　All day long he feels greedy,
　　　　but a righteous person gives and does not
　　　　　hold back.

21:25–26 Laziness will kill me because I won't ever get what I need. Compel me to hard work and generosity.

27 The sacrifice of wicked people is disgusting,
　　especially if they bring it with evil intent.
28 A lying witness will die,
　　but a person who listens to advice will continue
　　　to speak.
29 A wicked person puts up a bold front,
　　but a decent person's way of life is his own security.

21:29 Wicked people have to pretend to be brave, but a life of doing good makes me truly secure.

30 No wisdom, no understanding, and no advice
　　⌐can stand up⌐ against the LORD.
31 The horse is made ready for the day of battle,
　　but the victory belongs to the LORD.

21:30 No amount of human wisdom or understanding or advice can stand up to you!

22 1 A good name is more desirable than great wealth.
　　Respect is better than silver or gold.
2 The rich and the poor have this in common:
　　the LORD is the maker of them all.
3 Sensible people foresee trouble and hide ⌐from it⌐,
　　but gullible people go ahead and suffer
　　　⌐the consequence⌐.
4 On the heels of humility (the fear of the LORD)
　　are riches and honor and life.

22:1 Help me live in a way that earns me a good reputation.

22:2 You made both the rich and the poor. You love us all the same.

22:3 Help me be smart enough to see trouble coming and take shelter. Don't let me be stupid and try to stand up to a storm.

5 A devious person has thorns and traps ahead of him.
　　Whoever guards himself will stay far away from them.
6 Train a child in the way he should go,
　　and even when he is old he will not turn away from it.
7 A rich person rules poor people,
　　and a borrower is a slave to a lender.
8 Whoever plants injustice will harvest trouble,
　　and this weapon of his own fury will be destroyed.
9 Whoever is generous will be blessed
　　because he has shared his food with the poor.

22:6 Use me to train my children in the way they should go. Even in their old age they won't turn away.

22:9 I'm glad for the blessings you promise me when I'm generous. I'll share with the poor the abundance you've already given me.

10 Drive out a mocker, and conflict will leave.
　　Quarreling and abuse will stop.
11 Whoever loves a pure heart and whoever
　　　speaks graciously
　　has a king as his friend.
12 The LORD's eyes watch over knowledge,
　　but he overturns the words of a treacherous person.

22:11 Make me pure of heart and gracious in speech.

22:13 Lazy people make up all kinds of excuses not to get up and go to work. Fill me with passion and purpose.

22:17–19 I open my ears to the words of wise people. I open my mind to the knowledge you impart. I'll memorize your words so they stay on the tip of my tongue. Then I'll trust you fully.

22:22–23 The poor and oppressed make easy targets. But if I harm them you'll defend them.

22:24–25 I can't let myself be best friends with hotheads. It's too easy to pick up their bad habits.

22:29 Teach me to be efficient and get real work done. That will prepare me for greater responsibility.

23:1–3 There's no free lunch when I eat with important people. Give me good manners and wisdom in the gifts I accept.

¹³ A lazy person says,
"There's a lion outside!
I'll be murdered in the streets!"
¹⁴ The mouth of an adulterous woman is a deep pit.
The one who is cursed by the LORD will fall into it.
¹⁵ Foolishness is firmly attached to a child's heart.
Spanking will remove it far from him.
¹⁶ Oppressing the poor for profit
⌐or⌐ giving to the rich
certainly leads to poverty.

Listen to My Advice

¹⁷ Open your ears, and hear the words of wise people,
and set your mind on the knowledge I give you.
¹⁸ It is pleasant if you keep them in mind
⌐so that⌐ they will be on the tip of your tongue,
¹⁹ so that your trust may be in the LORD.
Today I have made them known to you, especially to you.
²⁰ Didn't I write to you previously with advice
and knowledge
²¹ in order to teach you the words of truth
so that you can give an accurate report to those
who send you?

Living With Your Neighbor

²² Do not rob the poor because they are poor
or trample on the rights of an oppressed person at
the city gate,
²³ because the LORD will plead their case
and will take the lives of those who rob them.
²⁴ Do not be a friend of one who has a bad temper,
and never keep company with a hothead,
²⁵ or you will learn his ways
and set a trap for yourself.

²⁶ Do not be ⌐found⌐ among those who make deals with
a handshake,
among those who guarantee other people's loans.
²⁷ If you have no money to pay back a loan,
why should your bed be repossessed?
²⁸ Do not move an ancient boundary marker
that your ancestors set in place.
²⁹ Do you see a person who is efficient in his work?
He will serve kings.
He will not serve unknown people.

23 ¹ When you sit down to eat with a ruler,
pay close attention to what is in front of you,
² and put a knife to your throat if you have a
big appetite.
³ Do not crave his delicacies,
because this is food that deceives you.

⁴Do not wear yourself out getting rich.
Be smart enough to stop.
⁵ Will you catch only a fleeting glimpse of wealth
before it is gone?
It makes wings for itself like an eagle flying into
the sky.

23:4–5 Warn me when I wear myself out getting rich. Make me smart enough to stop. Wealth doesn't last.

⁶Do not eat the food of one who is stingy,
and do not crave his delicacies.
⁷ As he calculates the cost to himself, this is what
he does:
He tells you, "Eat and drink,"
but he doesn't really mean it.
⁸ You will vomit the little bit you have eaten
and spoil your pleasant conversation.

23:6–8 I want to be truly generous when I share. I'm happy to see others enjoy what I give them. Alert me so I can repent of any reluctance I feel.

⁹Do not talk directly to a fool,
because he will despise the wisdom of your words.
¹⁰Do not move an ancient boundary marker
or enter fields that belong to orphans,
¹¹ because the one who is responsible for them
is strong.
He will plead their case against you.

23:9 Fools don't listen to wisdom. Tell me when I'm wasting words.

23:10 I won't cheat my neighbors or steal from the needy. You're their defender.

Learning From Your Father
¹²Live a more disciplined life,
and listen carefully to words of knowledge.
¹³Do not hesitate to discipline a child.
If you spank him, he will not die.
¹⁴ Spank him yourself,
and you will save his soul from hell.

23:13 Teach me how to discipline my children. Let them experience your love and firmness through me.

¹⁵My son,
if you have a wise heart,
my heart will rejoice as well.
¹⁶ My heart rejoices when you speak what is right.

23:15–16 My parents rejoice when they see my wise heart. Help me to not disappoint them.

¹⁷Do not envy sinners in your heart.
Instead, continue to fear the LORD.
¹⁸ There is indeed a future,
and your hope will never be cut off.

23:17 I choose to live for you with total respect rather than envy people who do wrong.

¹⁹My son,
listen, be wise,
and keep your mind going in the right direction.
²⁰ Do not associate with those who drink too
much wine,
with those who eat too much meat,
²¹ because both a drunk and a glutton will
become poor.
Drowsiness will dress a person in rags.

23:19–21 Your wisdom keeps my mind going in the right direction. Guard me from people who drag me to drunkenness or greed or laziness.

²² Listen to your father since you are his son,

23:23 I'm determined to get wisdom, discipline, and understanding. When I get hold of them I'll never let them go.

23:26 I freely give you my whole heart. Your ways make me exceedingly happy.

23:29–30 Drinking too much brings trouble and misery, quarrels and complaints, pointless wounds and bloodshot eyes. Carve those facts in my mind.

23:31–33 Wine sparkles in the glass and goes down smooth, but then it bites like a poisonous snake. It blurs my vision and makes my mouth say embarrassing things. Carve those facts in my mind.

23:34–35 Too much wine makes my body heave as if I'm riding ocean waves. Someone could punch me but I wouldn't feel pain. I'd just want another drink. Carve those facts in my mind.

24:1–2 I won't envy evildoers or wish I could hang out with them. In the end all they get is trouble.

24:3–4 Wisdom not only builds a house but fills it with lavish riches. Build me and fill me like that.

and do not despise your mother because she is old.

23 Buy truth (and do not sell it),
⌐that is,⌐ buy wisdom, discipline,
and understanding.
24 A righteous person's father will certainly rejoice.
Someone who has a wise son will enjoy him.
25 May your father and your mother be glad.
May she who gave birth to you rejoice.

26 My son,
give me your heart.
Let your eyes find happiness in my ways.
27 A prostitute is a deep pit.
A loose woman is a narrow well.
28 She is like a robber, lying in ambush.
She spreads unfaithfulness throughout society.

29 Who has trouble?
Who has misery?
Who has quarrels?
Who has a complaint?
Who has wounds for no reason?
Who has bloodshot eyes?
30 Those who drink glass after glass of wine
and mix it with everything.
31 Do not look at wine
because it is red,
because it sparkles in the cup,
because it goes down smoothly.
32 Later it bites like a snake
and strikes like a poisonous snake.
33 Your eyes will see strange sights,
and your mouth will say embarrassing things.
34 You will be like someone lying down in the middle of the sea
or like someone lying down on top of a ship's mast, saying,
35 "They strike me, but I feel no pain.
They beat me, but I'm not aware of it.
Whenever I wake up, I'm going to look for another drink."

24 1 Do not envy evil people
or wish you were with them,
2 because their minds plot violence,
and their lips talk trouble.

3 With wisdom a house is built.
With understanding it is established.
4 With knowledge its rooms are filled
with every kind of riches, both precious and pleasant.

⁵ A strong man knows how to use his strength,
 but a person with knowledge is even more powerful.
⁶   After all, with the right strategy you can wage war,
     and with many advisers there is victory.

⁷ Matters of wisdom are beyond the grasp of a
     stubborn fool.
 At the city gate he does not open his mouth.
⁸ Whoever plans to do evil will be known as a schemer.
⁹ Foolish scheming is sinful,
 and a mocker is disgusting to everyone.

¹⁰ If you faint in a crisis, you are weak.
¹¹ Rescue captives condemned to death,
 and spare those staggering toward their slaughter.
¹² When you say, "We didn't know this,"
 won't the one who weighs hearts take note of it?
 Won't the one who guards your soul know it?
 Won't he pay back people for what they do?

¹³ Eat honey, my son, because it is good.
 Honey that flows from the honeycomb tastes sweet.
¹⁴   The knowledge of wisdom is like that for your soul.
     If you find it, then there is a future,
         and your hope will never be cut off.

¹⁵ You wicked one,
 do not lie in ambush at the home of a
     righteous person.
 Do not rob his house.
¹⁶   A righteous person may fall seven times, but he gets
     up again.
     However, in a disaster wicked people fall.

¹⁷ Do not be happy when your enemy falls,
 and do not feel glad when he stumbles.
¹⁸   The Lord will see it, he won't like it,
     and he will turn his anger away from that person.

¹⁹ Do not get overly upset with evildoers.
 Do not envy wicked people,
²⁰   because an evil person has no future,
     and the lamps of wicked people will be snuffed out.

²¹ Fear the Lord, my son.
 Fear the king as well.
 Do not associate with those who always insist
     upon change,
²²   because disaster will come to them suddenly.
     Who knows what misery both may bring?

Learning From Wise People
²³ These also are the sayings of wise people:

24:5 Strong people often get what they want, but your knowledge makes me even stronger.

24:8 Even worse than doing evil is scheming ahead of time how to carry it out. Clear my mind when I start planning to sin.

24:12 I can pretend I've done no wrong, but you take note when I sin. You guard my soul, so you know the evil I've been planning. And you pay me back for whatever I do.

24:13–14 Your wisdom is like honey for my soul. I eat it because it tastes sweet. It gives me a hopeful future.

24:16–18 I might fall seven times, but each time you pick me up. If I'm glad when my enemy stumbles then my attitude has become the problem.

24:19–21 I won't lose sleep over the wicked or envy their success, because you say evildoers don't have a future. I'll keep living in awe of you.

24:23–25 You hate judges who

play favorites and call the guilty innocent. Everyone knows it's good to hold the guilty accountable.

24:26 Teach me to give answers as straightforward as a kiss on the lips.
24:27 Give me wisdom to know what I should do first, second, and third.

24:30–34 There's laziness all around me—lives overgrown with weeds and left unprotected from enemies. Let that be a lesson to me. Too much sleep, and poverty will overwhelm me.

Showing partiality as a judge is not good.

²⁴ Whoever says to a guilty person, "You are innocent,"
　　will be cursed by people and condemned by nations.

²⁵ But people will be pleased with those who convict a
　　guilty person,
　　and a great blessing will come to them.

²⁶ Giving a straight answer is ⌐like⌐ a kiss on the lips.

²⁷ Prepare your work outside,
　　and get things ready for yourself in the field.
　　　Afterwards, build your house.

²⁸ Do not testify against your neighbor without a reason,
　　and do not deceive with your lips.

²⁹ Do not say,
　　"I'll treat him as he treated me.
　　I'll pay him back for what he has done to me."

³⁰ I passed by a lazy person's field,
　　the vineyard belonging to a person without sense.

³¹ I saw that it was all overgrown with thistles.
　　The ground was covered with weeds,
　　　and its stone fence was torn down.

³² When I observed ⌐this⌐, I took it to heart.
　I saw it and learned my lesson.

³³ "Just a little sleep,
　　just a little slumber,
　　just a little nap."

³⁴ 　Then your poverty will come like a drifter,
　　　and your need will come like a bandit.

25 ¹These also are Solomon's proverbs that were copied by the men of King Hezekiah of Judah.

Advice for Kings

² It is the glory of God to hide things
　　but the glory of kings to investigate them.

³ ⌐Like⌐ the high heavens and the deep earth,
　　so the mind of kings is unsearchable.

25:4 Remove the impurities from my life. Mold me into your perfect shape.

⁴ Take the impurities out of silver,
　　and a vessel is ready for the silversmith to mold.

⁵ Take a wicked person away from the presence of
　　a king,
　　and justice will make his throne secure.

25:6–7 I won't assume I deserve a place of high honor. I'll let you invite me up to a better seat rather than set myself up to be put down.

⁶ Do not brag about yourself in front of a king
　　or stand in the spot that belongs to notable people,

⁷ 　because it is better to be told, "Come up here,"
　　than to be put down in front of a prince
　　　whom your eyes have seen.

⁸Do not be in a hurry to go to court.
What will you do in the end if your neighbor
disgraces you?
⁹ Present your argument to your neighbor,
but do not reveal another person's secret.
¹⁰ Otherwise, when he hears about it, he will
humiliate you,
and his evil report about you will never
disappear.

¹¹ ⌐Like⌐ golden apples in silver settings,
⌐so⌐ is a word spoken at the right time.
¹² ⌐Like⌐ a gold ring and a fine gold ornament,
⌐so⌐ is constructive criticism to the ear of one
who listens.
¹³ Like the coolness of snow on a harvest day,
⌐so⌐ is a trustworthy messenger to those who
send him:
He refreshes his masters.
¹⁴ ⌐Like⌐ a dense fog or a dust storm,
⌐so⌐ is a person who brags about a gift that he does
not give.

¹⁵ With patience you can persuade a ruler,
and a soft tongue can break bones.
¹⁶ When you find honey, eat only as much as you need.
Otherwise, you will have too much and vomit.
¹⁷ Do not set foot in your neighbor's house too often.
Otherwise, he will see too much of you and hate you.

¹⁸ ⌐Like⌐ a club and a sword and a sharp arrow,
⌐so⌐ is a person who gives false testimony against
his neighbor.
¹⁹ ⌐Like⌐ a broken tooth and a lame foot,
⌐so⌐ is confidence in an unfaithful person in a ⌐time
of⌐ crisis.
²⁰ ⌐Like⌐ taking off a coat on a cold day
or pouring vinegar on baking soda,
so is singing songs to one who has an evil heart.

²¹ If your enemy is hungry, give him some food to eat,
and if he is thirsty, give him some water to drink.
²² ⌐In this way⌐ you will make him feel guilty
and ashamed,
and the LORD will reward you.

²³ ⌐As⌐ the north wind brings rain,
so a whispering tongue brings angry looks.
²⁴ Better to live on a corner of a roof
than to share a home with a quarreling woman.
²⁵ ⌐Like⌐ cold water to a thirsty soul,
so is good news from far away.

25:8 I won't hurry to court. I don't want to be unnecessarily disgraced.

25:9–10 I won't tell another person's secret. I don't want to humiliate either of us.

25:11–12 I always want to speak the right word at the right time. I choose to welcome constructive criticism.

25:15 Teach me to let patience do its amazing work. Remind me that a soft word is stronger than I can imagine.

25:16–17 Give me good sense not to eat more sweets than I can stomach—and good sense not to overstay my welcome when I'm a guest.

25:21–22 Give me graciousness and generosity toward my enemies. I'll feed their hunger, quench their thirst, and trust you to change their hearts.

25:25 Send me good news I don't expect. It will be a cup of cold water to my thirsty soul.

25:26 When I give in to an evildoer I'm like a muddied spring. Purify me and help me stand up for what's right.

25:28 My lack of self-control exposes me like an unprotected city. Train me to take charge of myself!

26:1 No fool deserves honor. Help me rise above my foolishness.

26:3 I don't want to be a fool who needs harsh discipline. I'll respond quickly to your commands!

26:4 If I answer stupid with stupid, I've become a fool. Don't let me stoop to that.

26:11 Teach me to recognize stupidity the first time around, so I don't make the same mistake twice.

26:14–15 Wake me from my slumber when I make rest and recreation the most important part of my life.

26:16 Give me the sense to realize I'm never wiser than a group of sensible people.

---

²⁶ ⌊Like⌋ a muddied spring and a polluted well,
⌊so⌋ is a righteous person who gives in to a wicked person.

²⁷ Eating too much honey is not good,
and searching for honor is not honorable.^a

²⁸ ⌊Like⌋ a city broken into ⌊and⌋ left without a wall,
⌊so⌋ is a person who lacks self-control.

All About Fools

26 ¹ Like snow in summertime and rain at harvest time,
so honor is not right for a fool.
² Like a fluttering sparrow,
like a darting swallow,
so a hastily spoken curse does not come to rest.
³ A whip is for the horse,
a bridle is for the donkey,
and a rod is for the backs of fools.

⁴ Do not answer a fool with his own stupidity,
or you will be like him.
⁵ Answer a fool with his own stupidity,
or he will think he is wise.
⁶ Whoever uses a fool to send a message
cuts off his own feet and brings violence upon himself.

⁷ ⌊Like⌋ a lame person's limp legs,
so is a proverb in the mouths of fools.
⁸ Like tying a stone to a sling,
so is giving honor to a fool.
⁹ ⌊Like⌋ a thorn stuck in a drunk's hand,
so is a proverb in the mouths of fools.
¹⁰ ⌊Like⌋ many people who destroy everything,
so is one who hires fools or drifters.
¹¹ As a dog goes back to its vomit,
⌊so⌋ a fool repeats his stupidity.
¹² Have you met a person who thinks he is wise?
There is more hope for a fool than for him.

¹³ A lazy person says,
"There's a ferocious lion out on the road!
There's a lion loose in the streets!"
¹⁴ ⌊As⌋ a door turns on its hinges,
so the lazy person turns on his bed.
¹⁵ A lazy person puts his fork in his food.
He wears himself out as he brings it back to his mouth.
¹⁶ A lazy person thinks he is wiser than seven people
who give a sensible answer.

¹⁷ ⌊Like⌋ grabbing a dog by the ears,

---

^a 25:27 Hebrew meaning of this line uncertain.

ˌsoˌ is a bystander who gets involved in someone else's quarrel.
¹⁸ Like a madman who shoots flaming arrows, arrows, and death,
¹⁹ so is the person who tricks his neighbor and says, "I was only joking!"

²⁰ Without wood a fire goes out, and without gossip a quarrel dies down.
²¹ ˌAsˌ charcoal fuels burning coals and wood fuels fire,
so a quarrelsome person fuels a dispute.
²² The words of a gossip are swallowed greedily, and they go down into a person's innermost being.

²³ ˌLikeˌ a clay pot covered with cheap silver, ˌsoˌ is smooth talk that covers up an evil heart.
²⁴ Whoever is filled with hate disguises it with his speech,
but inside he holds on to deceit.
²⁵ When he talks charmingly, do not trust him because of the seven disgusting things in his heart.
²⁶ His hatred is deceitfully hidden, but his wickedness will be revealed to the community.

²⁷ Whoever digs a pit will fall into it. Whoever rolls a stone will have it roll back on him.
²⁸ A lying tongue hates its victims, and a flattering mouth causes ruin.

All About Life

27 ¹ Do not brag about tomorrow, because you do not know what another day may bring.
² Praise should come from another person and not from your own mouth, from a stranger and not from your own lips.
³ A stone is heavy, and sand weighs a lot, but annoyance caused by a stubborn fool is heavier than both.
⁴ Anger is cruel, and fury is overwhelming, but who can survive jealousy?

⁵ Open criticism is better than unexpressed love.
⁶ Wounds made by a friend are intended to help, but an enemy's kisses are too much to bear.ᵃ
⁷ One who is full despises honey, but to one who is hungry, even bitter food tastes sweet.

ᵃ 27:6 Hebrew meaning of "are too much to bear" uncertain.

26:18–19 When I say, "I was only joking!" I'm like a madman shooting flaming arrows of death. I'll say what I mean and mean what I say.

26:22 Confront me when I greedily swallow gossip. Slanderous words poison me and all of my relationships.

26:23–26 Smooth talkers conceal the evil in their hearts. They disguise the deceit inside them. Help me see through their charm. Then I'll know enough not to trust them.

27:1 I won't brag about tomorrow because I don't know what it will bring. But I count on you to go with me no matter what I face.

27:2 Alert me when I don't realize I'm boasting. I'll wait to hear praise from the lips of others.

27:5–6 Friends wound me to help me. But don't let me fall for enemies who blow me a kiss.

27:9–10 Perfume is sweet but a true friend is even sweeter. Teach me to value friends nearby who give me everyday help.

27:12 Let me see trouble coming and find a good place to hide.

27:14 I want to be a true blessing to all of my friends. Show me when my efforts fall short, and teach me fresh ways to love.

27:17 I need people to keep me sharp. Help me find friends and mentors and role models who will partner with me in following you.

27:20 I know my eyes can long for more and more of everything. I'll practice being content with what I have.

27:22 I'll submit to you and learn from you willingly. You won't need to crush me to rid me of stupidity.

27:25–27 Open my eyes to all the resources you've given me.

[8] Like a bird wandering from its nest,
  so is a husband wandering from his home.

[9] Perfume and incense make the heart glad,
  but the sweetness of a friend is a fragrant forest.[a]
[10] Do not abandon your friend or your father's friend.
  Do not go to a relative's home when you are in trouble.
    A neighbor living nearby is better than a relative
    far away.

[11] Be wise, my son, and make my heart glad
  so that I can answer anyone who criticizes me.
[12] Sensible people foresee trouble and hide.
  Gullible people go ahead ⌐and⌐ suffer.
[13] Hold on to the garment of one who guarantees a
    stranger's loan,
    and hold responsible the person
      who makes a loan in behalf of a foreigner.
[14] Whoever blesses his friend early in the morning with
    a loud voice—
  his blessing is considered a curse.

[15] Constantly dripping water on a rainy day is like a
    quarreling woman.
[16] Whoever can control her can control the wind.
    He can even pick up olive oil with his right hand.[b]

[17] ⌐As⌐ iron sharpens iron,
  so one person sharpens the wits of another.
[18] Whoever takes care of a fig tree can eat its fruit,
  and whoever protects his master is honored.
[19] As a face is reflected in water,
  so a person is reflected by his heart.
[20] Hell and decay are never satisfied,
  and a person's eyes are never satisfied.
[21] The crucible is for refining silver and the smelter
    for gold,
  but a person ⌐is tested⌐ by the praise given to him.
[22] If you crush a stubborn fool in a mortar with a pestle
    along with grain,[c]
  ⌐even then⌐ his stupidity will not leave him.
[23] Be fully aware of the condition of your flock,
  and pay close attention to your herds.
[24] Wealth is not forever.
    Nor does a crown last from one generation to
    the next.

[25] ⌐When⌐ grass is cut short, the tender growth appears,
  and vegetables are gathered on the hills.

[a] 27:9 Or "is sincere advice."
[b] 27:16 Hebrew meaning of this line uncertain.
[c] 27:22 Hebrew meaning uncertain.

²⁶ Lambs ⌐will provide⌐ you with clothing,
and the money from the male goats will buy
a field.
²⁷ There will be enough goat milk to feed you,
to feed your family,
and to keep your servant girls alive.

They're gifts from you to keep me alive.

28

¹ A wicked person flees when no one is chasing him,
but righteous people are as bold as lions.
² When a country is in revolt, it has many rulers,
but only with a person who has understanding
and knowledge
will it last a long time.
³ A poor person who oppresses poorer people
is like a driving rain that leaves no food.
⁴ Those who abandon ⌐God's⌐ teachings praise
wicked people,
but those who follow ⌐God's⌐ teachings oppose
wicked people.
⁵ Evil people do not understand justice,
but those who seek the Lord understand everything.
⁶ Better to be a poor person who has integrity
than to be rich and double-dealing.

⁷ Whoever follows ⌐God's⌐ teachings is a wise son.
Whoever associates with gluttons disgraces his father.
⁸ Whoever becomes wealthy through ⌐unfair⌐ loans
and interest
collects them for the one who is kind to the poor.
⁹ Surely the prayer of someone who refuses
to listen to ⌐God's⌐ teachings is disgusting.
¹⁰ Whoever leads decent people into evil will fall into
his own pit,
but innocent people will inherit good things.

¹¹ A rich person is wise in his own eyes,
but a poor person with understanding sees right through
him.
¹² When righteous people triumph, there is great glory,
but when wicked people rise, people hide themselves.
¹³ Whoever covers over his sins does not prosper.
Whoever confesses and abandons them receives
compassion.
¹⁴ Blessed is the one who is always fearful ⌐of sin⌐,
but whoever is hard-hearted falls into disaster.

¹⁵ ⌐Like⌐ a roaring lion and a charging bear,
⌐so⌐ a wicked ruler is a threat to poor people.
¹⁶ A leader without understanding taxes ⌐his
people⌐ heavily,
but those who hate unjust gain will live longer.
¹⁷ A person burdened with the guilt of murder

28:1 I'm bold as a lion but only because you back me up. No matter what I face I won't flee in fear.

28:2 Bring our country together. Give us leaders who get us all going in the right direction.

28:5 Keep me from thinking only about me. Teach me about justice. Show me what I can do to make the world more just.

28:8 If I gain wealth unfairly, I know you'll give it to someone else—someone who is kind to the poor.

28:9 My prayers disgust you if I refuse to follow your teachings.

28:11 Having a lot of money doesn't mean someone is wise. I'll listen to anyone who has genuine understanding.

28:13–14 As long as I hide my sin I won't prosper. So I'll confess and abandon everything that goes against your commands. I trust in your compassion. I'm blessed to have a healthy fear of sin.

will be a fugitive down to his grave.
No one will help him.

28:18 Honesty keeps me safe. Dishonesty always puts me in a precarious place.

[18] Whoever lives honestly will be safe.
Whoever lives dishonestly will fall all at once.

28:19 You provide me with plenty when I work hard. Show me when my dreams are unrealistic.

[19] Whoever works his land will have plenty to eat.
Whoever chases unrealistic dreams will have plenty of nothing.

28:20–21 Let me enjoy the blessings of being regarded as trustworthy. Teach me to not play favorites but to show fairness to everyone.

[20] A trustworthy person has many blessings,
but anyone in a hurry to get rich will not escape punishment.
[21] Showing partiality is not good,
because some people will turn on you even for a piece of bread.
[22] A stingy person is in a hurry to get rich,
not realizing that poverty is about to overtake him.

28:23 Nobody will take me seriously if I make a habit of flattery. Train me to offer helpful criticism in the right time and right way.

[23] Whoever criticizes people will be more highly regarded in the future
than the one who flatters with his tongue.
[24] The one who robs his father or his mother
and says, "It isn't wrong!" is a companion to a vandal.

28:25–27 Greed urges me to stir up fights to get what I want. But I'll trust you to prosper me. I'll rely on you to guide me. I'll look for ways to give to the poor.

[25] A greedy person stirs up a fight,
but whoever trusts the LORD prospers.
[26] Whoever trusts his own heart is a fool.
Whoever walks in wisdom will survive.
[27] Whoever gives to the poor lacks nothing.
Whoever ignores the poor receives many curses.

[28] When wicked people rise, people hide.
When they die, righteous people increase.

29:1 I'll flex when you warn me and bend your way. Rejecting your warnings will break me beyond repair.

29 [1] A person who will not bend after many warnings will suddenly be broken beyond repair.

29:2 Build up your people to be your righteous and wholehearted followers. We'll all rejoice to see what you do!

[2] When righteous people increase, the people ⌐of God⌐ rejoice,
but when a wicked person rules, everybody groans.
[3] A person who loves wisdom makes his father happy,
but one who pays prostitutes wastes his wealth.
[4] By means of justice, a king builds up a country,
but a person who confiscates religious contributions tears it down.

29:6 Sin pulls me in like bait in a trap. Alert me to the dangers of temptation. I'll run away and be glad!

[5] A person who flatters his neighbor
is spreading a net for him to step into.
[6] To an evil person sin is bait in a trap,
but a righteous person runs away from it[a] and is glad.

29:7 I understand the just complaints of the poor. I'll defend

[7] A righteous person knows the just cause of the poor.
A wicked person does not understand this.
[8] Mockers create an uproar in a city,

[a] 29:6 Hebrew meaning of "runs away from it" uncertain.

but wise people turn away anger.

the needy every chance I get.

⁹ When a wise person goes to court with a stubborn fool,
he may rant and rave,
but there is no peace and quiet.
¹⁰ Bloodthirsty people hate an innocent person,
but decent people seek ⌊to protect⌋ his life.
¹¹ A fool expresses all his emotions,
but a wise person controls them.
¹² If a ruler pays attention to lies,
all his servants become wicked.

29:11 Train me to keep my emotions in check. Teach me the right time and way to express them.

¹³ A poor person and an oppressor have this in common:
The LORD gives both of them sight.
¹⁴ When a king judges the poor with honesty,
his throne will always be secure.

29:14 You'll make me secure when I treat the poor with honesty. Help me see when I'm anything less than honest.

¹⁵ A spanking and a warning produce wisdom,
but an undisciplined child disgraces his mother.
¹⁶ When wicked people increase, crime increases,
but righteous people will witness their downfall.
¹⁷ Correct your son, and he will give you peace of mind.
He will bring delight to your soul.

29:17 I'll choose to discipline my children for their long-term good. In the end I'll enjoy peace of mind.

¹⁸ Without prophetic vision people run wild,
but blessed are those who follow ⌊God's⌋ teachings.
¹⁹ A slave cannot be disciplined with words.
He will not respond, though he may understand.
²⁰ Have you met a person who is quick to answer?
There is more hope for a fool than for him.
²¹ Pamper a slave from childhood,
and later he will be ungrateful.ᵃ

29:18 Speak to your people and lead us. We'll follow you wherever you want us to go.

²² An angry person stirs up a fight,
and a hothead does much wrong.
²³ A person's pride will humiliate him,
but a humble spirit gains honor.

29:22–23 I'll cool my temper rather than do wrong. I'll silence my pride before I humiliate myself.

²⁴ Whoever is a thief's partner hates his own life.
He will not testify under oath.
²⁵ A person's fear sets a trap ⌊for him⌋,
but one who trusts the LORD is safe.
²⁶ Many seek an audience with a ruler,
but justice for humanity comes from the LORD.
²⁷ An unjust person is disgusting to righteous people.
A decent person is disgusting to wicked people.

29:25 Fear will trap and destroy me. I'll trust in you and live unafraid.

29:26 Everyone looks to powerful people for justice. But I'll rely on you for real help.

30
¹ The words of Agur, son of Jakeh. Agur's prophetic revelation.

Agur Speaks About God

[To God]

This man's declaration:

30:1–3 I feel weary when I lack a living knowledge of you. I haven't mastered your wisdom and can't claim great human understanding. I'm more like a

---
ᵃ 29:21 Hebrew meaning uncertain.

dumb animal than a human being.

"I'm weary, O God.
I'm weary and worn out, O God.
² I'm more ⌊like⌋ a dumb animal than a human being.
I don't ⌊even⌋ have human understanding.
³ I haven't learned wisdom.
I don't have knowledge of the Holy One.ª

[To the audience]

30:4 You dwell in heaven and come down to earth. You created earth from end to end. You are God's Son.

⁴"Who has gone up to heaven and come down?
Who has gathered the wind in the palm of his hand?
Who has wrapped water in a garment?
Who has set up the earth from one end to the other?
What is his name or the name of his son?
Certainly, you must know!

30:5–6 Your every word proves true. I can't add a single thought to what you say.

⁵"Every word of God has proven to be true.
He is a shield to those who come to him
for protection.
⁶Do not add to his words,
or he will reprimand you, and you will be found to
be a liar.

A Prayer
[To God]

30:7–9 Keep me in a place where I need you—make me not too rich or too poor. If I have too much I won't rely on you. If I have too little I'll grow desperate and sin.

⁷"I've asked you for two things.
Don't keep them from me before I die:
⁸ Keep vanity and lies far away from me.
Don't give me either poverty or riches.
Feed me ⌊only⌋ the food I need,
⁹ or I may feel satisfied and deny you
and say, 'Who is the Lord?'
or I may become poor and steal
and give the name of my God a bad reputation.

Against Slander
[To the audience]

¹⁰"Do not slander a slave to his master.
The slave will curse you,
and you will be found guilty."

Four Kinds of People

30:11–14 Make me fully devoted to my whole family. Keep changing me until I'm truly unsoiled. Challenge me when I look down on others. And soften my sharp words.

¹¹A certain kind of person curses his father
and does not bless his mother.
¹²A certain kind of person thinks he is pure
but is not washed from his own feces.ᵇ
¹³A certain kind of person looks around arrogantly
and is conceited.
¹⁴A certain kind of person,
whose teeth are like swords
and whose jaws are ⌊like⌋ knives,

ª 30:3 Or "holy ones."
ᵇ 30:12 Blunt Hebrew term but not considered vulgar.

devours oppressed people from the earth
and people from among humanity.

Human Bloodsuckers
[15] The bloodsucking leech has two daughters—
"Give!" and "Give!"

Four Things That Are Never Satisfied
Three things are never satisfied.
Four never say, "Enough!":
[16] the grave,
a barren womb,
a land that never gets enough water,
a fire that does not say, "Enough!"

Disrespectful Children—Their Punishment
[17] The eye that makes fun of a father and hates to obey
a mother
will be plucked out by ravens in the valley and
eaten by young vultures.

Four Things of Intrigue
[18] Three things are too amazing to me,
even four that I cannot understand:
[19] an eagle making its way through the sky,
a snake making its way over a rock,
a ship making its way through high seas,
a man making his way with a virgin.

About the Woman Who Commits Adultery
[20] This is the way of a woman who commits adultery:
She eats, wipes her mouth,
and says, "I haven't done anything wrong!"

Four Things That Are Intolerable
[21] Three things cause the earth to tremble,
even four it cannot bear up under:
[22] a slave when he becomes king,
a godless fool when he is filled with food,
[23] a woman who is unloved when she gets married,
a maid when she replaces her mistress.

Four Things That Are Small—Yet Smart and Strong
[24] Four things on earth are small,
yet they are very wise:
[25] Ants are not a strong species,
yet they store their food in summer.
[26] Rock badgers are not a mighty species,
yet they make their home in the rocks.
[27] Locusts have no king,
yet all of them divide into swarms by instinct.
[28] A lizard you can hold in your hands,
yet it can even be found in royal palaces.

30:15–16 Shield me from harsh demands that won't go away. Protect me from death and barrenness, from drought and raging fire.

30:17 Teach me to respect my father and mother. Don't let me lose my sight.

30:18–19 You created a world I can't begin to understand—a place of slyness and flight, of adventure and love.

30:20 Compel me to admit my sin. Don't let me get away with transgressions large or small.

30:24–28 Give me the wisdom I see in your creation. Teach me to plan ahead, to create a safe home, to work well with my companions, to be bold and daring.

30:29–31 Give me the dignity I see in your creation. When I feel beaten down, help me walk with self-respect.

Four Things That Move With Dignity

²⁹ There are three things that walk with dignity,
   even four that march with dignity:
³⁰   a lion, mightiest among animals, which turns away
         from nothing,
³¹   a strutting rooster,ᵃ
      a male goat,
      a king at the head of his army.ᵇ

30:32 Teach me humility when I get out of hand in honoring myself. I'll start by silencing my boasting mouth.

Keep Calm and Quiet

³² If you are such a godless fool as to honor yourself,
   or if you scheme,
      you had better put your hand over your mouth.
³³   As churning milk produces butter
            and punching a nose produces blood,
               so stirring up angerᶜ produces a fight.

31 ¹ The sayings of King Lemuel, a prophetic revelation,
      used by his mother to discipline him.

Advice to a Prince

² "What, my son?
   What, son to whom I gave birth?
   What, son of my prayers?
³   Don't give your strength to women
      or your power to those who ruin kings.

31:4–5 Remind me of the risks of alcohol—making me forget my own important decisions and causing me to lower my standards of how I treat others.

⁴ "It is not for kings, Lemuel.
   It is not for kings to drink wine or for rulers to
         crave liquor.
⁵   Otherwise, they drink and forget what they
            have decreed
         and change the standard of justice for all
            oppressed people.
⁶ Give liquor to a person who is dying
   and wine to one who feels resentful.
⁷   Such a person drinks
         and forgets his poverty
            and does not remember his trouble anymore.

31:8–9 I'll find ways to speak up for people who can't speak up for themselves. I'll defend the rights of the oppressed and needy.

⁸ "Speak out for the one who cannot speak,
   for the rights of those who are doomed.
⁹ Speak out,
   judge fairly,
      and defend the rights of oppressed and
         needy people."

A Poem in Hebrew Alphabetical Order

¹⁰ "Who can find a wife with a strong character?

ᵃ 30:31 Hebrew meaning of this line uncertain.
ᵇ 30:31 Hebrew meaning of "at the head of his army" uncertain.
ᶜ 30:33 In Hebrew there is a play on words in verse 33 where the same verb is used to express all three actions.

She is worth far more than jewels.
¹¹ Her husband trusts her with ⌊all⌋ his heart,
  and he does not lack anything good.
¹² She helps him and never harms him all the days of
  her life.

¹³ "She seeks out wool and linen ⌊with care⌋
  and works with willing hands.
¹⁴ She is like merchant ships.
  She brings her food from far away.
¹⁵ She wakes up while it is still dark
  and gives food to her family
    and portions of food to her female slaves.

¹⁶ "She picks out a field and buys it.
  She plants a vineyard from the profits she has earned.
¹⁷ She puts on strength like a belt
  and goes to work with energy.
¹⁸ She sees that she is making a good profit.
  Her lamp burns late at night.

¹⁹ "She puts her hands on the distaff,
  and her fingers hold a spindle.
²⁰ She opens her hands to oppressed people
  and stretches them out to needy people.
²¹ She does not fear for her family when it snows
  because her whole family
    has a double layer of clothing.
²² She makes quilts for herself.
  Her clothes are ⌊made of⌋ linen and purple cloth.

²³ "Her husband is known at the city gates
  when he sits with the leaders of the land.

²⁴ "She makes linen garments and sells them
  and delivers belts to the merchants.
²⁵ She dresses with strength and nobility,
  and she smiles at the future.

²⁶ "She speaks with wisdom,
  and on her tongue there is tender instruction.
²⁷ She keeps a close eye on the conduct of her family,
  and she does not eat the bread of idleness.
²⁸ Her children and her husband
  stand up and bless her.
  In addition, he sings her praises, by saying,
²⁹   'Many women have done noble work,
    but you have surpassed them all!'

³⁰ "Charm is deceptive, and beauty evaporates,
  ⌊but⌋ a woman who has the fear of the LORD should
    be praised.
³¹ Reward her for what she has done,
  and let her achievements praise her at the
    city gates."

31:10–12 Discipline me so I develop strong character. Make me worthy of the total trust of others. Every day of my life I want to be a source of help, not harm.

31:13–18 I can't provide for my family without your help. I need your strength to work hard and long. I need your wisdom to earn a living.

31:20–22 With your help I'll give generously to the oppressed and needy. I'll shelter my own family and keep them warm. I'll provide them with good things.

31:25–26 I dream of strength and nobility and optimism. I want wisdom for myself and others. I need watchful eyes for my family and energy for work. Increase those qualities in me.

31:27–30 Make me a blessing and not a burden. I want my work to stand out. Give me enduring character as I live in awe of you.

About the Author

Kevin Johnson is the bestselling author or coauthor of more than fifty books and Bible products for youth and adults. With a background as a youth worker, senior editor, and teaching pastor, he now pastors Emmaus Road Church in metro Minneapolis. He holds an MDiv from Fuller Theological Seminary and a BA in English and print journalism from the University of Wisconsin–River Falls. Kevin is married to Lyn, and they have three children. Learn more at www.kevinjohnsonbooks.com.

Watch for the complete

Pray the Scriptures Bible

coming Summer 2012.